✳ CELEBRATION FOR – JOURNEY OF *THE GREAT CIRCLE* ✳

This unique, heartfelt, and visionary book penetrates to the deepest questions of the human journey, and offers touching and inspiring poetic images to guide us. Oman Ken brings the wealth of his experience and deep insights as a welcome roadmap to awakening. I recommend Journey of *The Great Circle* to anyone dedicated to fathom the mysteries of life and advance on your own healing journey.

> --- Alan Cohen, bestselling author of **A Course in Miracles Made Easy**

In his book, **Journey of *The Great Circle*,** Oman brings forth "pearls" of wisdom - and has strung those pearls together in a compelling narrative and practice. Bottom line: If you find yourself going around in circles in life, go around THIS circle, and you will spiral to a higher and brighter view.

> --- Steve Bhaerman, aka Swami Beyondananda "cosmic comic" and co-author
> with Bruce Lipton of **Spontaneous Evolution: Our Positive Future and a Way
> to Get There From Here.**

Oman's book inspires us to embark on a sacred journey and exploration of what life is truly about - and what really matters. Here is a book that can be utilized every day to polish the Diamond of our Souls.

> --- Rama Jyoti Vernon, co-founder of **The Yoga Journal** and author of
> **Yoga: The Practice of Myth & Sacred Geometry**

With the poetry of a passionate artist - and the perspectives of an intuitive scientist, Oman Ken has written a visionary book. Utilizing his unique system of daily practices, he lays out the vision and pathway for a more peaceful and compassionate world.

> --- Reverend Max Lafser, Unity minister and former chairman of
> **The Center For International Dialogue**

I know first-hand the power and beauty of a 365 daily transformation practice. Oman's deep reflection and soul searching has devoutly created this profound and poetic work. Use this book as a daily practice to soar into the heights of your soul. You will forever be transformed.

> ---José R. Fuentes, Co-Founder and Facilitator of the Sedona Integral Group

Oman's book, Journey of *The Great Circle,* is too rich with meaningful poetic and creative thinking not to be experienced. Through his 365 contemplative exercises, he brings a great gift to the human family for our next leap in wholeness. I celebrate this new work, for I know the reader will be assisted in their spiritual unfoldment.

> --- Bruce Kellogg, Unity minister

Journey of *The Great Circle* is Oman Ken's epic masterpiece to passionately hone and master the best in us. Four seasonal volumes of brilliant creativity weaving consciousness, science, art, history, and evolutionary spirituality. Stunningly written and organized. You will be blessed.

--- *Enocha Ranjita Ryan, Transformational Healing Artist*

As a minister, I would highly recommend Oman's book to inspire other ministers with meaningful themes for Sunday talks. Each of the 365 contemplative narratives is rich with powerful ideas and inspiration. Oman's book is such a meaningful gift for humanity as well as a practical pathway to a better world at this crucial moment in human development.

--- *Marshall Norman, former Unity minister of Madison, Wisconsin*

JOURNEY OF
THE GREAT CIRCLE

DAILY CONTEMPLATIONS FOR CULTIVATING INNER FREEDOM
AND LIVING YOUR LIFE AS A MASTER OF FREEDOM

WINTER VOLUME

OMAN KEN

BALBOA.PRESS
A DIVISION OF HAY HOUSE

Balboa Press books may be ordered through booksellers or by contacting:

Balboa Press
A Division of Hay House
1663 Liberty Drive
Bloomington, IN 47403
www.balboapress.com
844-682-1282

Cover art designed by Oman Ken – and created by Mark Gelotte.

Graphic art designed by Oman Ken – and created by Mark Gelotte.

Photography of Oman Ken by Charles Ruscher

ISBN: 978-1-9822-7567-9 (sc)
ISBN: 978-1-9822-7568-6 (e)

Print information available on the last page.

Balboa Press rev. date: 12/07/2021

✳ CONTENTS ✳
Themes and Metaphors of Winter

December 21	Gifts of Winter	The Big Questions
December 22	Qualities Within the Seasons of Life	Iconic Images of Winter
December 23	The Great Story of Awakening	Story of the Hero's Journey
December 24	*Journey of Awakening*	The Eternal Storyteller
December 25	The Celebration of Christmas	Birth of the Christ Child
December 26	Natural Yearning For Inner Development	The Food of the Gods
December 27	*Spiritual Journey*	Concert Violinist

December 28	*The Great Circle*	The Concept of a Year
December 29	*The Great Circle* of Expansion and Expression	Flowers and Root Systems
December 30	*The Great Circle* of the Tao	A Day of Light and Darkness
December 31	Completion	Exploding Supernovas

✳ DEDICATION ✳

This book is dedicated to those who serve,
the people who contribute their creative gifts and talents
to the wellbeing of others,

the humble ones who give to others
without any need for reward or acknowledgement,

the courageous ones who have discovered
that to lovingly serve another person
is to serve everyone,
for in truth, we are one global family.

Humanity may possibly be on the verge
of making a quantum leap into a whole new paradigm,
a novel and emergent expression of magnificent evolutionary expansion,
and this expansion is taking place
via the direct realization of one's *True Nature*.

This evolutionary leap in consciousness that we're all awakening to
is "a universal gift",
the blessed and mysterious gift
of directly experiencing and knowing who we really are.

✳ WHAT IS – JOURNEY OF *THE GREAT CIRCLE* ✳

JOURNEY OF *THE GREAT CIRCLE* is a collection of 365 contemplative narratives designed as a daily transformative practice for the purpose of personal transformation. The annual collection of narratives is divided into four volumes, Winter, Spring, Summer, and Autumn each beginning on either the solstice or equinox. Each of the 365 narratives has a specific spiritual theme to help you gain a more expansive understanding of what really matters - and points you to how to live a life with peace of mind and inner freedom.

The various themes of the narratives involve insights from spirituality, quantum physics, the evolutionary perspective, the study of visionary archetypes, healing, and transformative practice. **Journey of *The Great Circle*** can be thought of as "a spiritual map of an awakening life".

A life of inner freedom is when one consciously realizes the perfection that's always unfolding within - and within all of life. Living with this awareness allows the natural states of peace, happiness, joy and harmony to effortlessly arise. It is a life of one who has devotedly learned to love others and all of life unconditionally - and who has gained the joyful awareness of serving the wellbeing of others. In these writings, one who attains this level of mastery is referred to as a **Master of Freedom**.

We are all natural-born storytellers with a mandate from *Life* to generate the most fulfilling and creative story of life we can imagine. Every day is a new opportunity to make our life story a little more glorious, a little more fulfilling, a little more creative. We are the authors of this story in every moment of our lives based on the intentions we choose, either consciously or unconsciously. For most people, in order to have the most glorious, fulfilling, creative, and peaceful life requires some form of spiritual practice necessitating conscious attention each day.

Journey of *The Great Circle* utilizes a transformative system of daily practices that can help you:

1) Experience a life of peace, happiness, joy, harmony, and fulfilling creative expression.

2) Prepare for the day's activities and surprises that await you so you can meet each situation from the "sanctuary" of heart wisdom, gratitude, and centeredness.

3) Connect to the inner guidance of the heart so you may live you life with ease and grace.

4) Learn to love every expression of life unconditionally.

5) Maintain a conscious alignment with *a Greater Power*. *A Greater Power* has been called myriad names, including but not limited to, *the Source of Life, the Infinite Presence of Love, God, the Great Spirit,* and *the Infinite Intelligence of the Universe.*

When **Journey of *The Great Circle*** is used on a daily basis it will help cultivate inner freedom and assist you in fulfilling your sacred destiny of an awakened life as a **Master of Freedom**.

Being authentically present is the direct experience
of "abiding at the very center of the Universe"
and aligning with *the Natural Intelligence of Life* so completely
that, in some extraordinary way,
one becomes "the hands and heart" of the entire Cosmos.

✳ PREFACE – THE GENESIS ✳

I WAS STANDING ALONE on a large wooden stage in front of a thousand people performing my original songs with my two dear companions - my acoustic guitar and my lyrical voice. I had also created a photographic slide show to visually animate the poetic images of my songs, which projected on a large screen behind me.

As the strings of my guitar rang out, I was offering the last song of a two-week concert tour where I had traveled through the lush Northwest in late spring. As the musical notes of this final composition came to an end, I felt something was very wrong. I could feel a turbulent energy within my ailing body crashing through every cell. My physical form was in some kind of crisis, and from that moment on, my life would never be the same.

The Story of How This Book Came To Be

Life seems to lead each of us on an adventurous journey in which we must ultimately make important choices based on the many possible roads and different turns that come before us along the way. When we were young, most of us conjured up some sort of future vision about how our life would unfold when we grew older. Yet usually for most of us, there was a plethora of surprises and unpredictable twists along life's journey. This book is the surprising result of one of those twists.

In 2005, after numerous years of steadily declining health, a mysterious illness had become a major challenge, and I became deeply frustrated and depressed. I lost most of my physical energy and was very fatigued and exhausted. A heat sensation would rush up into my head each day accompanied by reddish flushing of my chest, neck, and head. At times I felt an internal shaking in my body that was strange, frightening, and uncomfortable. Because of these curious symptoms, I had to adjust my entire life. My musical career came to a halt, and I had to adapt to a new expression of who I was and what I did. I was no longer able to tour around the country performing concerts and retreats with my music. I lost all motivation and energy to record music in my home studio as I did in previous years. And I was barely able to perform at short local events - such as conferences and weddings in order to pay monthly bills.

Because of these increasing physical challenges, I spent many years and lots of money seeing numerous doctors, naturopaths, nutritionists, chiropractors, hypnotherapists, spiritual counselors, health wizards, and a "host of pretty cosmic characters" to find a resolution to my situation. I did get a little help here and there, but for the most part, nothing seemed to work ongoing. My health kept declining slowly. I got very angry at life. At God. At the *Infinite Intelligence* that was supposed to be good and fair. What was happening to me did not feel fair.

I thought of myself as "a spiritual person" because I did a host of "spiritual things". I meditated every day, read spiritual books, attended self-help workshops, exercised regularly, ate a fantastic array of organic food, projected what I thought was a positive attitude toward life, served people with my uplifting music, donated money to environmental organizations - and therefore in my mind, I did everything "right". Why would someone like me, who is "spiritual" and is doing everything "right", suffer from a physical condition that felt so "wrong"? Over time, I was getting more and more depressed, even suicidal. After a long period of feeling this way, I got very tired of living a depressed life and decided to take more responsibility for my healing.

When I made this shift in awareness, one of the ways I chose to responsibly deal with my ongoing depression was to re-dedicate my life to my spiritual practice. I did this by spending more time in Nature, so I could deeply contemplate my personal situation. I wanted to find out what, if anything, I was supposed to learn about myself from this challenging opportunity I was dealing with.

At that time I had been living in Sedona, Arizona for eighteen years. I received the inner guidance to spend one day a week out in Nature alongside a beautiful wooded creek called Oak Creek and use this time to explore my inner spiritual quest. Each week at the water's edge I would spend five to seven hours in contemplation and inquiry, and then wrote down any insights or realizations. I wanted to use this time in Nature to gain insights about what I could discover about myself from my increasing health challenges and how they might relate to my life-long quest of spiritual awakening, however I understood it.

Thus this weekly ritual of sitting beside the creek, quieting my mind, and waiting began. And then insights started to come. And they continued to emerge each week with different spiritual themes and different life perspectives for me to consider. The thought came to me that it would be easier to remember these insights at a later time if I could find a simpler form to record them, rather than writing long paragraphs of prose as in a spiritual journal. Previously, I had done a lot of journal writing, but I noticed I had a tendency to not go back and read my journals very often. Therefore, I wanted to devise another way to record my thoughts.

I decided to use the basic circular form of the Native American medicine wheel with its four cardinal points and a center point. I picked four primary concepts of each theme or idea I was exploring during my contemplations and wrote them down in four short phrases or sentences in the location of the four cardinal directions (west, south, east and north).

I named these thematic circles Contemplation Circles. Each Contemplation Circle was focused around a spiritual theme that would help point me to *a Transcendent Reality* and to an expanded vision of living my life with inner freedom. I perceived these circles as spirtual maps of consciousness - or theme targets - or wheels of distinction that empowered and supported my spiritual journey and the restoration of my health. Through these ongoing contemplations, I have received beneficial insights that have served the wellbeing of my body, heart, and mind, and have helped me to expand the way I love and accept myself.

Over many years of working with these Contemplation Circles on a daily basis, I began to see applications for them in various aspects of my spiritual practice. They started to organically have a life of their own. I was inwardly guided regarding how to use them in contemplation practices, affirmative prayer, foundational transformative practices, and to gain ever-larger perspective of my life, including my physical challenges.

In 2007, I experienced a transformational workshop called the Big Mind Process facilitated by Genpo Roshi, a Buddhist teacher and author. I was deeply moved by the ability of this process to bring a person to a direct experience of profound states of transcendence so quickly and effectively. The next morning, I began to create my own Contemplation Circles around my experience of the Big Mind Process. It felt natural to use a set of specific circles in a sequential form in my daily meditations. The result was very powerful. The depth of my meditations took on a new level of sublime communion, and I began to notice a much greater experience of self-love and acceptance of my life.

I used this system of meditation for a year, continuing to receive fulfilling results - and was then guided to put this meditation process into a form that could be shared with others. The first book I wrote is called, **Master of Freedom**. This book was written as a universal creation story that portrays "The Great Story" of the creation of the Universe, the 13.8 billion year process of infinitely intelligent evolution. **Master of Freedom** is the archetypal story of life awakening throughout the Universe - in relation to our current human journey of transformation, the spirituality of humanity. It offers a poetic glimpse of our sacred destiny, which is to live an awakened life of inner freedom - and to learn to love all of life unconditionally.

Then in November of 2008, I was given the inner guidance to take 365 of my 400-plus Contemplation Circles and organize them in such a way as to write a thematic narrative for every day of the year. I started writing these narratives on December 21, 2008, the Winter Solstice. That year, I wrote a 350-word narrative for 365 consecutive days. This daily set of contemplative narratives, accompanied by its adjacent Contemplation Circle, I called **Journey of *The Great Circle***.

I do not call myself a spiritual teacher, nor am I some kind of healer, psychological counselor, or expert of esoteric spiritual studies. I am simply a conscious person who is passionate about living life fully and discovering what really matters, but also a person, like many, who has suffered a great deal during my life adventure. Yet by some form of *grace*, I have embraced the conscious awareness to take responsibility for my healing, and through inner transformative work have gained a greater experience of inner freedom.

Initially, I did not begin this time of deep contemplation in Nature with a pre-conceived idea to write a book. The creative process of these contemplations grew over time on its own, and I feel this book was written through me rather than by me. I was benefiting tremendously from these contemplations and insights, living with greater peace, happiness, joy, and harmony, and my guidance informed me to put them into a book for the benefit of others.

The Daily Practice of Being an Artist of Life

Journey of *The Great Circle* is a daily transformative program to assist people interested in developing larger perspectives of what life is truly about in order to cultivate an ongoing experience of inner freedom and an awareness of loving oneself and others unconditionally. It uses *the evolutionary perspective* to help create an understanding of the "Bigger Picture" of our human reality.

This system of contemplative practices focuses on the daily practice of being an *artist of life* in which a person lives in a state of inner freedom, maintains an ongoing alignment with *Life*, and learns to effectively contribute his or her creative gifts and talents in service to others - and to all of life. In this series of narratives, living in inner freedom is described as an awakened individual (referred to as a **Master of Freedom**) who has discovered how to live life masterfully and who has learned to respond to every experience with gratitude, surrender, and complete acceptance of what is.

The insights from **Journey of *The Great Circle*** assist in understanding that this universal awakening is a part of the intrinsic evolution that's taking place everywhere in the Cosmos. Thus it's taking place on our little blue planet - and is also taking place within you and me. Every person has the potential to be a conscious self-reflective human being becoming aware of the natural unfolding of evolutionary principles within the Universe and throughout the Earth. When we become aware of, and deeply study, *the evolutionary perspective* (the unfolding perspective of the Universe that has been naturally evolving for 13.8 billion years) and we perceive how we are all an integral part of this constant and ever-expanding evolution, we then begin to understand that this *journey of spiritual awakening* is one of the most natural processes unfolding within every human being. It is just one step in the never-ending unfolding journey within a vast Universe of Infinite Awakenings.

The Intention for Journey of *The Great Circle*

This book is designed to assist individuals to respond to life's challenges with harmony and grace, as well as to understand the blessing and obligation it is to contribute one's unique gifts and talents to the creation of a more glorious world. In other words, these narratives are designed to inspire people to cultivate inner freedom and to joyously offer their creative gifts to others as an *artist of life*.

My intention in sharing this book
is that it be helpful
in discovering the magnificence
of who you really are.

My hope
is that the contemplative practices in this work
may aid you
to more easily navigate your life
to a place of peace and inner freedom.

✳ INTRODUCTION – POLISHING THE DIAMOND ✳

Bringing Light to *the Art of Life*

IMAGINE WALKING THROUGH AN ART MUSEUM that displays many exquisite masterpieces of paintings and sculpture. Now visualize that it's late at night when all of the lights are turned off - and every room is completely dark. In this moment you would not be able to see anything in the museum. All of the magnificent works of art would be right in front of you, but without any light to illuminate them, you couldn't enjoy them.

Now imagine that you light a match. The sudden light from the match would allow you to get a glimpse of some of the artistic majesty around you. Yet if you turned on a strong flashlight, it would provide even more illumination for you to enjoy a bigger spectrum of the art collection. And, of course, if the main lights in the museum were suddenly turned on, you would be able to appreciate the total experience of beauty and grace from all the masterpieces around you.

Certainly before the overhead lights were turned on, the art and sculpture were right there close to you the entire time, but were veiled and hidden in the dark. But with the aid of the light, you were able to observe what was always present.

Similar to the lit match, the flashlight, or the main lights in the museum, ever-greater spiritual awareness (ever-larger perspectives of what our life is truly about and what really matters) is like a powerful light that comes into "the mansion of our heart and mind" to illuminate the reality we perceive. More expansive perspectives of reality transform "the darkness of our mind", so we can easily see the truth, goodness, and beauty that is always there. What is always present within us, and what *the Essence of Life* yearns for us to fully experience, is the radiant magnificence of who we really are. We are constantly being invited by *Life* to rediscover our ever-present magnificence - by turning on the light of our conscious awareness.

There is a constant stream of *Transcendent Energy*, a *Field of Unlimited Creativity*, which surrounds us and permeates within us in every moment. This *Boundless and Transcendent Creativity* is who we really are. Yet sometimes "the darkness" of our habitual belief in separation, fear, and other loveless thoughts can inhibit us from seeing our own beauty, our own "magnificent work of art". Every one of us is a living masterpiece that is ever-evolving, a creative work in progress. Our life is the outer creative expression of our inner development. We are continually learning to unveil the exquisite beauty and majesty of who we truly are. Each day we fashion the blank canvas of our life to create the next version of our masterpiece. Every day we're embarked on a journey of learning to artfully live our lives in a way that expresses the natural states of peace, happiness, joy, and harmony. These are the natural states of our *True Eternal Nature*.

Greater spiritual awareness is what naturally nurtures the creative artist within us - or what we can call *the artist of life*. There are many time-tested ways to cultivate *the artist* within us - and to turn on "the light of our spiritual awareness", including meditation, self-inquiry, deep contemplation, and devotional prayer - to name a few. Yet another important way is to fully recognize that in the present moment, our life is always unfolding perfectly just as it is - for life simply is the way it is. This sublime recognition is a radical acceptance of our life.

The Daily Practice of *the Art of Life*

Like being helplessly and powerfully drawn toward some mysterious invisible magnet, we seem to be constantly pulled by unseen forces that attempt to compel us to seek for something other than what we already are. Our modern society, as well as the unconscious people around us, sometimes tell us that we are not OK the way we are, that we are somehow flawed and need to be fixed, that something within us is not right, and that what is wrong in us must be changed into what others believe is right.

The unconscious result of our society's dysfunctional conditioning is that it keeps pulling us away from the creative power of the present moment. This kind of social conditioning persists in attempting to catapult us to some future reality where, at some illusory time, our lives will hopefully be fixed, changed, holy, or enlightened. It falsely promises that we will finally be transformed into what we've been taught by others to believe life should actually look like.

If we habitually succumb to "the mysterious pull of this magnet", this collective illusion propagated within our society, then we typically begin our personal quest to be fixed, or to rid ourselves of our flaws, by first trying to eliminate our suffering. And sometimes from a religious point of view, this illusory quest compels us to attempt the pursuit of spiritual enlightenment - or some kind of spiritual transformation, so we may someday be like the elevated saints and gurus we have learned to venerate.

Of course there is nothing wrong with gaining inspiration from the wealth of great spiritual wayshowers that have come before us, especially if they're pointing us to our own innate power and invincible *True Nature*. Yet seeking to be fixed, as if we were broken, can become the kind of illusory spiritual quest in which we join millions of other people across the globe in seeking something to magically transform our lives, but which in actuality, we already have and already are. *We already are, and have always been, the perfect expression of truth, goodness, and beauty that the Infinite Intelligence of the Universe perfectly unfolds within us through a natural process of universal and personal evolution.* We are all living in a boundless *Field of Unlimited Creativity* which is always present to further our inner development and spiritual evolution.

As we intentionally open our heart so we may explore an even deeper and more meaningful spiritual quest, we begin to feel the inner attraction of an authentic "spiritual magnet", our true *journey of awakening*. This *journey of discovery* is primarily about the full realization of who we really are. This "attraction" is the natural tug of *the Transcendent Impulse* within us. It is the natural impulse to learn that, in the present moment, our life is unfolding perfectly just as it is.

Over time we begin to recognize the perfection unfolding within the creative expressions in every form of life. We are part of that perfection which includes each living creature on our planet and every phenomenal structure within the Universe. This awareness allows us to be truly grateful for everything, to humbly surrender our attachments and resistance, to fully accept ourselves just as we are, and to celebrate the essential Oneness of which we are a part.

This is *Life's* universal invitation to love and accept ourselves completely and unconditionally with all of our individual flaws and personality traits. It's a heightened recognition that the challenging parts of our life are not problems, but rather sacred gifts we can use to "polish the diamond" within us. We use these gifts so we may transform into a more radiant expression of our highest self. We attain this awareness - not by being habitually attached to getting rid of our suffering or our challenges - but by embracing each challenge as "a gift in disguise" offered for our personal and collective transformation. These are life's exquisite opportunities to let our pain or suffering point us to what our life is truly about - and what really matters.

As we arrive at this level of spiritual awareness, we become immune to the societal influences and programming of "the magnet of dysfunctional conditioning". We then experience a transformative shift from living under the unconscious urge of constantly seeking for what we do not have - to celebrating the magnificence of who we already are and joyously living *the art of life*.

Being and *Becoming*

Living our lives in the present moment is where true creativity exists, as well as the genuine experience of unconditional love. Authentically living in present moment awareness, or Presence, allows us to be consciously aware of two fundamental and paradoxical streams of life that are constantly expressing within us: **Being** and **Becoming**.

Being is the absolute reality where everything in our life is unfolding perfectly just as it is. A life that is unfolding perfectly is one that lives in the sacred sanctuary of present moment awareness. With this awareness there's a knowing that because of the perfection in our life, there is nothing to do and nowhere to go, and that nothing needs to be changed, altered or fixed. **Being** is also an awareness of the Oneness within all of life, and in that Perfect Oneness rests the experience of true happiness and peace of mind.

At the same time, living in Presence allows us to experience the paradoxical and complimentary stream of life called **Becoming**. The journey of **Becoming** is the constant natural yearning within us to develop our highest potential, to strive for ever-higher levels of awareness, to expand into new horizons and uncharted territory of unlimited possibilities, and to poetically "reach for the stars". This ongoing personal growth and inner development comes from an intrinsic longing to contribute to the creation of a more glorious world within an awareness of joy and creativity, rather than from an awareness of needing to fix something that is wrong with us - or the unconscious attachment to relieve our suffering.

Cultivating Inner Freedom

There are many beautifully written self-help books, which certainly play an important role in elevating a person's conscious awareness and alleviating suffering. As it has been already stated, **Journey of *The Great Circle*** is not about helping you change the outer circumstances of your lives, fix your emotional or psychological flaws, or get rid of your problems. These writings aim to inspire you to live a life of devoted practice so as to cultivate inner freedom, self-love, and an unconditional love for all of life. Yet with this wealth of self-cultivation, the areas of one's life are constructively affected. This book is also designed to point you to the conscious awareness of your *True Eternal Nature*, the supreme holiness and magnificence of who you really are.

It's pretty obvious that everyone has their own set of difficult opportunities to deal with, and there doesn't appear to be any way to bypass life's many challenges. Some challenges can be very hard to cope with, yet challenge is one of the most natural parts of evolving life. For without the dynamic challenges, chaos, and turbulence within the Universe there would be no galaxies, nor stars, nor planets. Thus there would be no intelligent life on Earth, and there would be no conscious awakening within you and me.

Therefore, with intention, we can choose to use our challenges as sacred gifts in order to become ever more free. We can make use of these opportunities to consciously develop a more awakened awareness, for true healing is learning to maintain a perfect balance within us that supports the evolution of all of life. No matter how much money we have, how great our health may be, how wonderful our marriage or significant relationship is, or how successful our career may be unfolding, we will always be presented with challenging situations that will invite us to expand our ability to experience true inner freedom.

Inner freedom does not come from changing the external conditions of our lives, but is fostered from how we're able to respond to the events and challenges of our life from inside the chamber of our heart. The heart is the integral part of us we must keep open and aligned with *the Source of Life*, so the sublime energy of *Limitless Love* can continuously flow through us unimpeded.

Embodying Inner Freedom

Inner freedom is the unconditional love and acceptance of ourselves and others in which we fully realize that our life is unfolding perfectly just as it is. Since the nature of life is to move through continuous cycles of order and chaos, balance and imbalance, challenges will always be an intrinsic and important part of our ever-evolving life. A masterful ability to love and accept life just the way it is, simply witnessing these experiences without judgment, allows for inner freedom to be embodied within the everyday unfolding of life's constant stream of challenges and treasures.

Just as turning on the main lights in a darkened museum allows us to see all the artistic masterpieces present, as we illuminate the light of our own awareness to the supreme majesty and magnificence of who we are, we re-establish our ability to live in self-mastery. In these writings, a person who realizes and lives with this elevated awareness is referred to as a **Master of Freedom**.

Transformative Practice

This innate yearning to embody inner freedom and joyously express our unique creativity is enhanced by developing a system of personal practice that helps us consciously live our visionary intentions. Through the use of daily transformative practices, we "polish the diamond of our inner being" and use the personal expressions of our creativity to help manifest a more peaceful and compassionate world. Transformative practice is what establishes new belief systems, new world views, new perspectives of life, and new behavior. Practice is what also slowly eliminates destructive habits and dysfunctional patterns in our life.

As we develop a more expanded awareness, "life becomes practice" and "practice becomes life". And both our life and our practice are informed and guided by consciously living in a state of Presence, a state of present moment awareness. From this state, we practice *the art of life*, like a musician practices his or her instrument, or a painter practices his or her craft, to co-create with life in sculpting a more beautiful world. Whether we practice the piano or tennis, compose a symphony, develop a life-enhancing personality trait, or help to relieve hunger on our planet, transformative practice is all about living in the joy of being an *artist of life*. It's about jumping into the natural stream of evolving life that inwardly directs us towards truth, goodness, and beauty - and towards expressions of unconditional love and service to others.

The essence of this book is intended to inspire and provide the mechanisms for the power of daily practice. Each day presents a unique awareness perspective to contemplate regarding the nature of your life. Each day provides an opportunity to expand your awareness of what your life is truly about - and what really matters. It is of great benefit to bring these contemplations out into the glory of Nature - to sit next to a creek - or lie upon the earth at the top of a hill - or lean against a tall tree. As you exercise the "muscles" of your *body, heart, mind, and Spirit* each day with steady determination and commitment, you are assisting *Life* in creatively sculpting its next expression of awakening within you.

Remember that you already are, and have always been, a supremely gifted *artist of life*. There is no one else who can create the exquisite masterpieces which only you can create. So while you enjoy your daily practice as you read and contemplate each day's theme within this book of narratives, you are practicing *the art of life*. And remember that your daily practice is not only for your personal benefit. We are all intimately connected as one global family as we ascend the infinite ladder of awareness. Our daily practice benefits all the men, women, children, and myriad creatures of the world. Practice well.

You Are A Diamond

You are a perfect diamond
    Longing to become more perfect
        A luminescent jewel
            Shimmering upon the necklace of this ephemeral world
           Forged from the supreme fire
                Within the heart of the Universe

You are a multifaceted gem of sublime majesty and grace
    Through which Life focuses its celestial starlight
        So it may glisten endlessly within you

You are a beloved artist of life
    Fashioning unparalleled hues upon the blank canvas of each new day
        To create the next rendering of your magnificent masterpiece

You are an invincible prism of the Soul
    Chiseled into form so the Fullness of the Cosmos can savor
        More of the luminous spectrum of its sensual wonders and hallowed glories

You are an ascending aeronaut spiraling heavenwards
    Climbing the infinite ladder of possibility
        Navigating tumultuous storms and immaculate skies
            Terrestrial chaos and galactic order
                The sacred gifts you use to share the omniscient nature of your truest self

You are a sovereign sculptor of untethered intentions
    Each one polishing the ever-effulgent diamond of your life
        So you may launch new portals of pristine freedom
            For the invisible lines of destiny to dance through you

Your mission - to dance with the Light
    Your purpose - to polish the perfection
        Your meaning of it all - to give for the good of all

It's just what diamonds
    Who spend their life Being
        In the course of Becoming
            Do

All inward realizations of attaining higher stages of consciousness within an individual
eventually take form as outward expressions of transformation or healing
which mirror one's expanded awareness
or elevated level of development,
for the process of healing is one of the natural ways the Universe evolves
into further stages of consciousness - and ever-new realms of glory.

✳ HOW TO BENEFIT FROM THIS BOOK ✳

The Daily Narratives and Contemplation Circles

JOURNEY OF *THE GREAT CIRCLE* has been designed to provide a set of contemplative narratives of various spiritual themes to be used as a daily transformative practice for cultivating peace of mind and inner freedom. Engaging daily in this form of inner development, especially for an entire year, you will be inwardly pointed to the most natural ways to experience greater peace, happiness, joy, and harmony.

Each of the 365 contemplative themes has a narrative displayed on the left page and a corresponding Contemplation Circle on the right. The Contemplation Circle illustrates a short summary of the daily narrative in four concise statements or words. Each Contemplation Circle can be used to quickly reconnect and summarize the primary ideas that have been described in the narrative.

The Contemplation Circles are typically read in the clockwise direction starting with the north node (top quadrant) yet there are often variations of how the Circles can be read. Many have arrows pointing in a specific direction for further contemplation. Generally, the counter-clockwise direction of the Circles represents the evolution of consciousness, and the clockwise direction represents the evolution of creation.

The Four Seasonal Volumes

The complete set of 365 contemplative narratives has been divided into four seasonal volumes. Each has a specific theme for its series of daily practices. The Winter Volume is oriented toward practices for the **cultivation of spiritual wellbeing**; the Spring Volume for **wellbeing of the mind**; the Summer Volume for **wellbeing of the heart**; and the Autumn Volume for **wellbeing of the body**.

Each of the four volumes contains sixteen primary Contemplation Circles that are repeated in all four volumes. The specific Contemplation Circle is the same within each volume, but the narrative is different, allowing you to explore and gain a deeper understanding of the main theme.

How to Use the First Two Seasonal Narratives – December 21st and 22nd

The first two narratives of this volume, December 21st and December 22nd, explore the spiritual meaning and transcendent qualities of the winter season. Both of these narratives have two dates printed at the top of the page. This is because the winter solstice, the first day of winter, will usually occur on one of those two dates depending on the relationship of the Earth's orbit with the Sun for any given year. The title of the first narrative is written as "Gifts of Winter – December 21 or 22" and the second is written as "Qualities Within the Seasons of Life - December 21 or 22".

When the winter solstice takes place on December 21st, read the first two narratives as they are sequentially laid out. When the winter solstice occurs on December 22nd, read the narrative entitled "Qualities Within the Seasons of Life" first on December 21st, and then read "Gifts of Winter" on December 22nd, the actual day of the winter solstice for that year.

Transformative Practices

A primary intention of this book is to encourage the use of daily transformative practice as a means to discover effective ways to embody and anchor the ideas and concepts into the heart as a direct experience. Consistent self-cultivation is the center of spiritual development. Throughout each of the four volumes there are a series of transformative practices that may be incorporated into one's daily life. The prominent focus is based upon four foundational transformative practices. These are:

1) meditation, 2) contemplation, 3) appreciation, and 4) prayer.

It is suggested for the spiritual development of the reader that some form of each of these four practices be experienced frequently. Change usually happens slowly and incrementally through constant repetition on a daily basis. In order to master a sport, an art, a science, or a business, one must practice ardently. It takes this same effort to develop our spiritual nature.

You may be interested in exploring the suggested meditative practices in the narrative from January 14th called "Meditation Practices" in the Winter Volume or explore various meditation practices that you discover elsewhere. You can also explore a specific form of the practice of contemplation in the narrative from April 5th called "A Contemplation Practice" in the Spring Volume. Daily appreciation is seemingly straightforward, yet you may get additional inspiration from the July 6th narrative called "Spheres of Appreciation" in the Summer Volume. And you may deepen your exploration of the power of prayer in the October 8th narrative called "The Practice of Prayer" in the Autumn Volume.

Daily Affirmation Statements

At the top of each contemplative narrative is a short affirmation printed in italics. This affirmation expresses one of the key themes within the daily narrative. For best results, the affirmation can be repeated at various times throughout the day. In the back of the book, all affirmation statements are printed for each day within a given volume. They are designed to be copied onto a piece of 8.5" x 11" paper. You can cut along the dotted lines and then take the individual affirmation with you as a reminder of the theme you are embracing for that specific day.

Visionary Archetypes as Transformative Practice

A visionary archetype is similar to the image of a distant horizon, for it represents qualities and virtues of ever-higher levels of human consciousness that we can envision on our personal horizon, yet desire to embody right now in our life. It is a poetic image of our greater potential or possibility, which we have yet to realize, until we have bravely traveled past boundaries of our current beliefs about who we think we are.

Visionary archetypes are symbolic templates that point us to higher stages of inner development and to the qualities and realms of creative expression we strive to achieve. They can be thought of as pictorial representations of superior moral qualities which can empower and motivate us to reach for something greater in ourselves, a promise of a more positive future for our life.

We can use these archetypes as a spiritual tool and blueprint of potential to assist us in imagining a more perfect expression of ourselves, and to hold within us an expansive vision of what is possible. It is suggested that each person seek their own inner guidance regarding how to use these visionary archetypes as a means to envision and embody the highest possibilities of who they really are.

Throughout each volume there are four sets of visionary archetypes that can be used as a transformative practice to envision and embody one's creative potential and spiritual sovereignty. The four sets are: 1) The Archetypes of Spiritual Awakening, 2) The Archetypes of Life Mastery, 3) The Archetypes of Higher Knowledge, and 4) The Archetypes of Conscious Contribution.

The Archetypes of Life Mastery, the Archetypes of Higher Knowledge, and the Archetypes of Conscious Contribution are all visionary archetypes. The Archetypes of Spiritual Awakening are four archetypes that represent our *spiritual journey*, or *journey of awakening*. The ultimate culmination of our *journey of awakening* is consciously living a life of inner freedom represented by the archetype of the **Master of Freedom**. All of the other visionary archetypes are facets of our unlimited potential, pointing to our sacred destiny as a **Master of Freedom**.

A Tool of Inner Guidance

There are additional ways to benefit from this book other than consecutively reading the daily narratives. You can also utilize this book to find guidance and inspiration by opening any volume to any place within the seasonal narratives, reading that specific narrative, and discovering how the narrative applies to your life at that moment. In this way, **Journey of The Great Circle** becomes "a tool of inner guidance" and can be used when you need a form of spiritual guidance or when you are seeking a moment of inspiration for your day.

The Great Circle as "a Spiritual Map of an Awakening Life"

The Great Circle is a map of consciousness and creation. It is a way to clearly understand the dynamics at play in our world and in our life. **The Great Circle** illustrates how our <u>inner development</u> determines and gives creative shape to how our <u>external reality</u> is expressed in our life. It portrays the universal dynamics relating to <u>our inward expansion of awareness</u> mirrored as <u>our outward creative expression</u>.

The primary function of **The Great Circle** as a transformative tool is to simply portray a useful collection of thoughts and ideas for the purpose of deeply comprehending the nature of existence. With this awareness we develop a greater understanding of what our life is truly about and thus cultivate an unconditional love for each expression of life.

There are many examples of traditional iconic images that represent **The Great Circle**, such as the Yin Yang symbol, the Star of David, the Medicine Wheel, and the Sacred Cross. In this book, the following symbolic image, *"The Great Circle* Portal - a Window Into *Being* and *Becoming"*, is also used to visually illustrate **The Great Circle** as "A Spiritual Map of an Awakening Life".

This image has been placed at each chapter of the contemplative practices to subconsciously assist you in deepening your understanding of the universal dynamics that are at play in the world and in your life. It can also be used to cultivate a comprehension of your purpose in life, your life mission, the meaning of life, and an awareness of your *True Nature*. Here is the significance of the Circle:

First, there is both a vertical line and a horizontal line within the larger circle of the image. The vertical line represents *Being* - or *Infinite Intelligence* - or God *(the Divine Transcendent* aspect of life). The horizontal line represents *Becoming,* our *journey of inner development,* our *spiritual journey.*

Over the vertical line within the large circle there is a Vertical Infinity Sign (a figure eight) that perpetually descends to the bottom of the circle and then ascends to the top repeating continuously. This Vertical Infinity Sign represents the constant yearning of our current physical lifetime (bottom circle) to merge with *the Transcendent, the Source of Life* (top circle) and *the Transcendent* (top circle) that constantly yearns to manifest ever-new expressions of creativity in our current physical lifetime (bottom circle). This natural and constant yearning (which is both the longing for spiritual awakening and spiritual embodiment) exists within us and within all forms of life. It is called *the Transcendent Impulse.*

The Vertical Infinity Sign represents *the Transcendent Impulse* as the top circle merging with the bottom circle - Consciousness merging with Creation - God merging with the Universe - *Divinity* merging with humanity - *Spirit* merging with the body - *Infinite Intelligence* merging with the myriad forms of Nature - *The One* merging with the Many.

The top circle within the Vertical Infinity Sign is a cosmic tunnel, like an inter-dimensional portal or quantum vortex, constantly moving towards the center. The center of this circle represents God, *the Source of All That Is, Universal Consciousness.*

The bottom circle has a Black Centerpoint or Singularity which represents material form, the physical body, or a focused point of creative manifestation.

The thick black line from the center of the top circle to the center of the bottom circle represents the perpetual alignment and Oneness of our current physical incarnation with *the Divine Transcendent (God, Infinite Intelligence, the Source of Life).*

Master of Freedom Logo

This image represents our *Fully Awakened Self,* one's *True Eternal Nature* completely experienced and lived within one's physical body. It is the embodied realization of a person who lives a life of inner freedom, loves all of life unconditionally, and serves the good of all with their creative gifts and talents. It is every person's sacred destiny to embody the *Awakened Self* and fully experience life as a **Master of Freedom.**

Infinite Awakenings Logo

This image represents the perpetual evolution - or the constant "awakenings" - that naturally take place in every aspect of Nature symbolized by the diamond, the flower, the bird, and the human being.

At one time, millions of years ago, there was only a plethora of green vegetation on the planet. The beautiful manifestation of flowers had not yet arrived on the evolutionary scene. But over time and with gradual development, evolving life eventually found a way to empower a brand new emergent form to arise; the very first flower.

For the first flower to take shape on Earth, a radical shift in consciousness was required within the plant kingdom. This new expression of vegetative form could poetically be thought of as an "enlightenment" or "awakening" of the plant kingdom. A similar kind of radical shift in consciousness also occurred in the mineral kingdom with the first diamond - and millions of years later, in the animal kingdom with the first flight of a bird.

The same expansive evolutionary impulses in consciousness are happening right now throughout the world as they continuously have from the beginning of the Universe. Each person on the planet is now, consciously or unconsciously, evolving and developing into his or her destiny as an awakened human.

The Story of Awakening Within the First Narratives

In the conceptual design of **Journey of The Great Circle**, there is a poetic interweaving of themes within the first four contemplative narratives of each volume. Together these four narratives reveal "a hidden archetypal story" regarding every person's *spiritual journey of discovery*.

The first four narratives in the Winter Volume are:
1) Gifts of Winter
2) Qualities Within the Seasons of Life
3) The Great Story of Awakening
4) *Journey of Awakening*

The daily practice of contemplative narratives can easily be accomplished without the understanding of this conceptual design. Yet for those who are interested, the concept of how these four narratives are woven together is described at the end of the book in the section called "The Story of Awakening Within the First Narratives".

Life as Practice

One of the foundational themes within the contemplative narratives of **Journey of The Great Circle** is to experience the spiritual power of daily transformative practice. In order to embody something that we desire in our life, it usually requires dedicated practice and committed perseverance.

When we intend to align our awareness with *the Source of Life*, it also takes practice to embody this alignment as an ongoing experience in every moment. When we intend to be grateful for all that we're learning from every experience of our life, it takes practice. When we intend to live a life of inner freedom, it takes practice. When we intend to love all of life unconditionally, it takes practice.

If a person is committed to the practice of learning to play the piano, in the beginning it requires a lot of focused attention on every detail of how to move the fingers across the keyboard. Yet over time as one implements daily exercises and perseverance, eventually playing the piano becomes natural and effortless. It is as if some invisible *Field of Energy* is playing through the person - as the piano becomes a natural creative extension of his or her body.

The same thing occurs with spiritual practice. For with the daily dedication of placing our attention on the spiritual desires of our heart, we naturally and effortlessly learn how to respond to life's glories and challenges with ease, grace, and conscious responsibility. This is what these 365 daily contemplative narratives are designed to help you manifest in your life. There comes a sacred moment on our journey of discovery when we deeply recognize the authentic joy of practicing each day to be the best version of ourselves. And in that sublime moment, daily transformative practice becomes one of the most fulfilling and meaningful facets of our life.

Therefore practice with all the vibrant joy in your heart so you may walk through this life, gracefully and naturally, as a **Master of Freedom**.

The *spiritual journey* and the *quest for healing*
are like two interwoven vines
growing in "the garden of the gods"
spiraling together,
and weaving their way up the Tree of Life.

DAILY CONTEMPLATION PRACTICES FOR WINTER

1

THE DANCE
OF THE INFINITE
SEASONS

GIFTS OF WINTER

I expand my awareness of my True Nature and of what really matters through self-reflection.

For every person who lives in the northern hemisphere of the Earth,
It is, once again, the first day of winter - *the winter solstice*,
The hallowed celestial moment during the annual seasonal cycle
When the span of night is the longest during the entire year
And the daytime dons its shortest interval of the Sun's light.

It's the time of year when the path of the Sun, as it journeys overhead throughout the day
(From its early rising in the east until its setting upon the western horizon),
Is at its most southern point in the sky.

Today we are at a significant turning point in the perpetual Wheel of Seasons,
For from now until June, the light of day will get progressively longer with each sunrise
And as the solar energy gradually increases, the path of the Sun across the sky
Will begin to slowly return towards its most northern arc in the heavens.

A deeper meaning of this day points us to the birth of a new cycle for our inner development,
For from the symbolic ending of the autumnal period of diminishing light
Now comes a season of renewing our dedication to expand the *Light* within us.

Within all of us there is *a Transcendent Impulse* urging us to constantly develop our potential
And explore the unlimited possibilities for our future with each "turning of the wheel",
For the endless revolving of seasons unleashes inner yearnings to reach higher
And courageously journey to the next horizon of who we want to become.

Winter is a natural time to go within - and expand our awareness of what our life is truly about,
And this is heightened through self-reflection, contemplation, and spiritual inquiry.

It's a period of integrating the significant experiences we've encountered throughout the year
By taking the time for self-examination within the sanctuary of silence
As we attempt to embody what we've learned during past "seasons of our life".

We all have the intrinsic capacity to continually renew and rejuvenate ourselves
By **maintaining an alignment with *the Source of Life* and living with presence**,
And so the winter season symbolically summons us
To consciously re-establish this connection on a daily basis.

The same *Infinitely Creative Impulse* that has fashioned the stars in the Cosmos,
That catapults the planets around the Sun,
And that increases the solar light each day upon the Earth,
Is the same *Creative Impulse* which vibrates through our lives
Constantly inviting us to cultivate the conscious awareness
That every form of life is a unique expression of **One Unity**.

And so we can begin our celebration of this winter season by widening our lens of possibility
Through the simple practice of frequently asking ourselves a few life-defining questions:
Why am I here? - What really matters? - What is my life truly about? - Who am I?

Circle of the Gifts of Winter
(Transcendent Qualities Within the Seasons of Life)

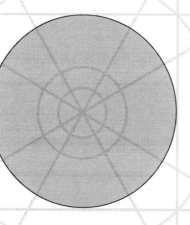

ALIGN WITH
"THE ONE"
A TIME OF SELF-RENEWAL
AND REJUVENATION
IN WHICH I STRENGTHEN
MY COMMITMENT
TO ALIGN EACH DAY WITH
"THE ONE" SOURCE OF LIFE

**CONTRIBUTION
TO ONESELF**
A TIME OF SELF-CARE
AS I ENTER SILENCE
AND SELF-REFLECTION
TO EXPAND MY AWARE-
NESS OF WHAT MY LIFE
IS TRULY ABOUT

ONENESS
A TIME OF DEEPENING
MY CONSCIOUS
AWARENESS THROUGH
CONTEMPLATION THAT
EVERY FORM OF LIFE IS
A UNIQUE EXPRESSION
OF ONE UNITY

**AWAKENED
PRESENCE**
A TIME THAT REMINDS ME
TO CULTIVATE MY ABILITY
TO LIVE MY LIFE
IN PRESENT MOMENT
AWARENESS
WITH EVERYTHING I DO

QUALITIES WITHIN THE SEASONS OF LIFE

Within the silent sanctuary of my heart Life is constantly inviting me to love unconditionally.

The season of winter has come yet again, with its numerous memories and iconic images
  Of gentle falling snow, silhouettes of barren trees, and still frozen landscapes.

And like other **seasons of the year**, winter also has its **characteristic qualities**
  Depicting "its distinctive essence of the season",
    Whereas together they express an expansive vision of a more awakened world
    Where people live from the heart - and cultivate their creative potential.

The history of our various cultural traditions is overflowing with rich symbolic stories,
  Colorful mythological tales that convey the archetypal *hero's journey*,
    And parables about the trials and tests within a person's *journey of discovery*.

Stories of *the hero's journey* have been told in this way since the dawn of humanity,
  And even though they only articulate a partial facet of the full nature of reality,
    They still offer us a vision of what *Life* is constantly inviting us to explore
    And assist us in recognizing the choices we must make
      To further our individual and collective *journey of awakening*.

In order to deepen our understanding of this *journey*
  (This perpetual progression forward along *the ever-unfolding spiral of life)*,
    We can intentionally create new archetypal stories, or modern creation myths.

These kinds of stories have the potential to aid us in making greater sense
  Of the meaning, purpose, and mission of our life.

There's *a Transcendent Impulse* within creation that constantly seeks greater development,
  And this same impulse, "this innate tug" that lies within each self-reflective human,
    Is the inward yearning of *the spiritual journey - the journey of awakening*.

It's *the sacred journey* in which we awaken to a deeper understanding of who we really are
  And discover our personal pathway to inner freedom.

Every person on Earth is embarked on this quest of inward expansion and outward expression,
  Of expanding our awareness of what really matters - and expressing our creative gifts.

The season of winter is a natural time on our journey for self-reflection and renewal,
  A time in which we find new strength and guidance by entering the silence within
    So as to receive further clarity regarding the next cycle that's to unfold in our life.

It's a time of personal integration, when we can learn to assimilate our past experiences
  That we've encountered throughout the seasons of the year by using our new insights
    To develop greater levels of understanding and compassion.

Within this inner sanctuary of silence, within the quiet cave of our heart,
  We can envision the next chapter of this unfolding story longing to be lived through us,
    The Great Story of Awakening which, for each one of us, is our sacred destiny.

Circle of Qualities Within the Seasons of Life

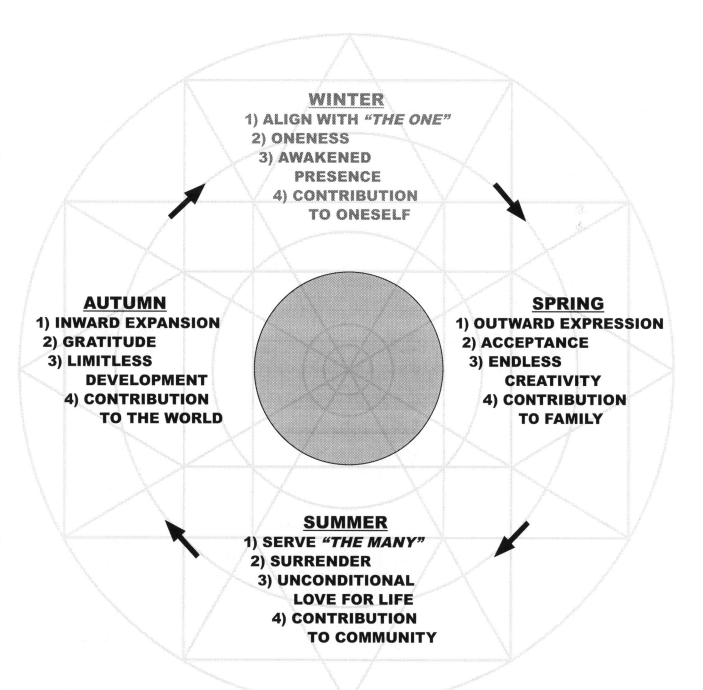

WINTER
1) ALIGN WITH *"THE ONE"*
2) ONENESS
3) AWAKENED
   PRESENCE
4) CONTRIBUTION
   TO ONESELF

AUTUMN
1) INWARD EXPANSION
2) GRATITUDE
3) LIMITLESS
   DEVELOPMENT
4) CONTRIBUTION
   TO THE WORLD

SPRING
1) OUTWARD EXPRESSION
2) ACCEPTANCE
3) ENDLESS
   CREATIVITY
4) CONTRIBUTION
   TO FAMILY

SUMMER
1) SERVE *"THE MANY"*
2) SURRENDER
3) UNCONDITIONAL
   LOVE FOR LIFE
4) CONTRIBUTION
   TO COMMUNITY

THE GREAT STORY OF AWAKENING

My external reality mirrors my internal awareness and reveals to me my path to inner freedom.

If you were to take time to enter the sanctuary of the heart, quiet your mind,
　　And consciously attune to the cycles of the Earth and "the natural pulse of existence",
　　　　You would hear *"the voice of Life"* whisper to you a magnificently simple story
　　　　　About *the journey of awakening* that you and everyone are embarked upon.

Most of the world's religious traditions have their own creation story - or "hero's journey" -
　　Which portrays their unique cultural perspectives regarding this inherent human quest.

The unfolding series of the first four daily contemplative narratives within this book
　　Illustrates an expansive vision of four important facets of our *spiritual journey*
　　　　Which have been shaped into "four chapters" of **The Great Story of Awakening**,
　　　　　And every "chapter" is made up of *four qualities* - one from each season
　　　　　　Pictured in the previous circle "Qualities Within the Seasons of Life".

As you observe *the contemplation circle* on the following page, the upper quadrant of the circle
　　Displays the chapter, or theme, of **The Great Circle** (see Dec. 28th)
　　　　Which affirms that *the journey of awakening* is our transformative quest
　　　　　To expand our awareness of what is true - and to learn to serve others.

The Great Circle is "a spiritual map of an awakening life" that defines our *journey of discovery*
　　As "our internal development that's mirrored in our life as our external reality",
　　　　And this chapter is the starting point for our individual and collective Great Story.

The next chapter, which is located in the right quadrant, (see Jan. 10th)
　　Portrays four **Pillars of Awakening** (powerful attributes for our personal transformation)
　　　　Which depicts qualities to exemplify (gratitude, surrender, acceptance, Oneness)
　　　　　In order to transform our suffering and our habitual thoughts of fear
　　　　　　Into an embodied experience of inner freedom.

As we move to the bottom quadrant,
　　We meet the third chapter that describes our Fully Awakened Self, (see Jan. 21st)
　　　　Our inner development that's reflected in our life as our creative gifts to others
　　　　　As we awaken to living each day in present moment awareness
　　　　　　Which is then expressed within a life of loving care and service,
　　　　　　　And this segment of our story is represented symbolically
　　　　　　　　As the chapter of the **Master of Freedom**.

Next we turn to the left quadrant, the chapter of the **Spheres of Contribution**, (see Jan 28th)
　　Where we investigate a deeper meaning for our life
　　　　As we respond each day to *the Transcendent Impulse* that's constantly inviting us
　　　　　To contribute our creative gifts and talents to the wellbeing of others.

When viewed in its entirety, these "four chapters" convey **The Great Story of Awakening**,
　　Which is a universal and essential story that all of humanity is being invited to embrace
　　　　And fortunately, many are now waking up to its vital message which whispers:
　　　　　"This is the journey of discovery everyone is ultimately destined to take".

Circle of The Great Story of Awakening
(My *Spiritual Journey* In Relation to the Infinite Seasons of Life)

THE GREAT CIRCLE
MY *JOURNEY OF AWAKENING*
IS TO MINDFULLY EXPAND MY
AWARENESS OF WHAT IS TRUE
AND SERVE THE GOOD OF ALL
+ + +
WIN - ALIGN WITH *"THE ONE"*
SPR - OUTWARD EXPRESSION
SUM - SERVE *"THE MANY"*
AUT - INWARD EXPANSION

SPHERES OF CONTRIBUTION
I RESPONSIBLY SUSTAIN
BALANCE REGARDING
MY CONTRIBUTIONS TO:
+ + +
WIN - MYSELF
SPR - FAMILY
SUM - COMMUNITY
AUT - THE WORLD

PILLARS OF AWAKENING
WITH DAILY PRACTICE
I TRANSFORM SUFFERING
INTO INNER FREEDOM
+ + +
WIN - ONENESS
SPR - ACCEPTANCE
SUM - SURRENDER
AUT - GRATITUDE

MASTER OF FREEDOM
ULTIMATELY I DISCOVER
HOW TO MASTER THE KEYS
TO LIVING AN AWAKENED LIFE
+ + +
WIN - AWAKENED PRESENCE
SPR - ENDLESS CREATIVITY
SUM - UNCONDITIONAL LOVE
AUT - INNER DEVELOPMENT

JOURNEY OF AWAKENING

The Infinitely Creative Impulse of Life constantly invites me to learn what my life is truly about.

Everything that humans have ever observed, from "the microscopic" to "the telescopic",
　　Is in a constant natural process of *awakening* to its next stage of creative expression.

Massive stars within our galaxy cycle through the various stages of their cosmic lives,
　　Some generating supernova explosions that produce *(awaken)* elementary particles.

At this moment, innumerable bacteria in every corner of the Earth
　　Are *awakening* novel symbiotic relationships with other more evolved forms of life,
　　　　Exploring how to co-create new interactions which have yet to be manifested.

Human history has revealed that nation states develop over long turbulent intervals of growth
　　As they encounter periods of brutality, war, and oppression,
　　　　Yet, in general, they arrive at a time of greater trust, agreement, and harmony,
　　　　　　And thus *awaken* to new pathways of global cooperation.

Similarly at a smaller level, communities transform themselves over many generations
　　From ethnocentric clans of people who display hateful and dysfunctional behaviors
　　　　To responsible peaceful villages of mature healthy adults.

And the individuals from these various communities are being continuously invited by *Life*
　　To respond to a natural yearning that beckons them to cultivate greater peace of mind.

As we observe this constantly evolving pattern of the Cosmos from a basic human perspective,
　　The inner developmental quest that humanity has been embarked on for millennia
　　　　Can also be seen as *a journey of awakening*.

Over time, this journey becomes conscious and intentional through a process of **development**,
　　Transforming our beliefs, discovering how to **master** a life of inner freedom,
　　　　And **contributing** our creative gifts and talents to the wellbeing of others.

Along the *spiritual journey*, we first learn to expand our awareness of what our life is truly about
　　And what really matters - as well as foster compassion and inclusion of all people.

Our inner development, in turn, helps us transform our fearful habits and loveless beliefs
　　Into more kind and caring ways of living our life.

Eventually with enough practice, enough inner growth - and with the blessings of *grace*,
　　We're able to embody this new awareness (the mastery of inner freedom) in our life.

The natural way to respond to our awakened awareness
　　Is to follow the guiding impulse within that directs us to contribute our gifts to others -
　　　　For this impulse is the same *Infinitely Intelligent Impulse* animating and directing
　　　　　　Every star, bacterium, animal, plant, and person into higher expression.

The Infinitely Creative Impulse of Life is always moving through us on our *journey of discovery*
　　Inviting us to *awaken* to our next glorious stage of ever-unfolding awareness.

Circle of the *Journey of Awakening*
(Key Stages of the Transformative Quest For Inner Freedom)

DEVELOPMENT
FIRST STAGE:
I EXPAND MY AWARENESS
OF WHAT MY LIFE
IS TRULY ABOUT AND
WHAT REALLY MATTERS,
FOSTER MORE INCLUSION
OF OTHERS, AND DEVELOP
MY UNLIMITED POTENTIAL

CONTRIBUTION
FOURTH STAGE:
AS I LIVE A LIFE OF INNER
FREEDOM, I CONTRIBUTE
MY CREATIVE GIFTS
AND TALENTS
TO THE GOOD OF ALL
- AND HELP CO-CREATE
A BETTER WORLD

TRANSFORMATION
SECOND STAGE:
I ENGAGE IN PRACTICES
THAT HELP ME TRANS-
FORM MY BELIEFS WHICH
NO LONGER SERVE *LIFE*
INTO MORE CARING,
COMPASSIONATE, AND
LOVE-CENTERED BELIEFS

MASTERY
THIRD STAGE:
I EMBODY THE MASTERY
OF LIVING A LIFE OF INNER
FREEDOM THROUGH MY
DAILY ALIGNMENT WITH
THE SOURCE OF LIFE AND
COMMITMENT TO TRANS-
FORMATIVE PRACTICE

THE CELEBRATION OF CHRISTMAS

Today I offer prayers of peace and harmony so I may help to strengthen a global field of love.

A few days have passed since *the winter solstice*, the annual birth of the winter season,
And with every consecutive dawning of the Sun, the solar light gradually increases,
While in a similar way, as we cultivate our love-centered awareness each day,
Our *inner light* increases as well - illuminating a path to our inner freedom.

A deeper meaning of Christmas can arise from our experience of this expanding light within us,
For the light of Christmas reminds us to humbly be the best version of ourselves
And its illumination points us to a hallowed recognition of who we really are.

This holy festival is a time for re-telling the biblical account of *the birth of the Christ Child*,
A story about the modest beginnings of a revered spiritual pioneer who dedicated his life
To his *journey of awakening* - and his *full embodiment of loving unconditionally*,
With hope that revisiting this archetypal story once again will inspire us
To renew our own dedication and commitment to spiritual freedom.

Christmas is also a time of year when many people find it easier to shift their attention
From their typical daily activities to a more compassionate awareness of others,
As kind individuals throughout the Earth focus their inner awareness
In ways that collectively help strengthen a vast global field of love.

The celebration of Christmas symbolizes "a time of new birth", or metaphorically,
It's the birth within us of higher consciousness formed by our inner development
That is born into our life from "the divine womb" of *Limitless Love*.

The Christmas season brings its familiar songs of hope that envision a future of possibility
Rekindling a renewed faith that we can collectively build a better global society,
That we can ultimately experience a world of peace, joy, and harmony,
And together as a family, we can help awaken humanity's higher potential.

The fulfillment of this potential manifests itself a bit more with the turning of each yearly cycle
And as every new season of winter regularly spins around *The Great Wheel of Life*
Endlessly unfolding an ever-growing spiral of greater inclusion and cooperation.

Yet in order to intentionally contribute to the advance of evolution along this spiral of progress,
It requires our commitment, responsibility, courage, and our personal choices
To consciously expand our awareness, keep our heart open,
And, each day, actively cultivate a life of care and service to others.

The spiritual journey is depicted by many religious traditions to be essentially simple in nature,
But, as most individuals on this journey have discovered, it's certainly not always easy.

Therefore, **the annual celebration of Christmas is a time for reminding ourselves**
To maintain an alignment with *"the Shining Star within"* all throughout the year
(In other words, with *the Infinite Presence of Love*),
So we might more fully offer to the world, the creative gifts and talents
Which *the Source of Life* is guiding us to share each and every day.

Circle of the Celebration of Christmas

COMPASSION
**A TIME OF YEAR
WHEN MANY PEOPLE
FIND IT EASIER
TO SHIFT THEIR ATTENTION
FROM THEIR TYPICAL
DAILY ACTIVITIES TO
A MORE COMPASSIONATE
AWARENESS OF OTHERS**

A FIELD OF LOVE
**A TIME
OF CO-CREATION WHEN
LOTS OF INDIVIDUALS
FOCUS THEIR INNER
AWARENESS IN WAYS
THAT COLLECTIVELY
STRENGTHEN A VAST
GLOBAL FIELD OF LOVE**

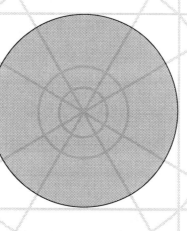

SERVICE
**A TIME THAT IS
AN ANNUAL REMINDER
OF THE COMMITMENT,
RESPONSIBILITY,
AND CHOICE TO EXPAND
MY AWARENESS,
KEEP MY HEART OPEN,
AND SERVE OTHERS**

A NEW BIRTH
**A TIME THAT SYMBOLIZES
A NEW BIRTH WITHIN ME
OF HIGHER CONSCIOUSNESS
FORMED BY MY INNER
DEVELOPMENT - THAT IS
BORN INTO MY LIFE
FROM "THE DIVINE WOMB"
OF *LIMITLESS LOVE***

A NATURAL YEARNING FOR INNER DEVELOPMENT

I feel a natural yearning within constantly inviting me to develop my unique creative potential.

Like the incessant current of an underground river invisibly coursing deep within the Earth,
There is an unseen guiding impulse flowing silently within each of us
Which arouses our desire to expand our awareness and develop our potential.

This natural yearning within us is the same intelligent force
That dwells within, and directs, the core of everything throughout the Universe.

It moves through the most distant galaxies, animates the innumerable stars and planets,
Pulses through each plant and animal, and lives within the heart of every human being.

For each unique expression of life to maintain its perpetual journey of evolving and developing,
It must nourish both its *interior dimension* - as well as its *exterior dimension*.

One vital way that life achieves "an internal form of nourishment" is through ongoing learning,
For the process of constant development is, metaphorically, "the nectar of the gods".

Life is continually in a natural process of "inwardly nurturing itself" by expanding awareness,
Developing its potential, learning new attributes, and seeking higher knowledge.

Over thousands of years, humans have explored three primary areas of development,
Three specific forms of this "nectar of the gods" through **deep investigations**
Of what is *true* - what is *good* - and what is *beautiful*.

Higher knowledge comes from our existential search for what we believe is *true* in our lives,
What we believe is *good* for all people, all creatures, and the planet,
And what we believe, observe. and express as *beauty*.

Humanity has achieved diverse ways to develop, such as **pursuing one's authentic interests**
And becoming a better, more creative person based on learning from one's experiences.

Development also comes from **heightening one's understanding of what life is truly about**
As well as **expanding one's awareness of what really matters**.

All of human culture has advanced due to the novel creativity within individuals,
And so another important means of development is by entering "the silence of the heart"
So we may align our awareness with the *Infinite Creativity* of the Universe
In order to **develop our unlimited creative potential**.

To flourish, life cannot remain stagnant and, thus, it inherently requires constant development
So it can maintain healthy balance - and flow like the endless current of a mighty river.

And since we, as human beings, require continual development to flourish as well,
Learning is a blessed privilege - a sacred gift of becoming the best version of ourselves.

If we intend "to sit at the banquet feast" and reap the perpetual bounty *Life* has to offer us,
We must taste "the nectar of the gods" through the joy of constant development.

Circle of a Natural Yearning for Inner Development

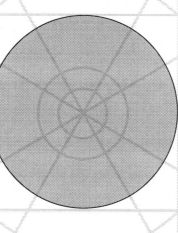

EXPAND AWARENESS
INNER DEVELOPMENT –
**HEIGHTENING MY
UNDERSTANDING OF WHAT
MY LIFE IS TRULY ABOUT
AS WELL AS EXPANDING
MY AWARENESS
OF WHAT REALLY MATTERS**

DEVELOP POTENTIAL
INNER DEVELOPMENT –
**ALIGNING WITH THE
INFINITE CREATIVITY
OF THE UNIVERSE
SO AS TO DEVELOP
MY CREATIVE
POTENTIAL**

DISCOVERY
INNER DEVELOPMENT –
**DEEPLY INVESTIGATING
WHAT I BELIEVE
TO BE *TRUE*, *GOOD*,
AND *BEAUTIFUL*
- MY DISCOVERY
OF HIGHER KNOWLEDGE**

AUTHENTIC INTEREST
INNER DEVELOPMENT –
**PURSUING MY AUTHENTIC
INTERESTS
- AND BECOMING A BETTER,
MORE CREATIVE PERSON
BASED ON LEARNING
FROM MY LIFE EXPERIENCES**

SPIRITUAL JOURNEY

I am on an inner quest to learn to love all people - and all of life - unconditionally.

Motivated people who desire *mastery* in a certain area of their life, such as playing the violin,
    Must usually embark on a journey of self-discipline that leads to their intended goal.

Of course, our life is a constant journey of discovery, personal growth, and inner development,
    And life can be thought of as a *spiritual journey* that leads to "the mastery of life itself",
        Where ultimately we experience sublime peace and true happiness.

Our **spiritual journey** (or what has also been called *"The Way"* in many religious traditions)
    Is our natural yearning - our quest - to live a life of inner freedom
        And represents the goal we seek that takes us to "a spiritual turning point"
        Where we genuinely desire to learn to love all of life more fully.

Sometimes, the process that brings us to this turning point is an experience of suffering,
    Or it may come from the blessing of heightened spiritual awareness,
        And, on occasion, it comes from a surprising and inexplicable gift of *grace*.

Life has its mysterious ways to shake us from the comfort of our everyday guarded thrones
    And direct our lives along a new and different path, leading us toward a higher pursuit.

It requires courage and determination to take our first conscious steps on the spiritual path
    As we satisfy our inherent need to find meaningful answers to life's Big Questions:
        "Why am I here?" - "What is my life truly about?"
        "What really matters?" - "Who am I?"

Asking these life-defining questions can initiate a pioneering adventure
    In which we begin to search for a larger meaning, purpose, and mission for our life,
        And as we take our initial steps toward freedom - **we begin to seek *"The Way"*.**

At first, we may seek the training, guidance, and disciplined practices of spiritual teachers
    Who help direct us on our *journey of awakening* - **we then follow *"The Way"*.**

Over time, we learn to also follow the inner guidance within our own heart
    As we become an example of living in love and serving others - **we live *"The Way"*.**

Then, from expanding our awareness of what is true, we fully embrace who we really are
    And awaken to an exalted experience of loving all people and all of life unconditionally,
        Thus with great perseverance, we ultimately realize - **we are *"The Way"*.**

Like the unfolding life journey of an accomplished concert violinist
    Who hears the violin for the first time and is captivated, one initially attempts to play it,
        Then later, one becomes a dedicated student that's focused on regular practice,
        And, in time, one draws on his or her expertise in order to teach others.

Eventually, there comes a sublime moment for this class of musician when one day,
    As the violinist progresses humbly into mastery, the instrument appears to play itself,
        For now it feels that the violin is being played by "the invisible hands of God".

Circle of the *Spiritual Journey*

AWAKENED ONE
(MASTER)
ULTIMATELY I AWAKEN TO
AN EXALTED EXPERIENCE
OF LOVING ALL PEOPLE
AND ALL OF LIFE
UNCONDITIONALLY
+ ENLIGHTENMENT +
+ + +
I AM "THE WAY"

BEGINNER
(SEEKER)
I INITIATE MY *SPIRITUAL*
JOURNEY BY SEEKING
ANSWERS TO LIFE'S BIG
QUESTIONS, AS WELL AS
A GREATER MEANING
AND PURPOSE OF MY LIFE
+ + +
I SEEK "THE WAY"

TEACHER
(EXEMPLAR)
OVER TIME, I BECOME
AN EXAMPLE OF LIVING
IN LOVE AND SERVING
OTHERS, AS I LEARN TO
FOLLOW THE GUIDANCE
WITHIN MY OWN HEART
+ + +
I LIVE "THE WAY"

STUDENT
(DISCIPLE)
I SEARCH FOR A PATH
OF INNER DISCOVERY
BY FOLLOWING THE
TRAINING, GUIDANCE, AND
DISCIPLINED PRACTICES
OF SPIRITUAL TEACHERS
+ + +
I FOLLOW "THE WAY"

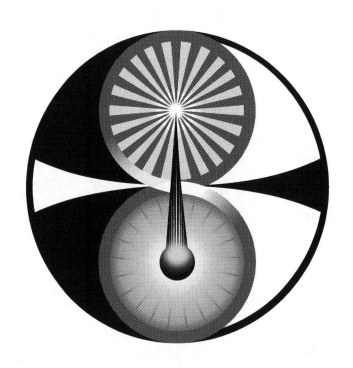

II

THE POETRY
OF
THE GREAT CIRCLE

THE GREAT CIRCLE

As I plant seeds of love in my inner awareness, they sprout forth out into the garden of my life.

Many people in our modern world (especially those with a tireless focus on Cartesian science)
 Have a way of describing reality by first separating things into smaller discrete parts
 And placing these isolated parts into special categories with their distinct labels.

These distinctive labels allow us to communicate with one another using a common language
 Consisting of definitive words that try to depict a certain segment of life as we see it.

Yet if we desire to portray in words "the nature of existence", we can do it more effectively
 When we sustain an awareness that each word we use, and everything it represents,
 Is an individual part of one whole interconnected and integrated system.

For example, in the past, many national leaders have had a tendency to see global problems
 In terms of disconnected political issues, economic issues, energy issues, social issues,
 And, therefore, tried to resolve each problem separately, distinct from the others.

Today many people now understand that in order to fully resolve the world's problems
 They must grasp and manage these challenges from a unified or integrated perspective.

Also in western medicine, doctors, in the past, have approached their attempts to heal people
 By focusing their allopathic practices on a particular and separate part of the body
 That appears to reveal a specific isolated symptom of imbalance.

Yet now, with a more advanced understanding of healing, many physicians see the entire body
 As an interconnected system that works together holistically, so as to yield true healing.

If we want to clearly communicate to others about "the universal dynamics at play in our lives",
 There's a benefit in portraying the individual and distinctive aspects of the dynamics
 As long as we maintain an awareness that all of these separate aspects
 Are, in truth, integral parts of one whole and unified totality of existence.

All of life (which includes every person) has within it an inward impulse that yearns to expand,
 To develop, to learn, and to evolve toward higher stages of consciousness.

The *Infinite Intelligence* within us mirrors our inward expansion as our outward expression
 Transforming our inner development (consciousness) into outer forms of our creativity,
 In other words - into the manifested contributions and gifts that we offer to others.

Four key factors (shown in the circle on the following page) are the dynamics within all of life
 Which are taking place in every galaxy, every star, every planet, every life form,
 And, therefore, are taking place right now within you and me.

A circle is a symbol that can represent the mystery of eternity, or unity without form,
 And like eternity, a circle has no beginning and no end.

Throughout history, the key dynamics of the ever-unfolding *mystery and paradox of existence*
 Have been described by some spiritual teachers and philosophers as **The Great Circle**.

The Great Circle
(A Spiritual Map of an Awakening Life)

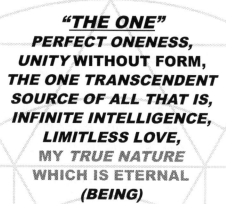

"THE ONE"
PERFECT ONENESS,
UNITY WITHOUT FORM,
THE ONE TRANSCENDENT
SOURCE OF ALL THAT IS,
INFINITE INTELLIGENCE,
LIMITLESS LOVE,
MY *TRUE NATURE*
WHICH IS ETERNAL
(BEING)

**INNER
DEVELOPMENT**
INWARD EXPANSION
OF MY AWARENESS
+
INTERIOR EVOLVING
CONSCIOUSNESS
+
MY SPIRITUAL
AWAKENING
(BECOMING)

**OUTER
TRANSFORMATION**
OUTWARD EXPRESSION
OF MY HEALING
+
EXTERIOR EVOLVING
CREATIVITY
+
MY CONSCIOUS
CONTRIBUTION
(BECOMING)

"THE MANY"
THE PERFECTION WITHIN
EACH FORM OF LIFE,
THE MANY UNIQUE
FORMS WITHIN NATURE,
INCLUDING MY BODY, ALL
UNFOLDING PERFECTLY
IN THE PRESENT MOMENT
(BEING)

THE GREAT CIRCLE OF EXPANSION AND EXPRESSION

As I expand my awareness of what is true, it is expressed in my life as peace and inner freedom.

The myriad types of flowers throughout the world are beautiful and unique innovations of Nature
Each with their own distinctive colors, captivating fragrances, and individual textures.

These floral creations (in which most point their blossoming petals toward the light of the Sun)
Initially emerged into the realm of Nature from the unseen depths of the underground
Where the dynamic force of life burst open their seeds (invisible to our eyes)
And pushed the tiny seedlings out into the light of day (the visible world).

When we try to describe "reality", it must include both an invisible and visible dimension,
Natural yearnings defined as **an inward impulse of expansion** (invisible awareness)
And **an outward impulse of expression** (the visible dimension of reality).

The union and integration of these two transcendent impulses which are constantly active in us
Can be identified as our *journey of awakening* - our **Journey of The Great Circle**,
Where **The Great Circle** illustrates "a spiritual map of an awakening life",
The primary universal dynamics that are at play in the world and in our life.

"The One" is a phrase that has been used to portray *the Infinite Intelligence of the Universe,*
In other words - *Universal Consciousness, the Source of All That Is, Limitless Love,*
And in many religious traditions, this *Natural Intelligence* is simply called God.

"The Many" is a phrase depicting the perfectly unfolding manifestations within all of creation,
Such as every galaxy, star, planet, life form, or particle of matter in the vast Cosmos,
And in relation to the present moment - the perfect unfolding of every person.

All the diverse manifested forms in the world have within them *an inward impulse* to develop,
To learn, to discover, and to reach for more expanded experiences of what is possible.

The inward impulse of expansion (that can also be referred to as *our inner spiritual journey*)
Is the natural yearning in us that seeks ever-greater awareness of what life is truly about
And describes how our consciousness always seeks to spiritually grow,
To expand our awareness, and to develop our potential.

The outward impulse of expression (that can also be defined as *our outer spiritual journey*)
Is the external expression of our life that reflects our inner development and expansion,
In other words - it is our unique creativity mirroring our expanding awareness
Which manifests as our creative gifts, talents, and contributions to others.

The visual image of **The Great Circle** on the following page
Is symbolically portrayed as four distinct dynamics within the four individual quadrants,
But expressed simply, it is the perpetual unfolding of all dynamics simultaneously
As one "Dance of Existence" - and as a Perfect Unity.

The entire evolving world we perceive with our eyes is like "the blossoming of a Great Flower"
That's birthed into the sunlight from the unseen inward depths of consciousness,
"The womb and fertile ground of *the Eternal Garden of Life*".

The Great Circle of Expansion and Expression
(The Universal Dynamics At Play In the World and In My Life)

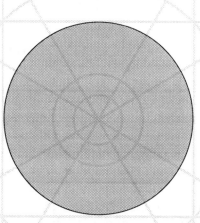

"*THE ONE*"
+ THE ONE SOURCE OF
  ALL THAT IS
+ INFINITE INTELLIGENCE
+ UNIVERSAL
  CONSCIOUSNESS
+ LIMITLESS LOVE
+ INFINITE PRESENCE
+ GOD

INWARD IMPULSE
OF EXPANSION
THE NATURAL YEARNING
WITHIN ME THAT SEEKS
GREATER AWARENESS
OF WHAT IS TRUE
+ CONSCIOUSNESS
SEEKING EVER-GREATER
GROWTH AND EXPANSION

OUTWARD IMPULSE
OF EXPRESSION
MY OUTER EXPRESSIONS
THAT REFLECT
THE INWARD EXPANSION
OF MY AWARENESS
+ MY CREATIVITY
MIRRORS MY EXPANDING
CONSCIOUSNESS

"*THE MANY*"
+ THE MANY FORMS OF
  LIFE WITHIN NATURE
+ THE UNIQUE AND
  PERFECTLY UNFOLDING
  MANIFESTATIONS
  WITHIN THE UNIVERSE
+ IN THIS MOMENT, WHO I
  AM - IS PERFECT

THE GREAT CIRCLE OF THE TAO

Within every new cycle of birth and death there is a perpetual continuity of Absolute Oneness.

Typically during the morning of each new day, we wake up to a dawn of fresh opportunities,
  And then in the later hours of evening, we lay our heads down for a time of renewal.

One complete spin of the planet Earth around its central axis (symbolizing wholeness)
  Can also be viewed as containing two separate aspects of reality,
    Which we commonly refer to as day and night.

Within "one full day" - or "one whole turning of the planetary wheel",
  We experience both the light and the dark of each twenty-four hour cycle.

We can use the above image of both *light* and *dark* existing within a single turn of the Earth
  As a way of understanding that the visual illustration of **The Great Circle**
    Is a symbol representing the fundamental unity of two complimentary dynamics,
      A universal dance of two seemingly separate impulses
        Moving seamlessly together as one harmonious whole.

These two polar impulses that exist within our reality are forever blended together as one,
  The inward impulse of expansion is merged with *the outward impulse of expression*,
    In other words - our **evolving consciousness** (our inner development)
      Is mirrored in our life as our **evolving creativity** (outer transformation).

Over time as our consciousness expands based on our inner development and life experiences
  Our heightened awareness is then mirrored in the world as our new creative expressions
    By the animating power of **"The One" (the Limitless Source of All That Is)**,
      And expressed as **"The Many" (the myriad forms of our creativity)**.

There are many rich spiritual traditions throughout human history
  That have created symbolic images to portray an interpretation of **The Great Circle.**

The ancient and well-known Chinese symbol of the Tao,
  Which merges together the harmonious energies of Yin and Yang, is one of them.

The word "Tao" in traditional Chinese philosophy means "the natural order of the Universe"
  And its iconic Yin - Yang symbol points to *the mystery and paradox of existence*
    Representing two different forces dancing in perfect balance,
      Two universal principles moving in complete harmony,
        Two essential aspects of the vast Cosmos merging as one.

The image of **The Great Circle** of the Tao on the following page
  Illustrates that within all beginnings and endings, within every cycle of birth and death,
    There is a perpetual continuity of Absolute Oneness.

And just as the Earth continues its ongoing spin along its axis
  Which generates both the light of day and the dark of night,
    So too "the Spiral of Life" is constantly turning like a Great Cosmic Wheel
      Generating its dual impulses so as to create its next glorious expression.

The Great Circle of the Tao

**THE SMALL
BLACK CIRCLE
REPRESENTS**
+ + +
"THE ONE"
*THE LIMITLESS SOURCE
OF ALL THAT IS*

**THE ASCENDING
WHITE AREA
REPRESENTS**
+ + +
MY EVOLVING
CONSCIOUSNESS
+ YANG +

**THE DESCENDING
BLACK AREA
REPRESENTS**
+ + +
MY EVOLVING
CREATIVITY
+ YIN +

**THE SMALL
WHITE CIRCLE
REPRESENTS**
+ + +
"THE MANY"
**THE MANY FORMS OF LIFE
UNFOLDING PERFECTLY**

COMPLETION

I let go of what limits me so I can receive the gifts of life that expand my awareness.

We have once again arrived at the last day of the Gregorian calendar year
　　And this common annual cycle has now wound its course to another ending.

For many people throughout the planet, there's a palpable feeling of **completion** in the air,
　　Which brings a sense of fulfillment, and a natural longing to give way to something new.

For most of us, certain beginnings and endings of cycles can be useful reference points
　　In the countless experiences which play throughout our lives,
　　　　For they reveal to us an intrinsic yearning to let go of what limits us
　　　　　　So we can receive the gifts of life that will expand our awareness.

In the last stage of its natural life cycle, a giant star will burn out and collapse upon itself
　　Letting go of the dynamic form it once had in order to produce a luminous supernova,
　　　　An enormous explosion with such power that it sends out elementary particles
　　　　　　Which travel in all directions "seeding the galaxy with new possibilities".

The basic elements born from these massive explosions are "the vast streams of stardust"
　　That are eventually sculpted into every human being and every other life form on Earth.

After a large star explodes, it then changes its outer material form like a cosmic chameleon
　　Reorganizing its stellar core into shapes like a rhythmic pulsar, or a new solar system,
　　　　Transmuting itself into a higher ordered configuration
　　　　　　As if it were "a huge solar caterpillar transforming into a celestial butterfly".

And we humans, on the final day of our lifetime, also change forms through a metamorphosis
　　In which our body's outer physical layer is released,
　　　　Leaving only the more subtle vibrational layers of our *Eternal Self* to carry on.

When we're capable of seeing the beginnings and ends of our biological human cycles
　　With a higher understanding and perspective of what our life is truly about,
　　　　Death becomes an *illusion* - and an experience as natural as breathing,
　　　　　　The silent pause between the in-breath and out-breath of our eternal life.

At this time in humanity's evolution, we're all being invited to release our loveless beliefs,
　　In other words - to let go of any old habitual patterns of fear or separation
　　　　In order to embrace the next higher stage of our ever-expanding awareness.

Some habitual patterns within our being that have been influencing us for a long time,
　　But have now out-lived their usefulness, are yearning to come to an end,
　　　　To die so to speak, so something brand new and more glorious
　　　　　　Can be born within the Universe through you and me for the first time.

Completion is a moment of conclusion in the fullness of time when one thing ends
　　In order to make way for the gift and blessing of something new
　　　　So we can support the continuum of perpetual development and creativity,
　　　　　　And, metaphorically, reach out and touch "another star in the heavens".

<u>Circle of Completion</u>
(In Relation to the Eternity of Life)

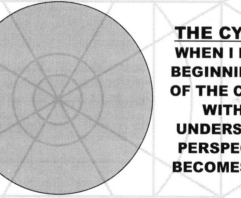

<u>CONTINUUM</u>
**COMPLETION IS
BOTH AN ENDING
AND A BEGINNING POINT
ALONG THE CONTINUUM
OF MY ETERNAL JOURNEY
OF CONSTANT GROWTH
AND DEVELOPMENT**

<u>CONCLUSION</u>
**COMPLETION IS
A MOMENT OF
CONCLUSION WHEN ONE
THING ENDS IN ORDER
TO MAKE WAY FOR
THE GIFT AND BLESSING
OF SOMETHING NEW**

<u>THE CYCLE OF LIFE</u>
**WHEN I PERCEIVE THE
BEGINNINGS AND ENDS
OF THE CYCLES OF LIFE
WITH A HIGHER
UNDERSTANDING AND
PERSPECTIVE, DEATH
BECOMES AN ILLUSION**

<u>CHANGE OF FORM</u>
**COMPLETION IS
THE NATURAL CHANGING
OF FORM AT THE END
OF A CYCLE OF NATURE
FROM ONE CREATIVE
EXPRESSION
TO ANOTHER**

BIRTH OF NEW POSSIBILITIES

Each morning gives me another opportunity to birth new possibilities and miracles in my life.

From the chaos of a turbulent storm comes, in due time, the emergence of still clear air,
From the depth of midnight's darkness comes the inevitable dawning of a new day,
And from the withering vegetation of late autumn
Comes the eventual sprouting of its potent seeds in early spring.

Every ending of a cycle or moment of completion along the many turns within the road of time
Has the potential of rekindling in us a set of new opportunities, a fresh spark of hope,
Which can launch the **birth** of unlimited possibilities and miracles in our life.

Birth can be thought of as a time of fulfillment from which a new beginning results
From the apparent ending or "death" of a previous cycle of life.

Examples of *birth*, or new beginnings, that can be observed within the natural cycles of Earth
(Such as the first light of day, the monthly cycle of the Moon, the origin of a season)
All seem to be outer signals which can motivate us to initiate inner development.

Each time the morning sunlight peeks over the distant horizon,
It offers us another opportunity to experience a new portal to our personal growth.

We self-reflective humans seem to be the only creatures on our planet that we know of
Who can intentionally contemplate upon the state of our inner wellbeing -
And how "a new beginning" or "end" has meaning for some aspect of our lives.

Our ability to do this as a device for learning is heightened by the conscious choices we make,
Especially the daily choice we make to align with *the Infinite Intelligence of Life*
So we may spend more of our time each day in heart-centered awareness.

As we align our awareness with *the Source of Life*, we support the vision of "a new birth in us"
Of a more awake and integrated self
That arises in us based on the level of our conscious awareness.

As we accept and embrace "the dance of change" that constantly permeates our life,
We learn to live in the present moment where **the natural stream of creativity**
Yearns to manifest our unique gifts and talents.

Today is the first day of the calendar year, an arbitrary **birth** in the infinite flow of time,
A moment when there seems to be a shared field of human awareness on our planet
That's collectively focused on beneficent change, progress, and possibility.

At this time, we all have been given an opportunity "to ride this mutual wave of momentum"
So we can further the contribution of our gifts to the ongoing development of humanity.

From the depth of midnight's darkness comes the dawning of a new day -
And from the depth of our heart-centered awareness aligned with *the Source of Life*
Comes a time **to *birth* and express new facets of our unlimited potential**
During this next annual cycle of our perpetual *journey of awakening*.

Circle of the Birth of New Possibilities

NEW BEGINNING
BIRTH –
A TIME OF FULFILLMENT
FROM WHICH A NEW
BEGINNING RESULTS
FROM THE APPARENT
ENDING OR "DEATH"
OF A PREVIOUS CYCLE

INITIATION
BIRTH –
THE INITIATING ENERGY
IN ME THAT EXPRESSES
NEW FACETS
OF MY POTENTIAL ALONG
MY PERPETUAL *JOURNEY*
OF AWAKENING

EMERGENCE
BIRTH – A NEW
EMERGENT EXPRESSION
OF A MORE AWAKE AND
INTEGRATED SELF THAT
ARISES IN ME BASED
ON THE LEVEL OF MY
CONSCIOUS AWARENESS

NEW CREATIVITY
BIRTH –
THE NATURAL STREAM
OF CREATIVITY
ORIGINATING IN ME
THAT YEARNS
TO MANIFEST MY UNIQUE
GIFTS AND TALENTS

NESTED SPHERES OF CONSCIOUSNESS

My consciousness is perpetually expanding along the arc of greater love and service to others.

In the early part of the twentieth century, scientists proved that all matter in the Universe
(Which most people at that time believed to be completely solid and dense)
Actually consists of 99.9999% empty space - with a tiny bit of "stuff" in it.

The tiny 0.0001% of "stuff" is made up of sub-atomic particles traveling at ultra-high speeds
And, in a manner of speaking, these particles are not solid material components either,
For they are the movement of quantum energy "blinking in and out of existence"
And seeming to mysteriously appear and disappear
Into a dimensionless void which has been called *The Unified Field*.

The Unified Field is a limitless field of all possibilities that is formless and unbounded
From which everything in the entire known Universe has emerged,
And many religious traditions speak of this *Field* simply as "God",
Or *the Divine Transcendent*.

The diverse voices of philosophy, spirituality, and science have used the word "consciousness"
In numerous ways to define various *nested facets of existence*,
Utilizing terms like *"Universal Consciousness", "Pure Consciousness"*,
"The consciousness of life", and "human consciousness", to name a few.

The word "nested" refers to *a set of consciousness spheres*, each emerging from a larger one,
Like *a set of Russian nesting dolls* that fit into one another as they get gradually bigger.

We can think of **Universal Consciousness** *(similar to the first and largest nesting doll in a set)*
As *the Infinite Intelligence* within the Cosmos that perpetually guides
The ongoing evolution and expansion of the entire Universe.

Some people then make a further distinction by referring to **the consciousness of life**
As the specific field of intelligent consciousness that shapes all biological life into form,
Which, over time, became self-aware *(the next smaller nesting doll in the set)*.

Human consciousness can be thought of as a specific sub-set of "the consciousness of life"
That intelligently directs the evolution and development of all human beings *(next doll)*.

Though it may serve us to make distinctions so we can converse about each nested aspect,
All **spheres of consciousness** are different emanations of **Universal Consciousness**.

Yet as we remember that the process of evolution in the Universe and in our world is ongoing,
We can trust and expect that there's a natural progression for human consciousness
That will continue evolving to its next stage of evolutionary unfoldment.

Therefore from this perspective, we can imagine that the destiny for all evolving human beings
Is to live **an awakened life** of inner freedom - and learn to love all of life unconditionally.

Many of the world religions and spiritual philosophies refer to our *destiny of spiritual awakening*
As true inner freedom - "the awakened consciousness of realizing who we really are".

Circle of the Nested Spheres of Consciousness

UNIVERSAL
CONSCIOUSNESS
THE INFINITE
INTELLIGENCE
WITHIN THE COSMOS
THAT PERPETUALLY
DIRECTS THE EVOLUTION
AND EXPANSION
OF THE ENTIRE UNIVERSE

CONSCIOUSNESS
OF LIFE
THE SPECIFIC SPHERE
OF CONSCIOUSNESS
THAT CREATIVELY
SHAPES ALL BIOLOGICAL
LIFE INTO DIVERSE
FORMS - IN WHICH SOME
BECAME SELF-AWARE

AWAKENED
CONSCIOUSNESS
THE SPHERE OF
CONSCIOUSNESS THAT
DIRECTS EVERY HUMAN
BEING TOWARD THEIR
DESTINY OF LIVING
AN AWAKENED LIFE
OF INNER FREEDOM

HUMAN
CONSCIOUSNESS
THE SPECIFIC SPHERE
OF CONSCIOUSNESS FOR
ALL SELF-REFLECTIVE
HUMAN BEINGS THAT
DIRECTS THE EVOLUTION
AND DEVELOPMENT
OF EVERY PERSON

THE THREE FACES OF GOD

I experience God as "The Transcendent" or "The Beloved" or "The Creation" - or all at once.

The chemical substance of water is a unique and essential component of the Earth,
    For without it, there couldn't have been *the creation of life* (at least not as we know it).

Water has a novel quality - for at specific low, medium, and high temperatures,
    It will exhibit one of three individual characteristics
        That take form as either 1) solid ice, 2) fluid liquid, or 3) gaseous steam.

In each of these three manifestations of water, it's still the same fundamental substance,
    But it is momentarily expressed in a completely different physical form.

Many spiritual explorers and religious mystics have reported
    Of their interior experiences of the divine in three distinct ways, or "three faces of God".

When the belief in a vast divine power first arose, **God was experienced as "The Creation"**,
    For early humans initially perceived divinity within the many forms of the natural world,
        Such as the Sun, Moon, or mountain, as they paid homage to *a Greater Power*,
            A supreme power they believed created everything on Earth.

Over time, as humans learned to develop intimate relationships, **God became "The Beloved"**
    Which was experienced as a direct and personal relationship with *a Supernatural Deity*
        With whom a deep intimate devotion and alignment could be cultivated.

Eventually, numerous sages, saints, and others began to have profound mystical experiences
    Of **God as "The Transcendent"** *(the Unbounded Ocean of Being)*
        In which God was directly experienced as a *Transcendent Oneness*,
            A realization of *Limitless Consciousness*,
                A sublime awareness of *Infinite Presence* or *Perfect Wholeness*.

So as to deepen our awareness, **the three faces of God** can be related to the forms of water
    Which, as has been stated, is one substance that can manifest in three distinct ways.

"The Transcendent" face of God (or *Limitless Consciousness*)
    Is analogous to an invisible ethereal steam that seems to permeate everything,
        God as "The Beloved" (or *a Supernatural Deity* one shares a relationship with)
            Can be thought of as the flow of warm fluid water,
                And God as "The Creation" (or *the Intelligence* of the Web of Life)
                    Can be represented by the solid stable crystals of frozen ice.

Everyday we typically experience these three individual forms of water in various ways,
    For example, as the solid ice in our refrigerators,
        The fluid water that flows out of our kitchen facets,
            And the gaseous steam that rises from our boiling teakettles.

Could it be that everyday we, also, have the opportunity to experience "the three faces of God"
    As **the mysterious merging and mystical integration**
        Of "The Transcendent", "The Beloved", and "The Creation"?

Circle of the Three Faces of God
(God May Be Experienced as 1ˢᵗ, 2ⁿᵈ, and 3ʳᵈ Person Perspectives)

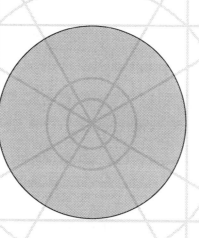

"THE MYSTERY"
(INTEGRATION)
GOD IS EXPERIENCED
AS THE MERGING OF
THREE DIVINE ASPECTS:
"THE TRANSCENDENT",
"THE BELOVED",
AND "THE CREATION"

"THE TRANSCENDENT"
(1ˢᵀ PERSON)
GOD IS EXPERIENCED
AS *TRANSCENDENT
ONENESS, PERFECT
WHOLENESS, LIMITLESS
CONSCIOUSNESS, BEING*

"THE CREATION"
(3ᴿᴰ PERSON)
GOD IS EXPERIENCED
AS *THE CREATIVE
INTELLIGENCE* THAT
MANIFESTS THE WEB OF
LIFE, THE PERPETUALLY
EVOLVING UNIVERSE

"THE BELOVED"
(2ⁿᴰ PERSON)
GOD IS EXPERIENCED
AS *A SUPREME DEITY*
WHOM I CAN CULTIVATE
A DIRECT AND PERSONAL
RELATIONSHIP WITH
- AND BE DEVOTED TO

GOD AS "THE MYSTERY"

I revel in the Mystery of the Universe so I may deepen the meaning and purpose of my life.

For over five centuries, there has been a wealth of discoveries within the fields of science
In which precise experimentation has led humanity to a vast spectrum of knowledge
About the intricate workings of the natural world and the Universe.

Yet it seems there will always be an endless *mystery* regarding what we still don't know
And, thus, scientists are driven to constantly explore the apparently limitless unknown.

In many of the creative arts, such as painting and writing,
The natural flow of creativity can lead an artist on a surprising adventure of *mystery*
As some artists marvel at how their creative expressions inexplicably unfold.

There are painters who artistically use their canvases as spontaneous journeys of possibility,
And literary writers who start their fictional manuscripts with an initial outline or concept
But have no idea where their characters will actually lead them within the story.

And those who sincerely study philosophy from "a Big Picture perspective of life"
Observe its premises and theories have been constantly progressing throughout history
Recognizing the future of its notions is a perpetual *mystery* to be revealed.

Yet within mysticism and spirituality, **God is probably the greatest *mystery* of all**,
Because from the dawn of time, God has been the Eternal Riddle, the Cosmic Enigma,
Which has puzzled humans since the nature of reality was first questioned.

Contemporary spiritual investigations into this ongoing pursuit
Of understanding the transcendent conundrum we call "God"
Have given us numerous revelations about God's mysterious *divine paradox*.

For example, some theologians have described God as the **integration** of a *Limitless Source*
That is sublimely one with all of the ever-evolving forms of the natural world,
Yet no matter how eloquently writers try to illuminate this paradox through words,
This mystical integration is still, and always has been, a *mystery*.

In relation to our common understanding of language using 1st, 2nd, and 3rd person vantages,
God can be experienced and expressed in **three distinct and unique perspectives**:
"The Transcendent", "The Beloved", and "The Creation",
And yet this hallowed merging of all three as one trinity is still a *mystery*.

God can also be seen as **the complete union of all seemingly separate material dualities**,
And yet this Ultimate Unity, this Oneness with All That Is, is nonetheless a *mystery*.

It can be transforming to embrace the notion that *mystery* is an essential part of our daily life,
For when we learn to accept that *mystery* and *paradox* are natural parts of who we are,
We open our hearts to greater possibilities of experiencing *miracles* in our life.

One of the *"miracles"*, or *"gifts"*, that humbly embracing the *Mystery* of the Universe leads us to
Is becoming ever more aware of the true meaning and purpose of our life.

Circle of God as "The Mystery"

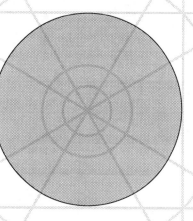

THE UNITY OF ALL DUALITIES
GOD, THE ULTIMATE UNITY OF ALL THAT IS, CAN BE KNOWN AS THE COMPLETE UNION OF ALL SEEMINGLY SEPARATE MATERIAL DUALITIES

TOTALITY
GOD CAN BE KNOWN AS THE TOTALITY OF ALL DIMENSIONS AND ALL VISIBLE AND INVISIBLE PHENOMENA WITHIN THE UNIVERSE

PERSPECTIVES
GOD CAN BE KNOWN AS THE MERGING OF 1ST, 2ND AND 3RD PERSON PERSPECTIVES: "THE TRANSCENDENT", "THE BELOVED", AND "THE CREATION"

INTEGRATION
GOD CAN BE KNOWN AS THE INTEGRATION OF A *LIMITLESS SOURCE* THAT IS SUBLIMELY ONE WITH ALL OF THE EVOLVING FORMS OF THE NATURAL WORLD

III

SPIRIT
AWARENESS
PRACTICES

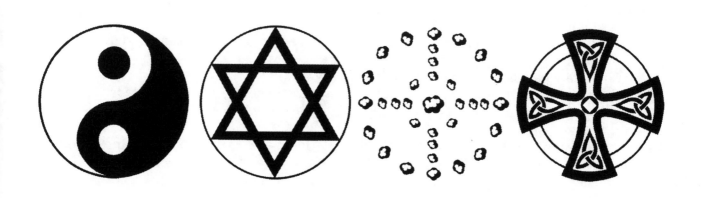

FOUNDATIONAL TRANSFORMATIVE PRACTICES

I use transformative practices to consciously transform the quality of my inner experience.

If you were to observe the continual swinging of a metal pendulum over a period of time
　　As it cycles back and forth inside a large grandfather clock,
　　　　You might become aware of the natural force that's attempting
　　　　　　To slow down the pendulum and return it to its stationary center point.

A pendulum oscillating within a clock is constantly seeking to reach a still point of no motion
　　And naturally tries to rest in a place of balance that resides at the middle of the swing.

Similarly, every one of Nature's vast creations has been formed by a *Natural Intelligence*
　　Which is always intending to bring any imbalanced experience back to "homeostasis"
　　　　(A word that describes a state of equilibrium and harmony with its environment).

For thousands of years, spiritual pioneers have explored the inner realms of consciousness,
　　And some have used their experiences to develop various transformative practices
　　　　Designed to assist others in maintaining high levels of peace and wellbeing.

These pioneers developed a number of "spiritual maps" with specific practices
　　That were aimed at helping other mystic journeyers cut through "the thick jungle of life"
　　　　And experience for themselves, a more peaceful "path through the maze".

Because of their insightful work, each of us can now find an easier shortcut to our destination
　　Which has been etched onto some contemporary "map of consciousness"
　　　　By a spiritual traveler who has previously investigated the territory.

One path on such a map is the simple, yet powerful practice of **appreciation** -
　　For being thankful that our life, in this moment, is unfolding perfectly just as it is
　　　　And being grateful for who we are, helps us cultivate a life of inner freedom.

Of course, one of the primary ways to consciously develop a "path of appreciation"
　　Is to keep our mind, our heart, and our eyes open
　　　　So we remain mindful to celebrate the everyday blessings that are all around us.

Another important path is the heartfelt practice of **prayer**
　　Which, in one particular form, is asking *Life* how we are to serve, and contribute to,
　　　　The wellbeing of others - and then courageously act on what we receive.

The practice of **contemplation** (reflecting on "the Big Questions" of what our life is truly about)
　　Is a method to foster a greater awareness of what is true - and what really matters
　　　　By using life-defining questions to access a wealth of higher insight.

And the key practice of **meditation** is a transformative vehicle
　　For entering the sublime field of inner silence so as to still our mind,
　　　　Consciously align our awareness with *Life,* and awaken to our *Eternal Nature.*

These **four foundational practices** serve as an invaluable "explorative map" for life's journey
　　And provide great support for guiding "the inner pendulum of our life to its center point".

Circle of Foundational Transformative Practices
(Primary Ways to Cultivate and Maintain Inner Freedom)

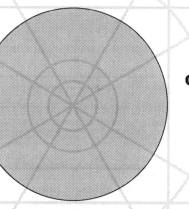

MEDITATION
THE PRACTICE
OF EXPERIENCING INNER
SILENCE SO AS TO STILL
MY MIND, ALIGN MY AWARE-
NESS WITH *THE SOURCE
OF LIFE,* AND AWAKEN
TO MY *ETERNAL NATURE*

PRAYER
THE PRACTICE
OF ASKING *LIFE*
HOW I AM TO SERVE,
AND CONTRIBUTE TO,
THE WELLBEING OF
OTHERS - AND ACTING
ON WHAT I RECEIVE

CONTEMPLATION
THE PRACTICE OF
CONSCIOUSLY EXPAND-
ING MY AWARENESS
BY REFLECTING ON
"THE BIG QUESTIONS"
REGARDING WHAT MY
LIFE IS TRULY ABOUT

APPRECIATION
THE PRACTICE OF BEING
THANKFUL FOR THE GIFTS
I RECEIVE EACH DAY,
BEING GRATEFUL MY LIFE
IS UNFOLDING PERFECTLY,
AND FULLY APPRECIATING
MYSELF FOR WHO I AM

GIFTS OF MEDITATION

The practice of meditation naturally leads me to the sublime realization of my Eternal Nature.

After learning to master the skill of crawling, a young child has an instinctual impulse
    To rise up on its two legs so that, while remaining in a standing position,
        The child can begin walking on its feet and move across the floor.

Time and time again, the child will fall attempting to conquer this new undertaking,
    Yet through sheer desire and determination, it will get up and try another time
        Getting more capable with each experience of *practice*.

Eventually the child progresses, becomes successful at this task,
    And learns to walk so proficiently, it becomes second nature to stroll down the street.

When we desire to initiate, or further develop, a particular skill
    (Such as learning a foreign language, expanding our abilities at the game of tennis,
        Or playing a musical instrument like a guitar),
            We must typically, to be successful, engage in a discipline of *practice*.

Practice is an important key to attaining our goals, for it's in our active participation with life
    And our commitment to developing ourselves through our mindful discipline
        By which we consciously advance our cultivation of individual skills.

If we intend to learn something that's "a bit more abstract",
    Such as how to awaken our consciousness to the truth of who we really are,
        Then *a system of practice* can also help point us in the direction of our intention.

Meditation is one of the time-tested transformative practices that helps us still our mind,
    Aids our inner development, points us to our *True Transcendent Nature*,
        And assists us to travel into silence beyond our thoughts
            So as to **align our awareness with *the Source of Life*.**

The practice of meditation has been used for centuries to provide many beneficial gifts,
    Such as **rejuvenate, relax, and relieve stress from the body, heart, and mind**.

It also **assists us in experiencing glimpses of expanded awareness**
    So we can access creative insights, intuition, and inner guidance.

Another gift of meditation is the ability to use this *practice*
    To help consciously **train ourselves to be mindful**
        So we can more easily keep our focused attention on our intended desire.

The only thing that's required by us to receive these various **gifts of meditation**
    Is to take the time, and expend the effort, of daily *practice*.

Meditation is a tool we use to naturally lead us to the sublime realization of our *Eternal Nature,*
    And with enough *practice* and commitment over time,
        Meditating eventually becomes "our every moment experience of living"
            And becomes as second nature as breathing - or walking down the street.

Circle of the Gifts of Meditation
(A Transformative Practice)

ALIGNMENT
MEDITATION
HELPS ME STILL MY MIND
SO I MAY ALIGN
MY AWARENESS WITH
MY *TRUE TRANSCENDENT*
NATURE,
THE SOURCE OF LIFE

REJUVENATION
MEDITATION
HELPS ME
REJUVENATE,
RELAX, AND RELIEVE
STRESS FROM
MY BODY, MY HEART,
AND MY MIND

MINDFULNESS
MEDITATION
HELPS ME TRAIN
MYSELF TO BE MINDFUL
SO I MAY MORE EASILY
KEEP MY FOCUSED
ATTENTION ON
MY INTENDED DESIRE

INTUITION
MEDITATION
HELPS ME EXPERIENCE
GLIMPSES OF EXPANDED
AWARENESS SO I MAY
ACCESS CREATIVE
INSIGHTS, INTUITION,
AND INNER GUIDANCE

SILENCE

I frequently renew and rejuvenate myself by spending time within the nurturing home of silence.

During the hush of winter, many of the tree branches within the woods
Are barren of the bright colorful leaves from autumn's cloak,
And the small grasses that cover the forest floor are brown and cracked.

At this time, scores of animals are hibernating in their dens
And the world seems as if, for a short span, it has halted its progression forward.

The season of winter is a phase within the annual cycle
When much of Nature's outer activity slows to an apparent standstill,
And life naturally turns inward in order to seek a period of rejuvenation.

The inherent impulse of winter's longing is fundamentally about reconnecting with *Being*,
In other words - realigning our awareness with the true essence of life
And rediscovering the freshness of renewal within the nurturing home of **silence**.

Yet many people in our, seemingly, fragmented modern culture have lost the understanding
Of how to sustain a vital alignment with *the Intelligence* of Nature
And to inwardly renew and nourish themselves in this way.

It's obvious that a significant portion of our conscious awareness each day
Is focused on our external world of activity and outward-directed creative expressions,
Yet another crucial factor of our awareness relates to our vast internal reality,
The experience of our inner world, which is critical to our wellbeing.

This interior factor also requires its own form of "nourishment" to keep us properly balanced,
For our internal awareness yearns to develop, "to drink from the chalice of renewal",
And to feast from the silence that's always present at *"the banquet table of Life"*,
Which can also be called the invisible wellspring of our unlimited creativity.

**Silence is experienced when we align our personal awareness with *Pure Awareness*,
The Infinite Presence of Love, in a sacred moment of stillness**.

From time to time, we may experience **a sublime moment of this ever-present silence
When our mind suddenly stops for a brief instant while letting go of all thoughts,
Such as during the surprise of beatific awe - or startling humor**.

Furthermore we undergo **periods of rejuvenating silence every night when we sleep
From the experience of deep rest as our mind releases conscious awareness**.

**And silence can also be known when our mind has surrendered all of its attention
Within the present moment, where there is no linear time**.

The familiar images of winter, the barren trees, hibernating animals, and brown grasses,
All have the potential to remind us of our own intrinsic ability to turn inward
And align ourselves to the natural cycles that perpetually point us
To the sublime field of silence - "the creative womb of our inner reality".

Circle of Silence
(The Creative Womb of My Inner Reality)

STILLNESS
I EXPERIENCE SILENCE
WHEN I ALIGN
MY PERSONAL AWARENESS
WITH *PURE AWARENESS,*
THE INFINITE PRESENCE
OF LOVE, IN A SACRED
MOMENT OF STILLNESS

SUBLIME MOMENTS
I EXPERIENCE SILENCE
WHEN MY MIND
STOPS FOR A SUBLIME
MOMENT DURING
A SURPRISE ENCOUNTER
OF BEATIFIC AWE
OR STARTLING HUMOR

PRESENCE
I EXPERIENCE SILENCE
WHEN MY MIND
HAS SURRENDERED
ALL OF ITS ATTENTION
WITHIN THE PRESENT
MOMENT, WHERE THERE
IS NO LINEAR TIME

DEEP SLEEP
I EXPERIENCE SILENCE
EVERY NIGHT
WHEN I ENCOUNTER
A STATE OF DEEP SLEEP
AS MY MIND
NATURALLY RELEASES
CONSCIOUS AWARENESS

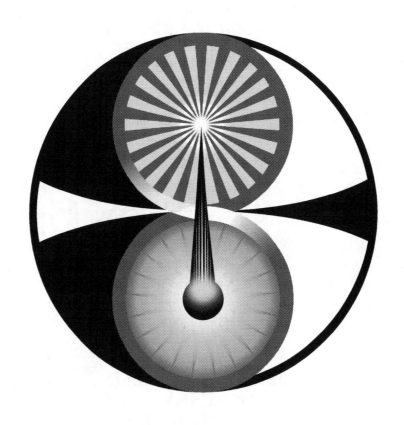

IV

THE SONG
OF EMBODIED
LOVE

THE NATURAL STATES THAT EMERGE FROM *BEING*

As I sustain an alignment with the Source of Life peace and joy naturally arise in my awareness.

When the steady current of a large river is prevented from flowing freely
    Because of the high retaining walls of a newly-constructed dam,
        Then the waters of the river cannot flow naturally
            And the vegetation downriver along its former banks will wither away.

Movement is an essential requirement for all organisms to continue living in a healthy way,
    And for the expressions of any form of life to maintain balance, it must circulate energy.

Yet at a future time, should the gates of the dam be opened - or the dam removed,
    The water from the river that has been "caged up" will be free to rush downstream
    And the original riverbanks will quickly regain their natural growth and vitality.

With the water moving once again, the river can glide around boulders and rocks
    Finding the easiest route to travel its *path of least effort*.

Each of us is also like "a river of energy" that seeks to remove any barriers to freedom
    And find *the natural path of least effort* that can help us maintain radiant wellbeing.

Every day we are invited by *Life* to be mindful to keep "our inner river of energy flowing"
    So the natural qualities of conscious living can effortlessly arise in our awareness.

When we intentionally sustain an alignment with *the Source of Life*,
    This sacred attunement enables **peace** to flow easily and effortlessly
        Through "the canyons of our hearts" as its most natural and intrinsic state.

Peace is what we spontaneously experience within our life
    When we have cultivated an awareness of *Limitless Love* and *Unbounded Eternity*.

As we learn to be aware of our Oneness with every person in our life - with all living creatures,
    This awareness enables us to unblock the self-made dams of fear, control, or approval,
        And to free us of any self-created stress or past trauma,
            Which then yields to the rising up of a natural state of **happiness**
        That streams unimpeded through our life.

Furthermore, when we develop a conscious awareness of *Absolute Perfection*
    And learn to fully experience that our life is unfolding perfectly in every moment,
        Joy naturally pours into the center of our being,
            For there is nothing constrictive in our consciousness to hold it back.

And as we discover how to support a healthy circulation of *Life Force energy* within us
    By nurturing our body with vital nutrients, exercise, and rejuvenative rest
        (While attentively listening and responding to the changing needs of our body),
        Greater **harmony** is felt in every chamber of our physical temple.

There is "a river of *Radiant Universal Energy*", "a living stream of *Vital Life Force*",
    That constantly yearns to flow through us as a natural state of *Embodied Love*.

Circle of the Natural States That Emerge From *Being*

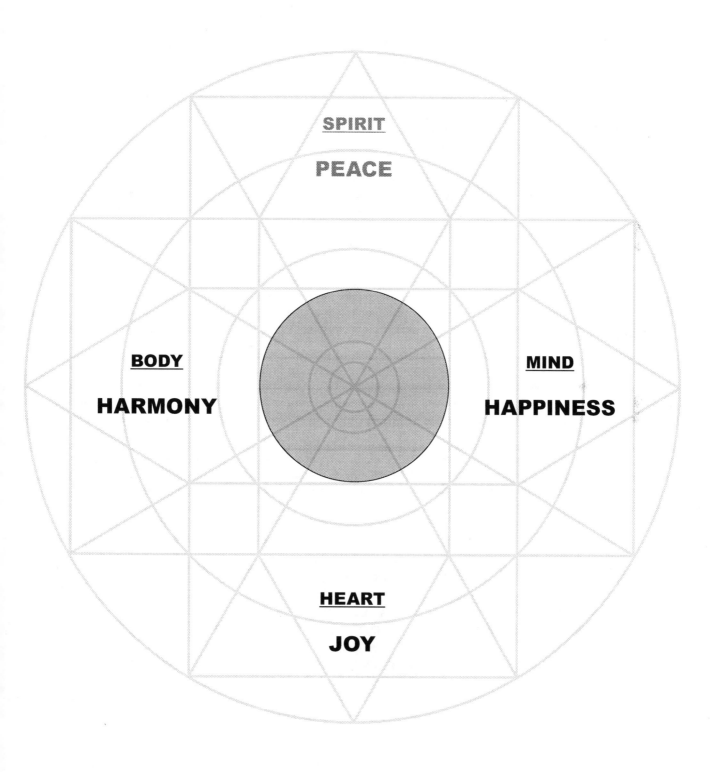

SPIRIT

PEACE

BODY

HARMONY

MIND

HAPPINESS

HEART

JOY

THE NATURAL STATE OF PEACE

Today I choose to live my life as a living expression of peace.

When you look at a photo of the Earth suspended against a starry background
    That was photographed by an astronaut while orbiting in space,
        The image of the planet seems to be shrouded in an air of peace and tranquility.

Within this iconic picture, everything on Earth appears to be in its right and proper place,
    For from this lofty altitude, there are absolutely no disturbances one can observe
        And thus from this grand perspective, all in the world
            Has the appearance of being in harmony and perfect balance.

In a similar way, there is a sanctuary of inner peace we can always access
    When we're able to perceive our personal lives from a big enough vantage point -
        But what exactly is, and how do we consciously embrace, this larger perspective?

If an astronaut in space returns to Earth and observes the actions of the world's governments,
    He or she would obviously be aware that there's still much conflict in certain countries,
        Yet most people who inhabit these nations proclaim they want to live in peace.

If the same astronaut then observed life of Earth from the perspective of some ethnic societies,
    He or she would see there's still much violence playing out in many areas of our planet,
        Yet the majority of citizens within these societies affirm they long to live in peace.

If this person then observed life from the vantage of a family dealing with very difficult problems,
    He or she would witness there's still much dysfunction acting out in certain communities,
        Yet most families declare, deep in their hearts, that they yearn to live in peace.

And surely from the personal perspective of so many individuals who are suffering in the world,
    There's still much ignorance and lack of awareness being experienced every day,
        Yet there are more people than ever before - who are now "waking up to peace".

Today, more of us are consciously choosing to live our lives from "the Big Picture perspective"
    In a manner celebrated by the Eastern sage Mahatma Gandhi when he reminded us,
        "We must be the change we wish to see in the world",
            In other words - we must each choose to be a living expression of peace.

We can all be engaged in finding better ways to peacefully live together on this planet
    And learn to embrace a larger understanding of what really matters,
        Which includes a deep compassion and respect for others
            So that our everyday lives can embody the change in perception needed
                To build a more peaceful and sustainable world.

Peace will naturally arise in our awareness when we hold **gratitude** within our heart each day,
    And when we **surrender** and harmonize with all that unfolds with absolute **acceptance**.

Could it be that in order to experience this **natural state of peace**, or "Big Picture perspective",
    We must look upon our world from "an inner space within the sanctuary of our heart"
        And from a larger vantage where we truly recognize - we are **one** with all of life?

Circle of the Natural State of Peace

ONENESS
PEACE –
THE NATURAL STATE
OF AWARENESS I FEEL
WHEN I EXPERIENCE
ONENESS WITH OTHERS
- AS WELL AS WITH EVERY
EXPRESSION OF LIFE

GRATITUDE
PEACE –
MY EXPERIENCE
WHEN I CONSCIOUSLY
LIVE IN GRATITUDE
FOR WHAT I'M LEARNING
FROM EVERYTHING
IN MY LIFE

ACCEPTANCE
PEACE –
MY EXPERIENCE
WHEN I ABSOLUTELY
ACCEPT THAT EVERY
SITUATION IN MY LIFE IS
UNFOLDING PERFECTLY
JUST AS IT IS

SURRENDER
PEACE –
MY EXPERIENCE
WHEN I LET GO
OF MY ATTACHMENTS
TO MY DESIRES
AND COMPLETELY
SURRENDER TO *LIFE*

PILLARS OF AWAKENING

I am aware of my Oneness with all of life.

One way of thinking about *spiritual awakening* is - "it's the natural evolutionary journey
    Of ongoing inner development that every person in the world is constantly embarked on"
        (Whether he or she is consciously aware of it or not).

Our *journey of awakening* can also be thought of as "a magnet from the future"
    Mysteriously pulling each of us towards it.

For *spiritual awakening* is every person's destiny - and arises from shifting one's awareness
    From the imprisoning bondage of the habitual drives of the ego
        (Which are focused around self-centered power, control, and fear)
            To the freedom and liberation of aligning with *the Source of Life*
            And serving the wellbeing of others.

So to support our awakening - *Life* may offer some experiences that shake us to our very core
    And "lead us to a sacred place" of intense breakdown - and profound breakthrough,
        A place where our heart opens to new possibility and greater awareness.

It's then, through *grace*, that *Life* presents to us the gift of a personal vision of hope,
    A glimpse of how it would feel for us to live in inner freedom (a life of spiritual mastery).

At times throughout our life, there are exalted moments of spiritual epiphany
    When we are blessed to receive such an expansive vision,
        A brief look at how it would feel to live in **a state of gratitude**
            For what we're learning from every experience we encounter.

Every so often, there are times when our heart suddenly bursts open
    And gets a sense of how it would feel to live each day
        Surrendering everything in our life to *the Infinite Presence of Love*,
            Discovering the most natural ways to flow with the changes of life
            And letting go of our attachments to our desires.

There are those moments when we experience an intuitive insight of how it would feel
    To **fully accept that our life is unfolding perfectly just as it is**
        And, ultimately, to **be aware of our Oneness with all of life**.

These elated epiphanies of *grace*, these extraordinary moments of awareness,
    Are like powerful magnets drawing us closer to "a turning point",
        A shift where we, more consistently, live with an awakened awareness.

These four fundamental qualities, **gratitude**, **surrender**, **acceptance**, and **Oneness**,
    Are referred to as **the Pillars of Awakening** that light the pathway of our journey
        So we may more clearly and consciously navigate the winding road of life.

It then becomes our responsibility to pursue this invitation to live a life of inner freedom
    By cultivating greater awareness of what is true - using daily transformative practices
        That help us embody and integrate these attributes into the fabric of our life.

<u>Circle of the Pillars of Awakening</u>
(Attributes For Cultivating Inner Freedom and a Life of Mastery)

ONENESS
I AM AWARE
OF MY ONENESS
WITH ALL
OF LIFE

GRATITUDE
I AM GRATEFUL
FOR WHAT I'M LEARNING
FROM EVERY
EXPERIENCE OF MY LIFE

ACCEPTANCE
I ACCEPT
THAT MY LIFE IS
UNFOLDING PERFECTLY
JUST AS IT IS

SURRENDER
I LET GO
OF MY ATTACHMENTS
AND SURRENDER MY LIFE
TO *A GREATER POWER*

ONENESS

The world I perceive with all of its myriad forms of life is one expression of universal energy.

At first glance, when you gaze up to behold the majesty of a tall snow-capped mountain,
It certainly appears to be solid and rigid.

But if you could look deeper into what it's fundamentally made of using the tools of science,
You would discover the mountain is formed out of various layers of rock strata
Consisting of diverse molecules patterned with numerous kinds of basic elements
That are each comprised of atoms surrounded by electrons
Which are shaped by invisible fields of limitless potential
All created from *photons of light*, or *radiant universal energy*.

These *photons of light* are constantly travelling at ultra-high speeds and are not solid particles,
For they are blinking in and out of material existence from the void of *The Unified Field*.

Furthermore, when you ponder the natural beauty of an oak tree
It too appears to be a physical structure that is dense and solid,
Yet, like a mountain, is made of diverse molecules from specific atoms
That are constructed from nuclei, electrons, and sub-atomic particles,
Which are also fundamentally *photons of light*, or *universal energy*.

In fact, science has shown that everything in the entire Cosmos exists in a Quantum Reality
In which every heavenly body such as stars and planets, as well as our physical bodies,
Plus every phenomenon in the material world of form
(From the smallest amoeba to the grandest galaxy cluster)
Is made, at its core, of the same radiant energy in constant motion.

Everything that exists is fashioned out of *photons of light* that coalesce into different forms,
In other words, the world with all its myriad forms is one expression of *universal energy*.

All creative manifestations on our planet occur within this **one Quantum Reality**
As a celestial dance of cosmic energy forming into different structures and shapes
Which have been perpetually evolving into the novel expressions of Nature.

We can make attempts to describe **Oneness** in numerous ways, such as **Ultimate Reality**
In which every form of creation is a unique expression of *one Unity*.

It can be described as **Transcendent Reality in which the Universe and everything in it**
Is comprised of *one Universal Love*, and many people simply call this *Love* - "God".

And **Oneness** can be described as **Infinite Reality in which each expression of life**
Is an integral part of *one unfolding never-ending spiral of Consciousness*.

Could it be that no matter what special name we choose to give this reality,
When we look at a tall snow-capped mountain, we are looking at the Oneness of *Life*,
When we enjoy the beauty of an oak tree, we are seeing the Oneness of *Life*,
And when we gaze into the eyes of other human beings,
We are gazing into the eyes of *the Limitless Expressions of Life*?

Circle of Oneness

UNITY
ONENESS DESCRIBED AS
ULTIMATE REALITY
IN WHICH EVERY
FORM OF CREATION
IS A UNIQUE
EXPRESSION
OF *ONE UNITY*

CONSCIOUSNESS
ONENESS DESCRIBED AS
INFINITE REALITY
IN WHICH EACH
EXPRESSION OF LIFE
IS AN INTEGRAL PART
OF *ONE UNFOLDING*
NEVER-ENDING SPIRAL
OF CONSCIOUSNESS

QUANTUM ENERGY
ONENESS DESCRIBED AS
QUANTUM REALITY
IN WHICH ALL
OF THE MANIFEST
WORLD OF FORM IS MADE
OF THE SAME *UNIVERSAL*
ENERGY (LIGHT)
IN CONSTANT MOTION

UNIVERSAL LOVE
ONENESS DESCRIBED AS
TRANSCENDENT REALITY
IN WHICH
THE UNIVERSE,
AND EVERYTHING IN
IT, IS COMPRISED
OF *ONE UNIVERSAL LOVE*

PILLARS OF SELF-LOVE

Loving myself unconditionally is the same as fully loving each unique expression of creation.

For a moment, imagine you are standing alone at the center of a crossroad in a rural area
　　Where two highways intersect at a perfect 90-degree angle.

Now, of the four distinct pathways that emerge out from the central heart of the crossroad,
　　Visualize you are facing the north leg, while directly behind you is the southern route,
　　　To the right of you lies the eastern highway as it shoots off across the horizon,
　　　　And on your left, the road to the west reaches onward into the distance.

Since all four roads go to "the corners of the world" from where you stand (poetically speaking),
　　Let's assume you're standing at the center of "your world", i.e. "your current worldview",
　　　And it's up to you to choose where the next step of "your journey" will take you.

Similarly, our *journey of awakening* presents many diverse spiritual paths for us to choose from
　　And while different paths take us in different directions, they all arrive at the same place,
　　　The sublime sanctuary within us that unwaveringly knows who we really are.

Each of the four **Pillars of Awakening** described in a previous narrative (see January 10th)
　　(Which have been recognized as **gratitude**, **surrender**, **acceptance**, and **Oneness**)
　　　Have various revelatory themes and concepts that support our *journey*
　　　And are essential for us to travel down our *pathway of awakening* -
　　　　For each pillar points us in the direction of our *Eternal Nature*,
　　　　　Which, at its essence, is *an Ocean of Limitless Love.*

Limitless Love is the same unbounded essence within us that we refer to as *the love of self*,
　　Because to love ourselves unconditionally is actually the same as loving all of creation,
　　　For in a very literal but unfathomable way - *we are the Universe.*

One powerful aspect of these four spiritual pathways of *self-love* is **being grateful**,
　　Grateful for what we're learning from every experience of life.

Another states that an important facet of *self-love* is **surrendering** everything in our life
　　To *a Greater Power* - and letting go of our attachments to our desires.

Self-love can also be thought of as **accepting** that our life is unfolding perfectly just as it is
　　No matter what blessings or challenges life may present to us.

And from a spiritual perspective, *self-love* is feeling completely loved by *Life* just as we are
　　Knowing we are interconnected and **one** with all of the myriad creations of the world.

In relation to our daily *journey of awakening*, no matter what direction we point ourselves,
　　Whether down the path of gratitude, surrender, acceptance, or Oneness,
　　　These pillars simply point us back to the very center of who we really are
　　　　Which, ultimately, is *the Unbounded Love of Self* (or *Love of All That Is*).

Are we willing to now stand at the many crossroads of our life and gaze out in all directions,
　　Yet only perceive and experience the *Infinite Presence of Love* wherever we look?

Circle of the Pillars of Self-Love
(In Relation to the Pillars of Awakening)

ONENESS
I AM LOVING MYSELF
EVERY TIME
I FEEL INTERCONNECTED
AND ONE
WITH ALL OF
THE MYRIAD CREATIONS
OF THE WORLD

GRATITUDE
I AM LOVING MYSELF
EVERY TIME
I FEEL GRATEFUL
FOR WHAT
I'M LEARNING FROM
EACH EXPERIENCE
OF MY LIFE

ACCEPTANCE
I AM LOVING MYSELF
EVERY TIME
I ACCEPT
THAT MY LIFE
IS UNFOLDING
PERFECTLY
JUST AS IT IS

SURRENDER
I AM LOVING MYSELF
EVERY TIME
I LET GO
OF MY ATTACHMENTS
AND SURRENDER
EVERYTHING IN MY LIFE
TO *A GREATER POWER*

REVERENCE

Today I honor the sacredness and beauty of each unique expression within the Web of Life.

If the electric power in your home goes out suddenly during a storm,
    Having a flashlight nearby that has a strong beam of light
        Can help you find your way through the darkness.

The light bulb in the flashlight will continue to send out a bright beam
    As long as its internal batteries are sufficiently charged with electrical power.

But, over time, as the batteries begin to slowly lose their charge,
    The light beam you depend on during moments of emergency
        Will start to gradually get dimmer and dimmer until, at one point,
            When the batteries are depleted, the light will no longer shine.

If you intend to keep the beam strong
    So a working flashlight will be there in times of need,
        You must, of course, maintain the electrical charge of its batteries.

Similarly, when "our internal battery is charged" from our alignment with *the Source of Life,*
    This sublime connection empowers us to feel a natural **reverence for life**
        That radiates through our heart with respect, awe, humility,
            And appreciation for others - and for all creatures of the Earth.

When we're consciously plugged into this *Infinite Source of Power,*
    Our **reverence for life** acts as "a spiritual beam of veneration",
        "A grateful stream of radiance" illuminating our inner world
            And shining "a light of clarity" giving greater meaning to everything we do.

The quality of reverence can be thought of as **a feeling of honor and respect**
    For the sacredness and beauty within each facet of life.

It is **a feeling of awe that we experience when we're in emotional alignment**
    With life's exquisite creations.

If our connection with this *Unlimited Power Source* should begin to diminish
    From a lack of attention, or lack of conscious awareness,
        Our degree of reverence for the wonder and glory of life can decrease as well.

Reverence can also be thought of as a feeling of being humbled
    By the magnificence and majesty of the world we live in.

Furthermore, the experience of reverence is a feeling of appreciation
    For each unique form within the intricate Web of Life.

Could it be that when we sustain **a deep reverence for all of life**
    Through our mindfulness of honoring others and the natural world,
        "The light of our reverence" will help illuminate our way through the darkness
            So we may more easily discover "the ascending path to our true home"?

Circle of Reverence

AWE
REVERENCE –
A FEELING OF AWE
THAT I EXPERIENCE
WHEN I'M IN EMOTIONAL
ALIGNMENT WITH LIFE'S
EXQUISITE CREATIONS

APPRECIATION
REVERENCE –
A FEELING
OF APPRECIATION
FOR EACH UNIQUE FORM
WITHIN THE INTRICATE
WEB OF LIFE

SACREDNESS
REVERENCE –
A FEELING OF HONOR
AND RESPECT
FOR THE SACREDNESS
AND BEAUTY WITHIN
EACH FACET OF LIFE

HUMILITY
REVERENCE –
A FEELING
OF BEING HUMBLED
BY THE MAGNIFICENCE
AND MAJESTY
OF LIFE

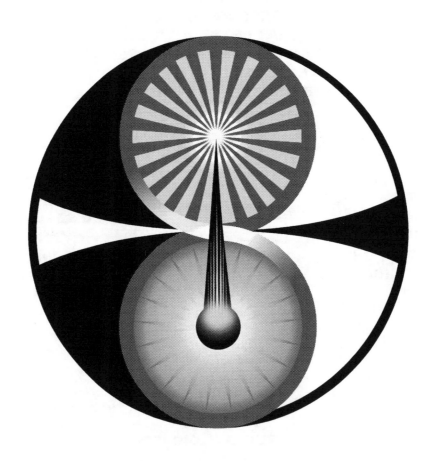

V

SPIRIT AWARENESS PRACTICES

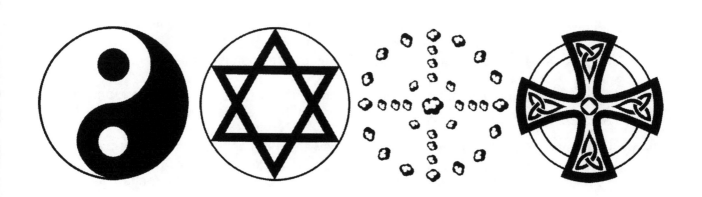

JANUARY 14
MEDITATION PRACTICES

I relax into the ocean of silence within me so I may directly experience my Eternal Nature.

Many people are familiar with, or have actually experienced, the practice of meditation,
  And it's generally known that the basic technique for meditation is simple,
    Yet the required concentration and focus can be quite demanding.

The practice of meditation is not complicated and is essentially as follows:
  First, find a place that's quiet where you can relax in a comfortable sitting position,
    Typically on a chair, a couch, or a high pillow.

Then with your eyes closed, keeping your spine straight,
  And with your hands gently resting on your lap,
    Begin to point the attention of your mind
      To "a spaciousness of silence" deep within you.

There are many different kinds of **meditation practices**
  That have been devised and tested for thousands of years by sincere spiritual seekers
    Which can help point you to *the ever-present stillness*
      Found in the silent gaps between your thoughts.

For example, you could choose to focus your inner awareness
  By silently **counting each breath** as it effortlessly moves in and out,
    Counting slowly from 1 to 10 while synchronizing a number with your breathing,
      ("1" with the in-breath, "2" with the out-breath, "3" with the in-breath, etc.)
        Repeating this sequence over and over for ten to thirty minutes.

Another meditation practice is to keep the concentration of your inner attention
  On **a sacred mantra or spiritual word** such as the ancient Sanskrit word "Om",
    Or more common phrases like "I am one with God", "I am *Limitless Love",*
      Or "I Am That I Am".

A further technique is to **consciously keep the mental focus of your inner awareness**
  On the circular rhythm of your incoming and outgoing breaths
    As you breathe slowly and naturally without any pauses between breaths.

There will, most likely, be many thoughts coursing through your mind that shall come and go
  Like soft clouds passing within a blue sky as they float by in a gentle wind.

When your attention strays from your practice and new thoughts appear (as they certainly will),
  You simply return your awareness to your *mantra,* your *breath,* or your ***witnessing,***
    Or whatever technique you are using - and continue on with your inner focus.

In the silent gaps between our passing thoughts
  Lies the direct experience of our *True Nature, the Eternal Self* that we really are,
    Waiting and eager for us "to sail upon its *Unbounded Ocean".*

The gifts of meditation are not achieved in the forceful accomplishment of a desired goal,
  But simply in the willingness to practice - and to surrender into the ocean of silence.

Circle of Meditation Practices
(Four Closed-eye Sitting Techniques)

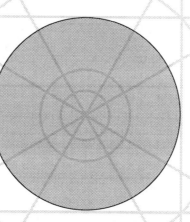

MANTRA MEDITATION
SILENTLY REPEAT A MANTRA OR SPIRITUAL PHRASE IN YOUR MIND'S EYE SUCH AS *"OM MANI PADME HUM"*, *"GOD IS LOVE"*, OR *"WHO AM I?"*

COUNTING MEDITATION
COUNT SLOWLY FROM 1 TO 10 WHILE SYNCHRONIZING EACH NUMBER WITH THE BREATH ("1" WITH THE IN-BREATH, "2" WITH THE OUT-BREATH, ETC.)

BREATH MEDITATION
CONSCIOUSLY KEEP THE MENTAL FOCUS OF YOUR INNER AWARENESS ON THE CIRCULAR RHYTHM OF YOUR INCOMING AND OUTGOING BREATHS

SILENT WITNESS MEDITATION
LET GO OF ALL TECHNIQUES RELATED TO FORMAL PRACTICE AND SIMPLY SIT QUIETLY AS THE SILENT EVER-PRESENT WITNESS OF YOUR LIFE

GOALS OF MEDITATION

In the spaciousness of silence lies my sacred communion with the Omniscient Source of Life.

If you desire to embark on a long journey to some far off place,
   Our modern world provides many different modes of transportation
      From which you can choose to travel the required distance.

For example, you can either walk the entire length of your journey,
   Or experience the adventure on a bicycle, or set out in a car, bus, train, boat, or plane.

You might even get there by riding a saddled horse through some pastoral countryside,
   Or by soaring through the clouds in a hot air balloon.

Yet if your goal was to achieve your intended destination in the shortest time possible,
   Then it's obvious you would want to choose the fastest mode of travel over others.

Regarding our *spiritual journey*, **meditation** is a transformative practice we can use
   That is a powerful vehicle to quicken our progress along our *journey of awakening*.

There are numerous ways we can benefit from this revered practice,
   In other words - there are **certain goals of meditation** we can achieve
      Should we realize the personal discipline to consistently practice.

The first and primary way of stating the goal of meditation
   Is that we practice meditation **to align our awareness with *the Transcendent***,
      In other words - with the eternal and unbounded aspect of our being.

In *the spaciousness of silence,* which is experienced within the gaps between our thoughts,
   Lies the promise of a sacred communion with *the Infinite Presence of Love*.

The practice of meditation is a tool to help us maintain our alignment with *the Source of Life*
   By opening up "portals of union" that link the absolute dimension of *the Transcendent*
      With the relative dimension of the outer material world of form,
         Much like opening the front door of a house
            Allows the inside of the house to be linked with the outside world.

Another goal of meditation is **learning to more fully accept each experience of our life**
   Just as it is, independent of external conditions,
      For we use this practice to strengthen our attitudinal muscles
         And, thus, deepen our awareness that our lives are unfolding perfectly.

Meditation also **helps us learn to surrender absolutely everything in our life -**
   All of our concepts and beliefs, all of our attachments, and all of our judgments,
      While a further goal is **to learn to cultivate a rich feeling of gratitude**
         For the blessed gift of simply being alive.

Thus, if we desire to find "the most effective path we can take" on our *journey of awakening*,
   Many dedicated spiritual seekers have discovered that daily meditation
      Is one of the best practices for cultivating the realization of who we really are.

Circle of the Goals of Meditation
(In Relation to the Pillars of Awakening)

ONENESS

I MEDITATE
SO I MAY ALIGN
MY AWARENESS WITH
THE TRANSCENDENT,
WITH THE ETERNAL
AND UNBOUNDED
ASPECT OF MY BEING

GRATITUDE

I MEDITATE
SO I MAY LEARN
TO CULTIVATE
A RICH FEELING
OF GRATITUDE
FOR THE BLESSED GIFT
OF SIMPLY BEING ALIVE

ACCEPTANCE

I MEDITATE
SO I MAY LEARN
TO ACCEPT EACH
EXPERIENCE OF MY LIFE
JUST AS IT IS, AND
ACCEPT THAT MY LIFE IS
UNFOLDING PERFECTLY

SURRENDER

I MEDITATE
SO I MAY LEARN TO
SURRENDER EVERYTHING
IN MY LIFE - ALL OF MY
CONCEPTS AND BELIEFS,
ALL OF MY ATTACHMENTS,
ALL OF MY JUDGMENTS

CULTIVATING AN AWARENESS OF ONENESS

I enter the sublime sanctuary of inner silence so I may directly experience my Eternal Nature.

Numerous cultures from around the world have contrived groups of **classical elements**
  Which, based on universal principles, are sets of the simplest essential parts
    Of which anything is fundamentally made.

There are ancient, medieval, and modern elemental systems - yet a common system
  Is one in which there are four basic elements: ***Earth***, ***Water***, ***Air***, and ***Fire***.

In one system, the element *Earth* is connected to the body represented in the west,
  Water is coupled with the heart in the south, *Air* with the mind in the east,
    And *Fire* is the element aligned with *Spirit* in the north.

Within this arrangement, the archetypal element that represents the current season of winter
  Is *Fire* in the north - and we will explore this element in terms of cultivating Oneness.

Fire symbolizes *"the Spark of Light"* that exists at the core within everything in the Cosmos,
  The perpetual movement of *Life Force energy* within all of manifest creation.

The element of *Fire* expresses itself as the quantum blaze at the nucleus of each atom,
  The molten furnace within the belly of the Earth,
    The immense luminosity at the heart of every Solar System,
      And the radiant *Divine Light* at the apex of our *Souls*.

This *"Spark of Light"* shining within everything we see in our world is the one *Universal Power*,
  The *Wholeness* that lives in every form of creation - in other words, *the Oneness of Life*.

The use of words can only point us in the direction of philosophically knowing this *Oneness*,
  Yet in order to fully realize it, a direct experience beyond our rational mind is required.

A key way to **cultivate an awareness of *Oneness*** so we may truly embody it in our daily life
  Is to practice being aware of this *Wholeness* within our **body**, **heart**, and **mind**.

When we take time to feel any sensation or pain in our **body** - and let go of any resistance to it,
  This awareness exercise can then assist us in being more present in our body
    So the ***Infinite Presence*** within us can be experienced as *Oneness*,
      As the *Unbounded Ground* of our being.

Completely feeling each diverse emotion within our **heart** as it arises
  Without placing any judgments on our emotions as "good or bad", "right or wrong",
    Can help us be more present to the ***Limitless Love*** that always pulses within us.

And by entering the sanctuary of silence - and aligning our awareness with *the Source of Life*,
  We can transcend our **mind** and directly experience our ***Eternal Nature***.

Could it be that by consciously heightening our awareness of *"the Spark of Light"* within us
  (The fiery movement of *Life Force energy* permeating within us and all of creation),
    Oneness can be experienced as *the Infinite Presence of Love* in every moment?

Circle of Cultivating an Awareness of Oneness
(Transformative Practices)

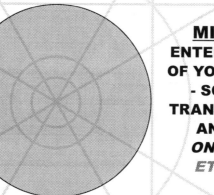

SPIRIT
ONENESS IS CONSTANTLY
PERMEATING WITHIN
ALL OF CREATION
AND IS EXPERIENCED AS
INFINITE PRESENCE,
LIMITLESS LOVE,
YOUR ETERNAL NATURE

BODY EXERCISE
FEEL ANY SENSATION
OR PAIN IN YOUR BODY
WITHOUT RESISTANCE
- SO THAT IN THE
PRESENT MOMENT, YOU
MAY KNOW *ONENESS* AS
INFINITE PRESENCE

MIND EXERCISE
ENTER THE SANCTUARY
OF YOUR INNER SILENCE
- SO THAT YOU MAY
TRANSCEND YOUR MIND
AND EXPERIENCE
ONENESS AS YOUR
ETERNAL NATURE

HEART EXERCISE
COMPLETELY FEEL
EACH DIVERSE EMOTION
WITHOUT JUDGMENT AS IT
ARISES - SO THAT IN THE
PRESENT MOMENT, YOU
MAY KNOW *ONENESS* AS
LIMITLESS LOVE

VI

ARCHETYPES OF SPIRITUAL AWAKENING

VISIONARY ARCHETYPES

Today I use my creative imagination to envision and embody the person I want to become.

Ever since people began to contemplate the spiritual, sages and mystics from around the world
Have been asking the existential question, *"Who am I?"* as a way of discovering
The deeper esoteric truth regarding the mystery of one's *Eternal Nature.*

And to attempt to resolve this perennial question, they sought for the blessing
Of a direct personal experience of their *Eternal and Unbounded Self.*

As these mystics asked this timeless question - which led them to transcendent experiences,
What was made clear was - *who they really are is the perfect union of the Source of Life
Merged as one with their human form (i.e. their body, heart, and mind).*

Another way of stating this is: *our True Nature is eternal and perfect, yet at the same time,
We naturally long to expand our awareness so we may help build a more perfect world.*

The constant expansion of our awareness (our innate yearning to reach for something greater)
Can be analogous to walking across the face of the Earth
And traveling to some distant place we've observed on the horizon,
A point that's a long way ahead of us, as far off as we can possibly see.

Yet as we finally arrive at "the horizon point" that has been our intended destination all along,
There's always another, even more distant, horizon we can catch sight of
Which is waiting somewhere far away over "the next valley of possibility".

The way we will describe **a visionary archetype** is similar to the image of "a distant horizon",
For it represents qualities and virtues on ever-higher levels of human consciousness
That we can envision on our "horizon", yet desire to embody right now in our life.

It is **a poetic image of our greater potential or possibility, which we have yet to realize**,
Until we have bravely traveled to "the place within the heart" where we have yet to go,
In other words, past boundaries of our current beliefs about who we think we are.

Archetypes are **symbolic templates that point us to higher stages of inner development
And to the qualities and realms of creative expression we strive to achieve.**

They can be thought of as **pictorial representations of superior moral qualities
Which can empower and motivate us to express something greater in ourselves,
A promise of a more positive future for our life.**

We can use this form of an archetype as **a sacred tool and blueprint of potential
To assist us in imagining a more perfect expression of ourselves
And to hold within us an expansive vision of what is possible.**

Visionary archetypes are "beneficent vehicles of awareness" we can use
To help us travel swiftly and boldly on our ever-unfolding life journey
To reach for, and touch, "the future horizons of possibility in the distance"
And help us answer the ageless question regarding who we really are.

Circle of Visionary Archetypes
(A Transformative Practice For Embodying Beneficial Qualities)

SYMBOLIC TEMPLATE

VISIONARY ARCHETYPE – A SYMBOLIC TEMPLATE THAT POINTS ME TO THE BENEFICIAL QUALITIES AND HIGHER STAGES OF INNER DEVELOPMENT I DESIRE TO ACHIEVE

POETIC IMAGE OF POSSIBILITY

VISIONARY ARCHETYPE – A POETIC IMAGE I USE TO INVOKE IN ME A SENSE OF MY GREATER POTENTIAL OR POSSIBILITY, WHICH I HAVE YET TO REALIZE

BLUEPRINT OF POTENTIAL

VISIONARY ARCHETYPE – A VISUAL BLUEPRINT OF MY FUTURE POTENTIAL THAT HELPS ME IMAGINE A MORE EXPANSIVE VISION OF WHAT IS POSSIBLE FOR MY LIFE

PICTORIAL REPRESENTATION

VISIONARY ARCHETYPE – A PICTORIAL REPRESENTATION OF SUPERIOR QUALITIES THAT MOTIVATES ME TO EXPRESS SOMETHING GREATER IN MYSELF

GIFTS OF THE ARCHETYPES

I use my imagination to envision greater possibilities for my future - and the future of the world.

A laser is a device that takes unfocused dispersed light
    And then, through a process of optical amplification,
        Channels the dispersed photons of light in a manner
            In which they are transformed into coherent beams of focused luminosity.

These coherent beams converge in such a way
    That specific lasers can even project an image of focused light on the face of the Moon,
        A distance that's approximately 239,000 miles from Earth.

Certain kinds of *archetypes* can be thought of as "mental lasers" or "internal points of focus",
    And by using them as symbolic images that represent our abundant future possibilities,
        They can help focus our intention of manifesting more of our unlimited potential.

Thus, when we take the time to consciously activate an empowering intention
    Using the transformative tool of *a visionary archetypal visualization*,
        And simultaneously fuel this intention with an elevated emotion such as joy,
            We can blend these two components to initiate a dynamic process
                Of embodying the qualities that the archetype represents to us.

This creative process of using our imagination produces an inner marriage of heart and mind,
    The merging of our *heartfelt emotion* with our *focused intention*,
        And invites us to open ourselves to receive the transformative gifts of this union.

The evocative images of certain visionary archetypes can assist us
    To connect with an invisible *morphogenetic field* of heightened awareness
        Where we access beneficial qualities we desire to bring into our life.

A morphogenetic field is a phrase used in developmental biology and consciousness studies
    That proposes there is a tangible field of energy that's generated by all things,
        Both physical structures and even mental constructs
            Which serves to organize the structure's characteristics and patterns.

When we consciously align ourselves to *the morphogenetic field of a specific archetype*,
    We begin a process of personally resonating to it and bringing into our awareness
        The visionary qualities and characteristics which the archetype symbolizes.

Using archetypes, we can **focus our attention on attributes of expanded awareness**
    Which has the potential to cultivate higher stages of our inner development
        And access entire new levels and areas of our creative expression.

Archetypes may also awaken previously inactive DNA connections of human abilities
    Which are potential in us, but have not yet been outwardly expressed.

These **gifts of the archetypes** can help us take our dispersed thoughts and feelings
    And consciously focus them into "coherent laser beams of creative imagination"
        So as to illuminate our path along our ever-unfolding *journey of awakening*.

<u>Circle of Gifts of the Archetypes</u>
(The Benefits of Using Visionary Archetypal Visualization)

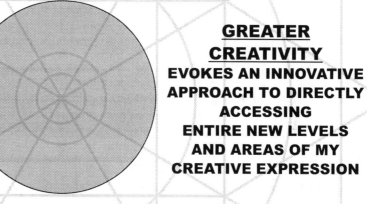

<u>INNER DEVELOPMENT</u>
FOCUSES MY ATTENTION
ON VARIOUS BENEVOLENT
ATTRIBUTES
OF EXPANDED AWARENESS
SO I MAY CULTIVATE
HIGHER STAGES
OF INNER DEVELOPMENTw

<u>HEIGHTENED</u>
<u>AWARENESS</u>
CONNECTS ME WITH
A MORPHOGENETIC
FIELD OF HEIGHTENED
AWARENESS WHERE
I CAN ACCESS
BENEFICIAL QUALITIES

<u>GREATER</u>
<u>CREATIVITY</u>
EVOKES AN INNOVATIVE
APPROACH TO DIRECTLY
ACCESSING
ENTIRE NEW LEVELS
AND AREAS OF MY
CREATIVE EXPRESSION

<u>NEW POTENTIAL</u>
MAY AWAKEN PREVIOUSLY
INACTIVE CONNECTIONS
OF HUMAN ABILITIES
WITHIN MY DNA WHICH ARE
POTENTIAL IN MY BEING,
BUT HAVE NOT YET BEEN
OUTWARDLY EXPRESSED

THE GREAT CIRCLE OF THE ARCHETYPES

I use my imagination to envision my life advancing to my next horizon of creative possibility.

Today we return to the foundational theme of **The Great Circle**, (see Dec. 28th)
　　Which portrays the universal dynamics at play in the world and in our lives,
　　　　And we shall symbolically associate the four primary dynamics within this circle
　　　　　　With four specific sets of visionary archetypes.

There is a transcendent yearning existing within all forms of life (and thus within every person)
　　That naturally longs to learn, expand, and awaken to higher stages of development
　　　　Through *the innate universal impulse* we refer to as **evolving consciousness.**

The Infinite Intelligence of the Universe manifests the inner expansion of our consciousness
　　By mirroring our new awareness into the world as our outer creativity and contributions
　　　　Through the act of *universal expression* that's referred to as **evolving creativity**.

The Great Circle can be thought of as *"The Great Spiral of existence perpetually evolving",*
　　For as we inwardly expand our **consciousness** and learn what our life is truly about**,**
　　　　It follows that **Limitless Love** outwardly mirrors our **creativity** within our life.

Over many eons, we humans have cultivated the evolutionary gift of self-reflective awareness
　　And this awareness has the potential to collectively advance human culture forward
　　　　As we learn to be agents of spiritual transformation - and service to one another.

By choosing life-enhancing transformative practices which aid us in developing our awareness,
　　Such as using specific visionary archetypes that help us imagine who we can become,
　　　　We support the cultivation of our inner freedom.

These archetypal templates can be intentionally applied to envision a better world
　　And to guide our mind and heart to our next horizon of creative possibility
　　　　For our own inner development and healing, as well as the healing of the planet.

In the following circle, each of the seasons are represented by a set of visionary archetypes
　　Which portrays natural qualities inherent within a particular season.

The Archetypes of Conscious Contribution (related to **spring**)
　　Can be used to consciously imagine "our heart being guided down the sublime road"
　　　　Of contributing our creative gifts in service to the wellbeing of others.

The Archetypes of Life Mastery (related to **summer**)
　　Can be used to envision ourselves at "the banquet table of heightened awareness"
　　　　And awaken the virtues in us that help cultivate the skills of conscious living.

The Archetypes of Higher Knowledge (related to **autumn**)
　　Can be used to visualize our lives as "a garden of unlimited possibilities"
　　　　Where we develop our potential - and rise to higher stages of consciousness.

The Archetypes of Spiritual Awakening (related to **winter**)
　　Can gently point each of us toward our "date with destiny" as a **Master of Freedom.**

The Great Circle of the Archetypes

WINTER

ARCHETYPES OF SPIRITUAL AWAKENING
ALL FOUR REPRESENT MY *JOURNEY OF AWAKENING* LEADING TO MY DESTINY AS A "MASTER OF FREEDOM", A LIFE IN SERVICE GUIDED BY *LIMITLESS LOVE*

AUTUMN

ARCHETYPES OF HIGHER KNOWLEDGE
EACH ONE REPRESENTS A NATURAL LONGING TO DEVELOP MY POTENTIAL AND HIGHER STAGES OF EVOLVING CONSCIOUSNESS

SPRING

ARCHETYPES OF CONSCIOUS CONTRIBUTION
EACH ONE REPRESENTS A NATURAL LONGING TO CONTRIBUTE MY GIFTS AND EXPRESS MY EVER EVOLVING CREATIVITY

SUMMER

ARCHETYPES OF LIFE MASTERY
EACH ONE REPRESENTS THE KEY VIRTUES, VALUES, AND QUALITIES THAT HELP ME CULTIVATE INNER FREEDOM AND EMBODY MY DESTINY OF LIVING AN AWAKENED LIFE

ARCHETYPES OF SPIRITUAL AWAKENING

I am on a quest to learn to love unconditionally - and to fully experience a life of inner freedom.

There is a famous Chinese proverb that states
"A journey of a thousand miles begins with the first step".

Whenever we embark on a new life adventure which has lots of potential challenges
    We may find that at the start of our undertaking, we are uncertain of how it will turn out,
        And yet there's power in having the courage to take the first step.

The most important journey we'll ever make is our *spiritual journey,* our *journey of awakening,*
    Our personal quest to love unconditionally - and to fully experience a life of inner freedom,
        For once we consciously take the initial steps of this *journey of discovery,*
        We begin a transformative investigation of who we really are.

If we're able to sincerely listen, we will hear "the whisper of a natural yearning deep within"
    Inviting us to learn what our life is truly about - and what really matters,
        A depth of inner guidance that leads us to self-examination and self-inquiry.

The Archetypes of Spiritual Awakening depicted in the Contemplation Circle on the next page
    Are poetic descriptions of primary stages of consciousness along our *spiritual journey*
    And are key steps we must take on our inner journey of personal transformation.

The circle visually illustrates the various stages of our journey
    And provides "a map of the interior territory" each of us must eventually travel.

The first stage, or initial "rung" along our ever-unfolding "ladder of consciousness",
    Can symbolically be portrayed as **the Young Awakening Self**.

This stage refers to the young and unconscious part of us that's initially self-centered
    And which is largely focused on our individual emotional and psychological survival,
        The aspect within us that dysfunctionally maneuvers the intricate pathways of life
            Through control of others, attachment, approval, personal power, or fear,
        Yet, over time, becomes aware of a yearning to spiritually awaken.

The next stage, the archetype of **the Compassionate Heart**, describes a world-centered person
    And represents the part of us that, through much personal development,
        Has found a gift in being grateful for what we're learning from every life experience,
        Has opened our heart to compassion and care for others,
            And has become aware of the responsibility to serve the good of all.

The most important key to our awakening, ***Infinite Presence***, refers to our *Transcendent Self,*
    Our *True Nature* which is eternal and unbounded,
        And it is this *Awakened Presence* that animates and directs every facet of our life.

Ultimately, we must journey "the thousand steps", or simply "the one next step that's required",
    To the sublime place within us where we integrate our life of service with *Limitless Love,*
        Where our **Compassionate Heart** is fully merged with ***Infinite Presence***,
        As we embrace our sacred destiny as a **Master of Freedom**.

Circle of Archetypes of Spiritual Awakening
(My Spiritual Journey of Personal Transformation)

MASTER OF FREEDOM
MY AWARENESS AS I LIVE AN AWAKENED LIFE OF INNER FREEDOM - AND LOVE UNCONDITIONALLY + MY COMPASSIONATE HEART FULLY MERGED WITH *INFINITE PRESENCE*

YOUNG AWAKENING SELF
THIS IS MY LEVEL OF AWARENESS WHEN I AM SELF-CENTERED, FOCUSED ON APPROVAL, ATTACHMENT, CONTROL, SELF-POWER, OR FEAR, YET YEARN TO AWAKEN

INFINITE PRESENCE
"THE ONE", THE SOURCE OF LIFE, UNIVERSAL CONSCIOUSNESS, GOD, INFINITE INTELLIGENCE, LIMITLESS LOVE, THE TRANSCENDENT SELF, MY ETERNAL NATURE

COMPASSIONATE HEART
MY LEVEL OF AWARENESS AS I CONSCIOUSLY LIVE A WORLD-CENTERED LIFE THAT IS COMPASSIONATE, CARING, GRATEFUL FOR LIFE, AND IN SERVICE TO THE GOOD OF ALL

MASTER OF FREEDOM

It is the destiny of all people, and thus my destiny as well, to live an awakened life.

It is the destiny of a baby bird to hatch from the protective shield of an egg,
Gain strength from the nourishing food provided by the parent birds,
And eventually leap courageously from its nest to soar high above the trees.

It is the destiny of a caterpillar larva to grow - and reach its full expression
So it can, one day, crawl to the place on a tree or rock where it will form its cocoon
And be transformed into a butterfly to take wing through the skies.

It is also the destiny of every one of us to respond to our natural inner yearning
To cultivate a higher awareness that will correct any unloving beliefs we have
So we may transform our unconscious habits, prevail over self-imposed fears,
Free ourselves from suffering, and ultimately awaken to who we really are.

The Intelligent Force of Life that animates all people with this powerful innate longing
Is constantly inviting us to expand our awareness of what is true,
Cultivate our greatness, express our creativity, and embrace our limitless nature.

In order to consciously transform our personal lives from a life of suffering and self-limitation
To a life in which we experience inner freedom and peace of mind,
We must boldly act on this *invitation* by participating in *a journey of discovery.*

It is our *journey of awakening* - where we inwardly align our awareness with *the Source of Life*
As we outwardly **share our unique creative gifts and talents**
In ways that contribute to a better, more enlightened world.

It is **accepting that our life is unfolding perfectly just as it is,**
Living in the present moment, and being aware of our Oneness with all of life.

Our *awakening journey* is also about constantly expanding our awareness,
Developing our unlimited potential, and awakening to our *True Eternal Nature.*

This is our *journey of life mastery* as we learn to compassionately serve the wellbeing of others
And **love the people in our life unconditionally.**

This spiritual quest can be thought of as *a sacred divine marriage*, for it is the hallowed union
Of **the Servant of Love** within us completely integrated with **Limitless Love.**

It is the cultivation of our **Compassionate Heart** fully merged with **Infinite Presence**,
And this sublime union can be expressed in our daily life as a **Master of Freedom.**

The archetype of the **Master of Freedom** can also be described as our *Fully Awakened Self,*
Which is our awakened awareness of inner freedom and loving all of life unconditionally.

It is our destiny to embody our *Awakened Self*, to jump from "the nest of limitation and fear",
To benevolently transform ourselves within "the cocoon of *the Infinite Power of Love*",
And to leap confidently into "the unlimited skies of awakened living" that await us.

Circle of a Master of Freedom
(Living a Life of Inner Freedom and Loving Unconditionally)

AWAKENED PRESENCE
I AM IN ALIGNMENT WITH
INFINITE PRESENCE
AS I ACCEPT THAT MY LIFE
IS UNFOLDING PERFECTLY,
LIVE IN THE PRESENT
MOMENT, AND AM AWARE
OF MY ONENESS WITH ALL

LIMITLESS DEVELOPMENT
I AM IN ALIGNMENT WITH
INFINITE INTELLIGENCE
AS I CONSTANTLY
EXPAND MY AWARENESS,
DEVELOP MY POTENTIAL,
AND AWAKEN
TO WHO I REALLY AM

ENDLESS CREATIVITY
I AM IN ALIGNMENT WITH
THE SOURCE OF LIFE
AS I GENEROUSLY SHARE
MY CREATIVE GIFTS
AND TALENTS IN WAYS
THAT CONTRIBUTE
TO A BETTER WORLD

UNCONDITIONAL LOVE FOR LIFE
I AM IN ALIGNMENT WITH
LIMITLESS LOVE
AS I COMPASSIONATELY
SERVE THE WELLBEING
OF OTHERS
- AND LOVE ALL OF LIFE
UNCONDITIONALLY

UNCONDITIONAL LOVE

It is my spiritual destiny to love all people and every expression of life - unconditionally.

When a master musician skillfully plays a wooden flute
　　His or her breath naturally flows unimpeded through the instrument
　　　　So as to support the beautiful sounds and melodies the instrument can make.

But if an obstruction should get inside the hollow chamber of the flute,
　　The air from the musician's breath won't be able to flow through it
　　　　And, of course, its beautiful music cannot be enjoyed.

Metaphorically, each of us is like a wooden flute being played by *the Breath of Life*
　　Which constantly animates us and provides us energy
　　　　In order to express the infinite melodies of its *Universal Love*.

Yet *the Breath of Life* which naturally flows through us can be partially blocked, or obstructed,
　　Especially by certain kinds of unloving choices,
　　　　For example, by an unconscious choice that closes down our heart to another.

It can also be closed off by a habitual choice that inhibits us
　　From appreciating the unique beauty or creative expressions of another person
　　　　Because of our competitive behavior - or comparing ourselves with others.

Furthermore, the effortless flow of *Life Force energy* can be hindered by an illusionary belief
　　That we are separate from other people,
　　　　And that, because of our self-limiting habits based around fear and ignorance,
　　　　　　We selfishly think of only our own needs rather than the needs of others.

Unconditional love can be thought of as the most natural unobstructed flow of *Life energy*
　　That wants "to perpetually play its sacred melodies of the heart - through us".

It is **an exalted and absolute feeling of total gratitude for every aspect of another**,
　　As well as **completely letting go of all judgments of that person**
　　　　While we wholly support and empower them.

The unconditional love of another is **the ability to fully embrace and accept**
　　Every aspect of that person just as they are, as well as **the profound realization**
　　　　And sublime experience that we're truly one with them.

Yet in order to learn to unconditionally love all people,
　　We must also learn to courageously open our hearts to loving and accepting ourselves.

As we discover a deeper meaning for our life than merely to fulfill our own personal needs
　　And begin to grasp that "a much larger meaning of life is about serving others",
　　　　Then loving ourselves and the people around us unconditionally
　　　　　　Becomes the most natural gift we can offer to another.

Unconditional love is the boundless *Essence of Life* freely flowing through us unimpeded,
　　And this flow has the potential to turn each and every day into "a glorious love song".

Circle of Unconditional Love
(In Relation to the Pillars of Awakening)

ONENESS

UNCONDITIONAL LOVE FOR ANOTHER –
MY PROFOUND REALIZATION AND SUBLIME EXPERIENCE THAT I AM TRULY ONE WITH ANOTHER

GRATITUDE

UNCONDITIONAL LOVE FOR ANOTHER –
AN EXALTED AND ABSOLUTE FEELING OF TOTAL GRATITUDE FOR EVERY ASPECT OF A PERSON

ACCEPTANCE

UNCONDITIONAL LOVE FOR ANOTHER –
MY ABILITY TO FULLY EMBRACE AND ACCEPT EVERY ASPECT OF A PERSON JUST AS THEY ARE

SURRENDER

UNCONDITIONAL LOVE FOR ANOTHER –
COMPLETELY LETTING GO OF ALL MY JUDGMENTS OF ANOTHER AS I WHOLLY SUPPORT AND EMPOWER THEM

EVOLUTION OF AWAKENING

Evolution yearns for me to awaken to my True Nature as a vital part of a vast global awakening.

A tall tree is such a grand and magnificent expression of Nature,
  And yet its origins emerge from a tiny seed.

For a tree to fulfill its destiny it must journey through various stages of development
  Unfolding from seed underground, to sprout seeking light, to seedling stretching upward.

There's a natural impulse or *yearning* within a young seedling to shoot up strong and towering
  So it can, one day, send out its branches and grow leaves to capture the sunlight.

There is an innate *longing* within each of these stages for a new *awakening* of the next stage,
  And each new stage becomes an essential foundation for succeeding stages.

The various stages of a developing tree provide us with a powerful metaphor
  We can use to become aware of the natural stages of our own spiritual awakening.

The arrival of our human species was part of **a long series of *emergent awakenings***
  That have been taking place throughout evolution since the beginning of time.

After the dynamic birth of the Universe 13.8 billion years ago,
    Evolution *yearned* for the first massive explosion of a star, the first **supernova**,
      In order to create suitable chemical elements to shape the building blocks of life
        So the *awakening* of **biological life** could emerge.

Evolution then *yearned* for the first forms of life to manifest the necessary five bodily senses
  So the stage of *awakening* that included **self-awareness** could finally develop.

A further stage of *awakening* occurred as some animals became self-aware
  And developed highly evolved brains with new cognitive capacities,
    Which set the stage for **the human species** to emerge as a new form of life.

At present, for us to consciously contribute to the life-enhancing "direction of evolution's arrow",
  We each can further humanity's *global awakening* through our own *personal awakening*.

In order for this to happen, we're being invited every day to **maintain an alignment with *Life***
  So we can experience the individual wellbeing, balance, and vitality
    That enables us to truly serve our families, communities, and the world.

Based on evolutionary science, we now have more clarity of "the direction of evolution's arrow"
  And the higher stages of consciousness our human species is most likely evolving to
    And, thus, we can contribute our creative gifts to a future of greater cooperation
      By being aware to cultivate our own *awakening* - through serving others.

Evolution is *yearning* for people everywhere to have a direct experience of their *True Nature*
  (*The Limitless Essence* within every person which is eternal and unbounded)
    So that **the next *awakening*** (whatever unknown and glorious form it will take)
      Can one day burst into expression.

Circle of the Evolution of Awakening

AWAKENED HUMAN
EVOLUTION *YEARNED*
FOR THE FIRST HUMANS
TO HAVE EXPERIENCES
OF AWAKENING TO THEIR
TRUE ETERNAL NATURE
+FURTHER AWAKENINGS
CAN NOW EMERGE

FIRST SUPERNOVA
EVOLUTION *YEARNED*
FOR THE FIRST MASSIVE
EXPLOSION OF A STAR
TO CREATE THE BUILD-
ING BLOCKS OF LIFE
+BIOLOGICAL LIFE
COULD THEN EMERGE

SELF-AWARENESS
EVOLUTION *YEARNED*
FOR THE FIRST SELF-
AWARE FORMS OF LIFE
TO DEVELOP HIGHLY
EVOLVED BRAINS
+THE HUMAN BEING
COULD THEN EMERGE

BIOLOGICAL LIFE
EVOLUTION *YEARNED*
FOR THE EMERGENCE OF
THE FIRST FORMS OF LIFE
AND DEVELOPMENT OF
THE FIVE BODILY SENSES
+SELF-AWARENESS
COULD THEN EMERGE

ENLIGHTENMENT

I feel inner freedom in the moments I accept life just as it is and when I'm fully serving others.

Even before the earliest religions appeared thousands of years ago,
There have always been a few spiritual explorers who found it natural
To seek an experience of profound union with a transcendent power,
The direct realization of sublime Oneness with *All That Is*.

In numerous spiritual traditions, mystics and sages developed specific spiritual techniques,
Such as various types of meditation, that were practiced to transcend the mind
So as to realize this *Eternal Reality*, or what some call *the Presence of God*,
And ultimately merge their consciousness with this *Eternal Presence*.

A number of these traditions call this state of ultimate communion **enlightenment**,
A holy state of spiritual union in which a sincere seeker experiences Oneness with God.

Yet some seekers of truth believe that attaining this sacred union with *the Essence of Life*
Requires the physical body and material world to be disdained,
For particular Western religions deem the worldly realm to be sinful or unholy,
While in some Eastern traditions, this realm is referred to as "maya",
A Sanskrit word which means "illusion" or "what is not real".

In general, as humanity continues to evolve and develop ever-higher stages of awareness,
The natural impulse within every religious person to quest for *enlightenment* remains,
Yet for many spiritual seekers, one's understanding of what *enlightenment* is,
And "the Bigger Picture" of what it truly means, also continues to evolve.

Today there's a growing understanding by many that an evolved meaning of *enlightenment*
Is not only about one's personal *awakening* - or **awareness of Oneness with God**,
But that any sustained individual alignment with *Ultimate Reality*
Must also be embodied and grounded within one's physical body
And then shared collectively through the personal actions
Of serving the wellbeing of others.

In some contemporary spiritual groups, the concept of *enlightenment* is now perceived
As **a sustained experience of loving others and loving self unconditionally**
While serving the good within all of life.

Enlightenment is **the sublime embodiment of inner freedom** - which is living at a stage
Of spiritual consciousness where one abides in inner peace no matter what occurs.

With this larger perspective and expanded meaning of *enlightenment*,
It then becomes our personal responsibility to cultivate our spiritual awareness
So as to experience "the unfolding perfection" and **acceptance** of life just as it is,
As well as recognize that in those moments when we're truly aligned
And fully in love with all of life, we are enlightened.

Could it be that from this vantage point, *enlightenment* is simply just another natural step,
A rung of the ladder of perpetual evolving development within the epic journey of life?

Circle of Enlightenment

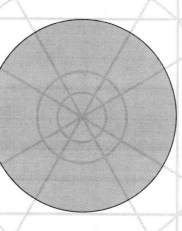

ONENESS
ENLIGHTENMENT –
A CONSTANT AWARENESS
OF MY ONENESS WITH
ALL OF LIFE, WHICH IS
SHARED COLLECTIVELY
THROUGH THE PERSONAL
ACTIONS OF SERVING THE
WELLBEING OF OTHERS

ACCEPTANCE
ENLIGHTENMENT –
A CONTINUOUS
RECOGNITION
OF THE ALL-EMBRACING
GRATITUDE,
ACCEPTANCE,
AND PERFECTION OF MY
LIFE - JUST AS IT IS

UNCONDITIONAL LOVE
ENLIGHTENMENT –
A SUSTAINED EXPERIENCE
OF LOVING OTHERS
AND LOVING MYSELF
UNCONDITIONALLY WHILE
SERVING THE GOOD
WITHIN ALL OF LIFE

INNER FREEDOM
ENLIGHTENMENT –
THE SUBLIME EMBODI-
MENT OF INNER FREEDOM,
WHICH IS LIVING
AT A STAGE OF SPIRITUAL
CONSCIOUSNESS WHERE
I ABIDE IN INNER PEACE
NO MATTER WHAT OCCURS

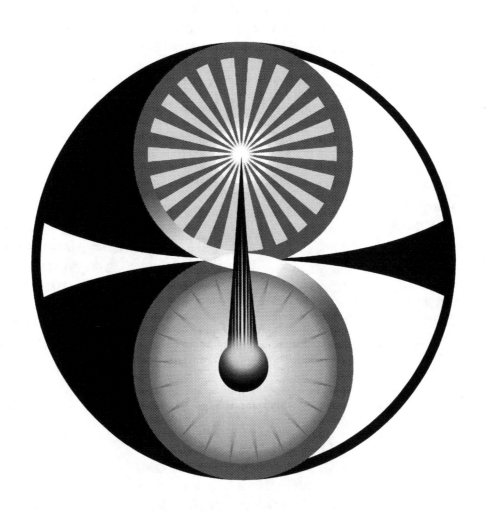

VII

SPIRIT
AWARENESS
PRACTICES

MINDFULNESS

The thoughts I consciously focus on grow stronger - as the ones I ignore gradually fade away.

Due to centuries of acquiring certain ancestral knowledge, many traditional farmers are aware
Of the subtle changing patterns within the seasons, of the various phases of the Moon,
And with this awareness, they have learned when it's best to plant their seeds.

They have also learned to recognize when the last spring frost has taken place
By observing the new buds on branches of specific trees and bushes,
And by watching particular seasonal activities of the local wild animals.

These farmers must consistently be mindful of these subtle nuances of Nature
So they can effectively know when to sow their crops.

Mindfulness is a valuable faculty to cultivate in every aspect of our life,
Yet many people don't ever think of being mindful about the content of their thoughts
Which are constantly passing in and out of their minds throughout the day
Because, most likely, they were never taught the benefit of doing so.

Our flow of thoughts arises from a number of sources, some from our inner awareness,
Some thoughts surface from past generations of our inherited programming,
And some even arise from the fields of mass consciousness that surround us
Which directly impact our mind and, thus, influence our personal thoughts.

When we become mindful of our thoughts each day,
In other words - **when we're aware of where we place the attention of our mind,
We can learn to choose the kind of thoughts we give attention to.**

Whatever thoughts we focus on will grow and prosper,
And whatever ideas we ignore and reject, in time, will wither and disappear.

**As we practice the simple act of witnessing our thoughts
And make this a conscious daily awareness exercise,
We can learn to live more fully in each moment and with more freedom**
Rather than focus on thoughts that habitually keep us in bondage.

**Mindfulness is a technique for observing the activity of our mind
So we may learn to cultivate an acceptance of life no matter what is going on**
And overcome our ingrained dysfunctional pattern of resisting life the way it is.

The practice of mindfulness can bring us to a greater discovery
Of how to **transform the perception of our current self-identity
From an experience of separation from others
To an authentic realization of our Oneness with all of life**.

Just as a farmer's crops which are nourished with attention grow stronger and healthier
While the ones which are overlooked and neglected wither away,
So too the thoughts we consciously focus on each day grow stronger
While the ones we ignore - gradually fade away.

Circle of Mindfulness
(A Transformative Practice)

AWARENESS
MINDFULNESS –
A TRANSFORMATIVE
EXERCISE
FOR BECOMING AWARE
OF THE KIND
OF THOUGHTS I GIVE
MY ATTENTION TO

PERCEPTION
MINDFULNESS –
A PRACTICE
FOR TRANSFORMING
THE PERCEPTION
OF MY SELF-IDENTITY
FROM AN EXPERIENCE OF
SEPARATION TO ONENESS

WITNESSING
MINDFULNESS –
A METHOD
FOR BRINGING
MY AWARENESS INTO
THE PRESENT MOMENT
BY WITNESSING
THE EVENTS OF MY LIFE

OBSERVATION
MINDFULNESS –
A TECHNIQUE FOR
OBSERVING MY MIND
SO I MAY CULTIVATE
AN ACCEPTANCE
OF LIFE NO MATTER
WHAT IS GOING ON

MINDFULNESS PRACTICES

Today I am mindful of the quality of my thoughts that I choose to focus my attention on.

If you have ever hiked through a high alpine wilderness
    And took some time to sit and watch the running water of a cold mountain stream,
        You would, most likely, have observed that the stream flowed continuously
            As if its current would never end.

Obviously, the ceaseless current of an alpine stream has a constant water supply,
    Yet if you were to gaze up at the tall mountaintops where its origins come from,
        The source of the stream would appear as if it arose out of nothing.

Many of the mystical religious traditions
    And some of the contemporary psychological sciences
        Have developed **specific practices and techniques**
            For helping a person learn how to be mindful
                Of the content and quality of his or her steady stream of thoughts.

These traditions have discovered pragmatic methods that an individual can practice in daily life
    To become more conscious of the incessant movement of thought within the mind.

For example, **Noticing Resistance** is an awareness practice
    Which can help us notice when our mind centers on a thought
        That's resisting some experience - because we want life to be different than it is.

Presence is a simple mindfulness exercise we can practice throughout the day
    Which helps us authentically live in the present moment
        By assisting us to be aware to put our complete attention
            On the activity we are currently engaged in.

Another valuable mindfulness practice is **Self-Observation**
    Which can be described as taking time at various periods of the day
        (Especially in the early morning or late evening) to become acutely aware
            Of our flow of thought, our passing emotions, and our physical sensations,
            As well as any negative reactions we may have to them.

Furthermore, there is a mindfulness practice referred to as **Witnessing**
    Which is the practice of identifying ourselves as *the Silent Witness*
        So as to watch the constantly changing events of our life without judgment.

This awareness practice can help us shift the focus of our self-identity
    From our egoic self-oriented nature to our *True Nature (the Eternal Self)*
        By embracing the part of us that simply witnesses
            The passing of each event we encounter without judging or resisting it.

Like enjoying the steady current of a mountain stream as it continuously passes by,
    How would our lives be enhanced if we were truly mindful throughout the day
        Of the constant stream of *Life Force energy* flowing within us
            Which appears to arise out of nothing?

Circle of Mindfulness Practices
(Transformative Awareness Exercises)

WITNESSING
THE PRACTICE
OF IDENTIFYING MYSELF
AS *THE SILENT WITNESS*
THAT WATCHES THE
CONSTANTLY CHANGING
EVENTS OF MY LIFE
WITHOUT JUDGMENT

SELF-OBSERVATION
THE PRACTICE
OF BEING AWARE OF MY
THOUGHTS, EMOTIONS,
AND PHYSICAL
SENSATIONS - AND ANY
REACTIONS TO THEM

NOTICING RESISTANCE
THE PRACTICE
OF NOTICING
WHEN MY MIND
CENTERS ON A THOUGHT
OF RESISTANCE TO
CERTAIN EXPERIENCES

PRESENCE
THE PRACTICE
OF BEING ATTENTIVE TO
LIVING IN
THE PRESENT MOMENT
BY FULLY FOCUSING ON
THE ACTIVITY I'M
CURRENTLY ENGAGED IN

WITNESSING AWARENESS

I witness without judgment the thoughts, emotions, and sensations that pass by my awareness.

Many people seem to enjoy the experience of "getting into someone else's skin"
    Or feeling what it's like "to face the seemingly impossible"
        By simply sitting back and spending time watching a feature-length movie.

When we go to a movie theater to view a film,
    We witness scores of shifting images that are projected on a flat white screen
        Where the images are constantly changing as they pass in front of us,
            While the actual screen on which they're projected remains unchanged.

We can use *the blank movie screen* as a metaphor for *the Transcendent*,
    The Source of All That Is, which is eternal and unchanging,
        Yet which witnesses all of the changing images that pass through our mind.

In other words, it is that which witnesses every thought, emotion, or sensation we experience,
    Which, like the passing film images, constantly come and go.

The existential question "Who am I?" points us to an *Absolute Reality* that does not change,
    That is eternal, unbounded, limitless, and **beyond form**.

Yet in the relative world of phenomenal form, the material reality we discern with our senses
    Is always in a process of change, a perpetual shifting of events that come and go,
        A realm where our physical body is born, has many life experiences
            And, in time, ceases to be.

Yet through our spiritual investigation of life - and ultimately through the blessings of *grace*,
    We can realize the aspect within us which never changes, which is transcendent,
        And which many theologians have referred to as *the Mind of God.*

We can also choose to practice embodying this *Eternal Reality*
    By consciously being aware each day of *the Witnessing Presence* within us,
        The sublime *Transcendent Presence* that knows - *I am not my body.*

The same is true for our emotions and our thoughts as they gently pass through us,
    Like vaporous clouds floating past a clear blue sky,
        For we are neither our emotions nor our thoughts.

When we consciously take the time to be aware of *the Witnessing Presence*
    That simply witnesses without judgment each experience of our life just as it is,
        We can discover for ourselves that who we really are
            Is not our body, or our various emotions, or our passing thoughts,
                But who we truly are is transcendent, eternal, and unbounded.

Just like everything that comes and goes within the material Universe,
    Our body sensations, our full spectrum of emotions, and our myriad thoughts
        Constantly come in and out of existence in a changing field of time,
            Yet our *True Nature* (what is witnessing these changes) remains forever.

Circle of Witnessing Awareness
(A Transformative Practice)

BEYOND FORM
I AM AWARE OF
*THE WITNESSING
PRESENCE*
WITHIN ME THAT IS
TRANSCENDENT,
ETERNAL, UNBOUNDED,
AND BEYOND FORM

BEYOND BODY
I AM AWARE OF
*THE WITNESSING
PRESENCE*
WITHIN ME
THAT KNOWS
WHO I AM
IS NOT MY BODY

BEYOND MIND
I AM AWARE OF
*THE WITNESSING
PRESENCE*
WITHIN ME
THAT KNOWS
WHO I AM
IS NOT MY THOUGHTS

BEYOND FEELINGS
I AM AWARE OF
*THE WITNESSING
PRESENCE*
WITHIN ME
THAT KNOWS
WHO I AM
IS NOT MY EMOTIONS

91

VIII

ARCHETYPES
OF CONSCIOUS
CONTRIBUTION

JANUARY 28

SPHERES OF CONTRIBUTION

There is a natural yearning in me to serve and contribute to the wellbeing of others.

If you were to look, either with a microscope or a telescope, at individual components of reality,
  You could notice each component of the Cosmos is a smaller *part* of a greater *whole*.

Yet no matter at what scale within the Universe you observe this, *the micro* or *the macro*,
  Each smaller *part* of the *whole* (larger system) is also *whole* and complete itself.

For example, a nucleus (which is *whole* itself) is part of an atom, an atom is part of a molecule,
  A molecule is part of an individual cell, a cell is part of an organic system,
    An organic system is part of an organism, and so on.

Each individual component or part of reality is vitally necessary to the whole system
  And brings greater fulfillment and possibility to the next larger level of expression,
    But only when and if it's in a healthy condition, in harmony with its environment,
      And in a state of functional balance.

Similarly, the numerous levels, or spheres, of how we humans *contribute to the greater whole*
  Also work in an unfolding nested fashion where each smaller sphere supports the next.

For many people, the natural response to the perennial question, *"What is the meaning of life?"*
  Has developed into the innate yearning to serve and contribute to the wellbeing of others.

Yet one thing we must keep in mind when we think about serving another person
  Is that it's also important to **contribute to our personal wellbeing** -
    In other words, to contribute to the care of our own health, happiness, and vitality
      So we're truly able to serve the wellbeing of someone else.

For when we are experiencing a place of wholeness and balance within ourselves,
  We can more effectively **contribute to our immediate and extended families**
    By supporting each of our "loved ones" in ways
      That help them feel safe, loved, empowered, and connected to *Life*.

It then follows that healthy productive families are much more capable
  To constructively **contribute to the co-creation of stronger vibrant communities**
    By helping cultivate integrous relationships, equal opportunities, and cooperation.

And, of course, strong communities support and build more collaborative societies,
  And more benevolent nations, **which eventually lead to a better world**.

These unfolding **Spheres of Contribution** can be understood in the reverse direction as well,
  For in order to best serve the world, it's imperative to have healthy communities.

To best serve our communities,
  It's important to foster healthy functional families.

And to best serve and contribute to our families and "loved ones",
  It is paramount to live a life of wellbeing and balance within ourselves.

Circle of the Spheres of Contribution

CONTRIBUTION TO ONESELF
I CONTRIBUTE TO THE CARE OF MY PERSONAL WELLBEING AND HAPPINESS SO I'M TRULY ABLE TO SERVE OTHERS

CONTRIBUTION TO THE WORLD
I CONTRIBUTE MY CREATIVE GIFTS AND TALENTS TO THE WELLBEING OF OTHERS SO I MAY HELP BUILD A BETTER WORLD

CONTRIBUTION TO FAMILY
I CONTRIBUTE TO MY FAMILY AND "LOVED ONES" BY HELPING THEM FEEL SAFE, LOVED, EMPOWERED, AND CONNECTED TO *LIFE*

CONTRIBUTION TO COMMUNITY
I CONTRIBUTE TO MY LOCAL COMMUNITY BY CULTIVATING INTEGROUS RELATIONSHIPS, EQUAL OPPORTUNITIES, AND COOPERATION

CONTRIBUTION TO ONESELF (PERSONAL WELLBEING)

Today I nourish my body, my heart, my mind, and my spirit so I'm truly able to serve others.

Building contractors know the importance of establishing a strong foundation
   At the base of any structure they intend to erect.

They recognize that it best "contributes to" the construction project
   To create a solid and well-built footing for the building
      Or else the proposed structure may one day falter.

When we typically use the word "contribute",
   We might think of an act of extending help or benefit to another person,
      Or to an external situation, or to the environment, through some specific deed.

The word "contribute" may also conjure up an image in our mind
   Of helping out a friend in need, volunteering at a community organization,
      Feeding the hungry, or giving money to some humanitarian cause.

And yet, the first time we're introduced to the phrase - **"contribution to oneself"**
   It may bring up a thought that someone is acting in a selfish or egotistical way
      And is only concerned with one's own self-centered needs.

Each of us (in our seemingly separate lives) is on an *inner journey of discovery*
   In which we're being invited to become aware of how interconnected we are,
      And that ultimately all of life, and every person in it, is truly **one *Eternal Self*.**

A gardener that properly nourishes the seeds of flowers, first generates healthy seedlings,
   Which then produce strong stems and leaves that, in time, create many new buds,
      And finally these buds blossom into colorful flowers.

In a similar manner, we are all "individual gardeners within the Garden of Earth",
   And, therefore, it's first necessary to consciously nourish the foundational seeds
      Of our personal body, heart, mind, and spirit
         So the larger "Garden of Life" can grow in a healthy and productive way.

Thus it's important to learn the benefits of *serving ourselves*,
   In other words - of contributing to a state of personal wellbeing and happiness
      As the basic foundation of our life in order to more effectively be of service to others.

Just like a well-built house requires a strong foundation
   Onto which to build the upper floors and roof,
      So too we need personal wellbeing as a solid platform
         To better fashion functional peaceful communities and nations.

By cultivating greater awareness of our **personal wellbeing**
   (Which can also be referred to as self-love)
      Using certain transformative practices listed in the circle on the following page,
         We can more easily support the essential building blocks
            That can ultimately help create a better world.

Circle of Contribution to Oneself
(Cultivating One's Personal Wellbeing)

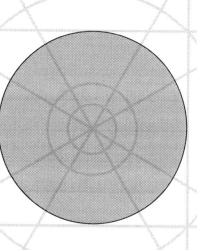

SPIRIT
1) PERIODS OF SILENCE
   AND MEDITATION
2) MINDFULNESS
   PRACTICE
3) PRAYER
4) FOLLOW, AND ACT ON,
   INNER GUIDANCE

BODY
1) PROPER NUTRITION
2) PHYSICAL EXERCISE
3) ADEQUATE REST
   AND RELAXATION
4) LIVE SIMPLY
   IN HARMONY
   WITH NATURE

MIND
1) STUDY WHAT REALLY
   MATTERS
2) CONTEMPLATION
3) CLARITY OF PURPOSE
   AND MEANING
4) IMAGINATION
   PRACTICES

HEART
1) GRATITUDE
2) SERVICE TO OTHERS
3) FULLY EXPERIENCE
   EMOTIONS
4) RELEASE THE
   SHADOW ASPECTS
   OF SELF

ARCHETYPES OF CONSCIOUS CONTRIBUTION

I consciously contribute my creative gifts and talents in ways that serve the good of all.

There is *a force of empowerment* that's available to us from certain archetypes
    When we use them as a way to embody a greater vision of who we can become.

As a reminder a visionary archetype (as defined in these narratives) is a symbolic visual image
    Representing noble qualities or characteristics that we desire to activate in our life,
        And through the power of our clear intention and focused attention,
            These archetypes can assist us to envision our potential
                And help us become a more conscious and compassionate human being.

When we bring the thought or picture of a visionary archetype into our awareness
    (And do this with intention as a conscious transformative practice),
        These images can support us in fueling our imagination
            In ways that aid us in manifesting our greater possibilities.

Furthermore, wherever we place the focused attention of our thoughts
    Is exactly the areas of our life where our consciousness will grow stronger.

When a person becomes aware of the natural inborn yearning to be of service
    As well as the desire to contribute his or her gifts and talents to the wellbeing of others,
        There are many types of symbolic images one could use to advance this desire.

In order to help guide us on a discovery of what truly matters regarding contributing our gifts,
    Four iconic images of the **Archetypes of Conscious Contribution** have been selected.

The archetype of **the Visionary Healer** can be represented by a well-crafted wooden flute
    In which "the Master Flute Player", symbolized by *the Infinite Presence of Love,*
        Breathes the music of beauty and grace into the "flute"
            To consciously assist healing and transformation within the world.

The Visionary Storyteller is an archetypal image symbolizing one who has the awareness
    To point others to their deepest and innermost connections with their *True Nature.*

It's one who supports others with their inner development
    By offering empowering stories that are inspired from "a Big Picture perspective"
        So as to help them expand their awareness of what really matters.

The archetype of **the Visionary Teacher** can be thought of as one who has climbed a tall tree,
    Who has gained the knowledge and experience from all of the lower branches,
        And now is able to motivate and inspire others from this much higher vantage.

It is one who is an example of living their life intentionally aligned with *the Source of Life,*
    Who learns what life is truly about, fosters beauty, and serves the wellbeing of others.

Finally, **the Visionary Leader** offers us the gift of seeing expanded possibilities of how to lead
    And is one who helps others gain awareness of how to embrace life and its challenges
        From a more inclusive perspective of life - and a sacred vision of who we really are.

Circle of Archetypes of Conscious Contribution

VISIONARY LEADER

IT IS THE PART OF ME THAT HELPS OTHERS EXPAND THEIR AWARENESS OF HOW TO BE A TRUE LEADER - AND TO EMBRACE LIFE AND ITS CHALLENGES FROM A MORE INCLUSIVE PERSPECTIVE AND VISION

VISIONARY HEALER

IT IS THE PART OF ME THAT HELPS OTHERS ATTUNE THEIR MIND, HEART, AND BODY WITH THEIR *ETERNAL NATURE* AND ALIGN WITH THE UNLIMITED SOURCE OF ALL HEALING POWER

VISIONARY TEACHER

IT IS THE PART OF ME THAT TEACHES OTHERS THROUGH EXAMPLE TO ALIGN WITH *THE SOURCE OF LIFE*, LEARN WHAT LIFE IS TRULY ABOUT, FOSTER BEAUTY, AND SERVE OTHERS

VISIONARY STORYTELLER

IT IS THE PART OF ME THAT SHARES WITH OTHERS EMPOWERING STORIES WHICH ARE INSPIRED FROM "A BIG PICTURE PERSPECTIVE" SO AS TO EXPAND AWARENESS OF WHAT REALLY MATTERS

VISIONARY LEADER

Today I make conscious choices that support the vision of a better world for all people.

In America during the mid 1800s, small groups of people set off in wagon trains
 And traveled long distances from the east toward the untamed lands of the Wild West.

Some wagon trains would send a few scouts to explore the area ahead of the main group
 Hoping to find information about the coming journey and to seek the best route forward.

Visionaries are "those who have traveled ahead of the rest" and have gained access
 To an expanded vision of what is possible - long before most others.

They are able to journey into "untamed territories" and courageously scout "unknown lands",
 While reporting back to others what they believe is the best path forward.

**A *visionary* is one with an awareness to perceive life from a bigger vantage than most,
 And who is increasingly cognizant of more inclusive perspectives of life.**

The word "visionary", used as an adjective, signifies a person who lives their life
 From these greater perspectives and, thus, a more refined level of human development,
 Since they have learned to respond to life in a way that includes all points of view
 While recognizing that serving the wellbeing of others
 Is an essential part of living a meaningful life.

Their expanded awareness allows them to use these larger perspectives to **help others
 Gain greater understanding of the nature of reality - and what life is truly about.**

It also provides them with **the enhanced clarity to hold a vision
 Of the constructive and beneficent possibilities for the future of humanity**
 And cultivate greater empathy for the difficult plight of others.

**We can use the archetypal image of the Visionary Leader
 To imagine various facets of the greater potential for our life**,
 To help us visualize the most empowering qualities we want to embody,
 To connect with an ever-expanding vision of who we can become,
 So we may effectively contribute our creative gifts and talents
 To building a more sustainable and peaceful world.

Acquiring larger **perspectives** of what really matters brings us to greater **understanding**,
 Which naturally points us to higher **visions** of possibility for ourselves and society.

Enlightened leadership can then be empowered and manifested into the world
 As in a conscious CEO of business, a visionary politician, or a community organizer, etc.

When we intentionally incorporate this archetype into our life as a daily transformative practice,
 It can assist us to be like a "scout" who travels far in front of the rest
 And to live our life based on an expanded vision of a better future
 Where we navigate our way through "the wilderness of an everyday world"
 To a new horizon of promise and inner freedom.

Circle of the Visionary Leader
(An Archetype of Conscious Contribution)

GUIDANCE
I HELP OTHERS
IMAGINE AND EMBODY
THEIR UNLIMITED
CREATIVE POTENTIAL
AND EXPAND THEIR
AWARENESS OF HOW TO
BE AN EFFECTIVE LEADER

PERSPECTIVE
I HELP OTHERS
PERCEIVE THE WORLD
AND ITS CHALLENGES
THROUGH THE VISIONARY
LENS OF INCLUSIVE
AND COMPASSIONATE
PERSPECTIVES OF LIFE

VISION
I HELP OTHERS
HOLD A VISION
OF THE CONSTRUCTIVE
AND BENEFICENT
POSSIBILITIES
FOR THE FUTURE
OF HUMANITY

UNDERSTANDING
I HELP OTHERS
GAIN A GREATER
UNDERSTANDING
AND AWARENESS
OF THE NATURE
OF REALITY - AND WHAT
LIFE IS TRULY ABOUT

PRIMARY PERSPECTIVES OF THE WORLD

I constantly expand how I perceive the world so I may learn to love others more fully.

Imagine for a moment you are standing in front of your home
    And as you look out into the neighborhood or area around you,
        You notice you can only see as far as the end of your street.

Now imagine climbing into the passenger basket of a large colorful hot-air balloon
    And, after lifting off the ground, you slowly rise 500 feet up into the sky
        So you can now gaze down at your whole neighborhood below you.

Then envision ascending another quarter-mile to observe the complete view of your town,
    Rising one more mile to see your entire state, fifteen miles to look at all of your country,
        And, finally, floating out into space to take in a full vista of the planet's majesty.

Obviously, your outlook becomes completely different and so much more expanded
    As you begin to observe life from ever-larger perspectives.

As humanity evolved through its various developmental stages over numerous centuries,
    The primary perspectives of how people viewed the world have evolved many times,
        Much like growing through the developmental stages from an infant into an adult.

When we were infants, our vantage of life was exclusively focused on our self-oriented world
    With the personal discovery of all its magical physical sensations and emotional stimuli,
        And everything we knew about life converged around ourselves and our needs.

As we grew into childhood, our expanding perspective of life began to include many others,
    Such as family and friends, and the feelings that arose from our encounters with them.

Behavioral scientists have observed that a newborn baby initially perceives
    That everything in its world, including its mother, is experienced as its personal self.

As the growing child has various life experiences, it's taught that it is separate from others,
    And that the world around it isn't just one whole personal "I" anymore, but has changed,
        For the child learns to divide life into *the different points of view* of "I", "**we**", and "it",
        Which include *the points of view* of personal, cultural, society, and nature.

Then with more life experience - and the awareness gained from learning what really matters,
    It eventually becomes apparent that life, and everything within it, is constantly changing,
        And that our **primary perspectives of the world** must constantly change as well.

We more easily embrace "the Big Picture of life" as we view the world from four perspectives:
    1) an interior / exterior perspective, 2) an individual / collective perspective,
        3) a three-viewpoint perspective, 4) an evolutionary perspective. (see circle)

Right now humanity seems like a young child that's learning to grow up and mature
    Sensing that, one day, when it's able to grasp a greater perspective of what really matters
    And gain a much more expansive vantage of where other people currently stand,
        It will use this maturity and wisdom to help create a more glorious world.

Circle of the Primary Perspectives of the World
(Four Points of View to More Clearly Understand My Life)

THE EVOLUTIONARY PERSPECTIVE
A PERSPECTIVE THAT IDENTIFIES MY NATURAL INNER DRIVE TO DEVELOP HIGHER LEVELS OF CREATIVITY, COMPASSION, INCLUSION, AND COOPERATION

INTERIOR / EXTERIOR
A PERSPECTIVE THAT IDENTIFIES THE INWARD IMPULSE OF EXPANDING MY CONSCIOUSNESS WHICH CORRELATES WITH MY OUTWARD IMPULSE OF EXPRESSING CREATIVITY

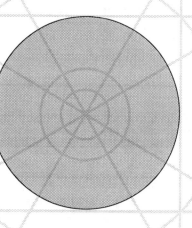

THREE-VIEWPOINT
A PERSPECTIVE THAT IDENTIFIES THREE FUNDAMENTAL WAYS TO VIEW MY WORLD:
1) "I" - PERSONAL,
2) "WE" - CULTURAL,
3) "IT" - DEPICTS BOTH SOCIETY AND NATURE

INDIVIDUAL / COLLECTIVE
A PERSPECTIVE THAT IDENTIFIES THE PERSONAL ASPECT OF MY INDIVIDUAL SELF WHICH IS DIRECTLY RELATED TO THE GROUP ASPECT OF MY COLLECTIVE SELF

SPIRITUAL UNDERSTANDING

A greater understanding of what really matters leads me to a greater attunement with my heart.

From historical anthropology, we can observe that the evolution of human development
Has progressed through specific *developmental stages* within a short period of time
Advancing through levels of development so much faster than any other species.

One reason it's postulated that humans have evolved so quickly compared to other animals
Is that the human species has developed the self-reflective attribute of **understanding**,
Which is the cognitive ability to cultivate a unique type of rational awareness.

In a brief amount of time that's said to be "an evolutionary blink of the eye",
We humans have expanded our knowledge of technology from stone axes and spears
To advanced computers and interplanetary space travel.

In our philosophical quest to understand the best ways to live together harmoniously,
Some nations have progressed through centuries of violence and brutal warfare
Yet over time, have evolved beyond war, slavery, oppression, authoritarian rule,
And have established democratic governance - as well as human rights.

In the area of spirituality, many religious groups have matured beyond their traditional creeds,
Like believing in a wrathful supernatural God who was feared and who punished sinners
To the belief in a benevolently *Natural and Loving Intelligence* that nurtures all of life.

Our constant exploration of how to creatively express ourselves (our sense of what is beautiful)
And how to embrace beauty and art continues to progress beyond previous limitations.

Over great spans of time, the human species has developed this unique ability *to understand*
Which enables us **to comprehend new levels of clarity about the nature of reality**
And to know that some particular idea or concept is inherently true.

Understanding is a cognitive tool we use that allows us to experience **brand new insights**
Leading to greater awareness of what our life is truly about - and what really matters,
Which empowers us to contribute more of our creative gifts to the progression of life.

A more expanded notion of understanding is **the direct experience of spiritual revelation**
That comes when we are truly aligned with, and guided by, *the Source of Life*.

This *higher insight of **spiritual understanding*** is an innate longing inviting us to live each day
With a willingness to keep our heart open, cultivate compassion, and serve others,
For it's the heart that is our *true power center* to help us manifest our greater potential.

And yet, the thoughts we hold in our mind can either expand our understanding - or diminish it,
Thus, when used correctly, the mind is a key tool that points us to loving unconditionally
And consciously realizing who we really are.

Greater understanding of what is - is a gift that can lead to a greater connection with our heart,
The sacred place within where we align with the ever-expanding possibilities for our life
And the unlimited potential of the person we are destined to be.

Circle of Spiritual Understanding

COMPREHENSION
SPIRITUAL UNDERSTANDING –
COMPREHENDING
NEW LEVELS OF CLARITY
ABOUT SOME ASPECT
OF THE NATURE
OF REALITY

INSIGHTS
SPIRITUAL UNDERSTANDING –
GAINING NEW INSIGHTS
AND AWARENESS
OF WHAT MY LIFE
IS TRULY ABOUT - AND
WHAT REALLY MATTERS

KNOWING
SPIRITUAL UNDERSTANDING –
ACQUIRING
AN INNER KNOWING
THAT SOME THOUGHT,
IDEA, OR CONCEPT
IS INHERENTLY TRUE

REVELATION
SPIRITUAL UNDERSTANDING –
THE DIRECT SPIRITUAL
REVELATION
THAT COMES WHEN
I AM ALIGNED WITH
THE SOURCE OF LIFE

VISION

Today I hold a vision in my mind that imagines the fully awakened person I am destined to be.

When professional architects design brand new buildings,
They first sketch their vision of what the structure will look like on a set of drawings
Which artfully represents the inspired images floating in their heads.

When an original creative idea for a new automobile is conceived,
A skilled car designer draws out detailed plans
Of how the vehicle is perceived within his or her mind.

When a quarterback intends his football team to work together as a flowing harmonious unit,
He tells his team, while in the huddle, to perform a specific pre-determined play
That he envisions will attain his goal.

In each case, the architect, car designer, and quarterback
Share with others on their team an image or vision of what is possible to achieve.

**We can use the attribute of *vision* in our everyday life as a clear image within our mind
Of a greater possibility of good for ourselves, others, or some aspect of the world.**

It is **a future positive goal along our journey of life that we're guided to achieve
Which can be visualized and comprehended, but which we have not yet attained.**

A *vision* is "a personal design or blueprint" we can use to help bring value to our world,
A visual idea or creative imagination of something to manifest at a future time.

It is something we can express into material form
By combining an elevated emotion with our focused intention of a greater possibility.

We can also **hold a *vision* in our mind as a lucid picture
Of a beneficial quality or higher potential of the person we want to become.**

Our *visions* basically come from two fundamental places within our human experience,
Either from our *self-centered awareness* - or our *world-centered awareness*.

When we were young, we learned to form *visions* (what we called desires) from our egoic self,
And these *visions* were predominantly generated to satisfy our *self-centered needs*.

With a lack of higher awareness, this type of *vision* attempted to fulfill our self-oriented drives
And fueled our individual desires for power, control, or approval from others.

A second type of *vision* arises from our eventual maturing into *world-centered awareness*
And from the inner guidance that comes due to our alignment with *the Source of Life*
Directing us to be attentive to concerns regarding the wellbeing of others.

As we discover how to deepen our attunement with this natural intelligent yearning within us,
We assist *"the Architect of Life"* to guide us with the *visions* or *"vehicles of possibility"*
That will help us "be part of a global team" in building a more peaceful world.

Circle of Vision

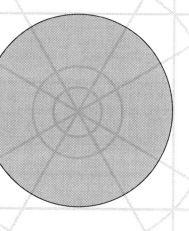

POSSIBILITY
VISION –
A CLEAR IMAGE
WITHIN MY MIND
OF A GREATER
POSSIBILITY OF GOOD
FOR MYSELF, OTHERS, OR
AN ASPECT OF THE WORLD

POTENTIAL
VISION –
A LUCID PICTURE
I HOLD IN MY MIND OF
A BENEFICIAL QUALITY
OR HIGHER POTENTIAL
OF THE PERSON
I WANT TO BECOME

GOAL
VISION –
A FUTURE POSITIVE
GOAL ALONG MY
JOURNEY OF LIFE THAT
I'M GUIDED TO ACHIEVE,
BUT WHICH I HAVE
NOT YET ATTAINED

IMAGINATION
VISION –
A VISUAL IDEA
OR CREATIVE
IMAGINATION
OF SOMETHING I COULD
BUILD OR MANIFEST
AT A FUTURE TIME

IMAGINATION

I use the unlimited power of my imagination to envision myself as the person I intend to be.

It can be very relaxing to lie on the ground, or sit in a lawn chair,
  And spend a few moments gazing up into a sky full of billowy clouds
    To watch pictorial images slowly taking form
      Within the moving patterns of white swirls against a blue background.

You might begin to imagine ancestral faces taking shape in the sky above you,
  Or you might see mighty sailing ships, or fierce dragons, or radiant angels,
    Appearing where, just a moment ago, there were only formless dancing clouds.

As a simple analogy, the thoughts we think that pass through our awareness
  Are like "internal clouds" which float through "the sky of our mind",
    And we have the power to use "the sculpting hands of our creative imagination"
      To consciously shape these passing thoughts into higher expression.

Our imagination can be utilized to picture and focus new mental images
  So as to positively influence a desired future outcome.

Imagination is the faculty of mind that combines our clear intention
  With an elevated emotion in order to help us manifest our desires.

There is a natural yearning within each of us (*the Infinite Intelligence* of the Universe)
  Which is constantly inviting us to keep our heart open
    So we may learn more conscious and virtuous ways to live our life
      And, thus, respond to the ever-widening **perspectives** that we discover.

Acquiring greater perspectives of what our life is truly about - and what really matters
  Can lead us to greater **understanding**, especially in relation to others,
    Which nurtures in us an experience of greater compassion and inclusion.

From this wider vantage that we gain from our investigation into life's universal questions,
  We can view "the greater horizon of our potential" and begin to crystallize this potential
    By forming a clear **vision** within our mind of what's possible for us to become.

The next step toward manifesting this vision as part of our personal reality
  Is to use the sculpting and focusing power of our creative **imagination**
    By energizing this vision with strong empowering emotions, such as a love for life.

Our imagination can also be a powerful tool we exercise to visualize maturing
  To higher levels of development through the use of certain archetypal images.

We can think of this as **our innate ability to draw on visionary images to focus our mind**
  On a specific vision of possibility in order to realize our greater potential.

Within the daily journey of our life there are many ways to use our natural gift of imagination
  As one of the most important tools we have to consciously re-create ourselves
    And to be the person we truly intend to be.

Circle of Imagination

VISUALIZATION
IMAGINATION –
A POWERFUL TOOL
OF THE MIND THAT I USE
TO VISUALIZE MYSELF
MATURING TO HIGHER
LEVELS OF DEVELOPMENT
AND EXPANDED AWARENESS

CLEAR INTENTION
IMAGINATION –
A FACULTY OF MIND
THAT COMBINES
MY CLEAR INTENTION
WITH AN ELEVATED
EMOTION IN ORDER TO
MANIFEST MY DESIRES

INNER FOCUS
IMAGINATION –
THE ABILITY TO
PICTURE AND FOCUS
NEW MENTAL IMAGES
SO I CAN POSITIVELY
INFLUENCE A DESIRED
FUTURE OUTCOME

VISION
IMAGINATION –
THE INNATE CAPACITY
TO FOCUS MY MIND
ON A SPECIFIC VISION
OF POSSIBILITY
IN ORDER TO REALIZE
MY GREATER POTENTIAL

IX

SPIRIT
AWARENESS
PRACTICES

PRIMARY TRANSFORMATIVE PRACTICES

I use transformative practices to assist Life in creating its next expression of awakening in me.

When body builders begin an exercise program to enlarge their muscles or shape their bodies,
> They typically start their training sessions with lighter weights
>> And gradually, over a period of time, add heavier weights to each exercise.

Usually in the first few days of training, no outer muscular development is observed,
> But with perseverance and ongoing daily practice,
>> They slowly increase the weights and, therefore, the resistance to their muscles
>>> Which, little by little, begins to affect the contours of their bodies.

With commitment and a good amount of work,
> Their bodies are progressively transformed into toned and sculpted physiques.

By using specific physical exercises, the outer body can be kept in good condition,
> While in regards to our inner lives, **primary transformative practices** can also be used
>> To help shape and develop the *heart, mind, and Spirit* aspects of our being.

Used as regular daily practices, these exercises can assist us to consciously transform our life
> From living within the illusion of fear to an authentic experience of inner freedom.

With dedication, they can aid in unshackling the grip of our unconscious self-oriented nature
> And support us in realizing our *Eternal Nature.*

The four foundational areas of our wellbeing - *body, heart, mind, and Spirit,*
> Each has its own set of transformative practices that can serve
>> To consistently cultivate in us a state of sustained wellbeing.

To nurture our spiritual wellbeing, meditation can be used as a fundamental daily practice,
> Yet other valuable practices are prayer, asking *Life* for inner guidance, and mindfulness.

Brain science has demonstrated the human mind has the capacity for unlimited learning
> That's enriched by contemplation, music training, imagination, and learning languages.

And, of course, our heart center also requires ways to sustain a state of health and balance,
> As does our physical body, of which exercise programs have already been mentioned.

In addition, there's great benefit toward accelerating the positive transformation of our life
> When we practice a little every day from all four of the foundational areas of wellbeing,
>> Which include the **body, heart, mind, and Spirit** *(see the following circle)*
>>> By choosing practices from each area that serve our individual needs.

All of the foundational practices support the others to enhance our overall transformation
> Working together as an integrated system of blossoming into our greater potential.

As we exercise the "muscles" of our *heart, mind, and Spirit,* as well as the muscles of our *body,*
> A little each day with steady determination and commitment,
>> We're assisting *Life* in creatively sculpting its next expression of awakening in us.

Circle of Primary Transformative Practices
(For the Four Foundational Areas of Wellbeing)

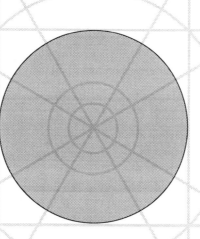

SPIRIT PRACTICES
+ MEDITATION
+ PRAYER
+ ASKING FOR GUIDANCE
+ MINDFULNESS
+ PRESENCE
+ WITNESSING
+ SELF-OBSERVATION

BODY PRACTICES
+ AEROBIC WALKING
+ YOGA
+ WEIGHT TRAINING
+ TAI CHI / QIGONG
+ BREATHWORK
+ NUTRITION
+ GARDENING

MIND PRACTICES
+ CONTEMPLATION
+ IMAGINATION
+ SPIRITUAL INQUIRY
+ STUDY INTERESTS
+ AFFIRMATIONS
+ MUSICAL TRAINING
+ LEARN LANGUAGES

HEART PRACTICES
+ APPRECIATION
+ SELF-LOVE
+ SERVICE TO OTHERS
+ FORGIVENESS
+ CULTIVATE CREATIVITY
+ EMOTIONAL RELEASE
+ TIME IN NATURE

CULTIVATING SPIRITUAL AWARENESS

Today I sit quietly in the silence of the present moment and align with the Source of Life.

When two pendulum clocks are fastened on a wooden wall adjacent to one another
So that they "feel", or respond to, the vibrations of the other directly through the wall,
Over a period of time the pendulum from one clock will start swinging
To the same rhythmic pulse as the other pendulum.

Eventually, the pendulums from the two clocks will swing together in perfect resonance
Becoming fully synchronized and aligned through the vibratory connection of the wall
That they're commonly attached to.

Similarly, if we desire to be in resonance with *Life* - and "feel" the pulse of *the Transcendent*,
We can choose to consciously place ourselves on *"the Wall of Spirit"*, so to speak,
In other words - re-establish an alignment with *the Source of Life*
Which is the foundation for truly **cultivating spiritual wellbeing**.

Yet *spiritual wellbeing* is a phrase that's a bit of an oxymoron,
Because, from an absolute perspective, *Spirit* by definition is *the Essence of Life*
That's eternal, unbounded, and unchanging,
And never in need of wellbeing or change of any kind.

But from the relative vantage of our daily life, it benefits us *to cultivate spiritual awareness*
So we can maintain a conscious alignment with *the Source of Life*
As well as learn to experience a life of inner freedom, of loving unconditionally,
And of contributing our creative gifts and talents to the wellbeing of others.

There is a major advantage in discovering how to maintain a conscious alignment,
A moment-to-moment resonance with *the Infinite Presence of Love*,
If we desire to intentionally embody greater peace, joy, and harmony.

The prominent spiritual traditions of the world have many time-tested techniques
Which sages and mystics of past and present ages have developed
That can help us nurture this transcendent attunement.

For example, a powerful way to **cultivate our spiritual awareness**
Is to enjoy **periods of silence each day**
Either through **meditation practice**, or by spending time in the hush of Nature,
Or by simply sitting quietly in the stillness of the present moment.

Experiencing silence can aid in sustaining an awareness of *the Infinite Intelligence*
Which continually informs our actions and choices, and animates our body and mind.

Other methods to maintain this alignment could include various **mindfulness practices**,
Prayer, and **the practice of attuning to our inner guidance**.

The specific technique or form of practice is not the important factor here,
Yet what's important is to find effective ways "to fasten ourselves to *the Wall of Spirit"*
So we can constantly feel, and respond to, a resonance with *the Mystery of Life*.

Circle of Cultivating Spiritual Awareness
(Transformative Practices)

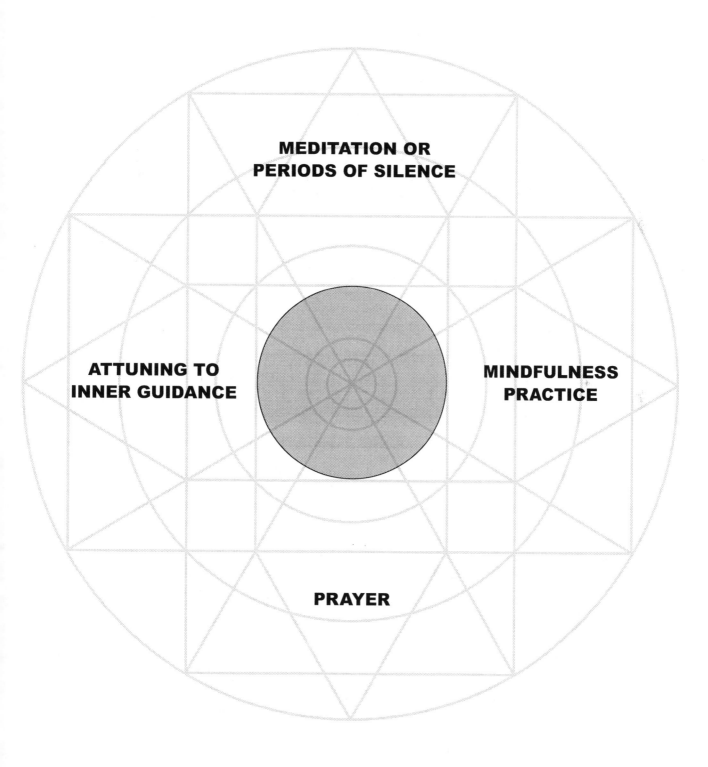

MEDITATION OR
PERIODS OF SILENCE

ATTUNING TO
INNER GUIDANCE

MINDFULNESS
PRACTICE

PRAYER

PRAYER

I willfully align my awareness with the Infinite Presence of Love - thus every moment is a prayer.

Every time we want to listen to a particular kind of music or news program on our car radio,
    We must make sure the channel button, that's connected to the radio's internal receiver,
        Is set properly so it's attuned to the specific frequency of our desired station.

Radio frequencies are constantly being broadcast through the airwaves in every direction,
    But our radio can't receive the appropriate signal of the station we desire
        Until we tune our receiver to a precise frequency.

We can think of **the practice of prayer** as analogous to tuning the receiver of a radio
    In that **prayer is the co-creative act of attuning, or aligning, our heart and mind**
        With *the Infinite Presence of Love (the Source of Life, God, Perfect Wholeness)*
        In order to assist others or ourselves in some beneficent way.

Prayer is the act of aligning with *the Natural Intelligence of the Universe*
    And compassionately "sending" the sublime energy of *Love* to another
        So as to help promote a return of balance or wellbeing to them.

When we pray for the wellbeing of another,
    We can create within our mind **a visualization of our goal**
        In which we become a vessel for the radiant force of *Limitless Love*
        To flow through us as it positively affects the energy field of that person.

Each time we pray authentically for others or ourselves, we become like *laser beams of Love*
    And, of course, laser beams are powerful beams of focused light rays
        In which all of the rays of coherent light are aligned in one specific direction.

When our sharply focused imagination converges and is aligned
    With the genuine compassionate feelings within our heart of serving another,
        This caring image has the potential to become a powerful influential stream
        In the unfolding of future possibilities.

Prayer can also become a natural daily expression of our conscious heartfelt intention
    To help restore the flow of wellbeing or peace to one who is in need.

Scientists have conducted numerous double-blind studies on the efficacy of prayer
    And many scientific studies have demonstrated the effectiveness and benefits
        For both the one who is being prayed for,
        As well as the one who is actually "doing the praying".

The transformative practice of prayer emerges out of our gratitude for life
    As we focus our intention on someone or some particular situation
        While "tuning our receivers to a channel of *Unlimited Creative Energy*"
        So *the Power of Love* can do its miraculous work.

When our awareness is truly aligned with *the Infinite Presence of Love,*
    Every moment of our life becomes a prayer.

Circle of Prayer
(A Transformative Practice)

ALIGNMENT
PRAYER –
A CO-CREATIVE ACT
OF ALIGNING MY HEART AND
MIND WITH *THE INFINITE*
PRESENCE OF LOVE
IN ORDER TO ASSIST
SOMEONE IN NEED

"SENDING" LOVE
PRAYER –
AN ACT OF COMPAS-
SIONATELY "SENDING"
THE SUBLIME ENERGY
OF *LOVE* TO ANOTHER
SO AS TO PROMOTE
A RETURN OF BALANCE

VISION
PRAYER –
A CREATIVE
VISUALIZATION
THAT HAS THE GOAL
OF HELPING BRING
GOOD, HARMONY,
OR HEALING TO OTHERS

INTENTION
PRAYER –
A CONSCIOUS
HEARTFELT INTENTION
TO HELP RESTORE
THE NATURAL FLOW
OF WELLBEING OR PEACE
TO ONE WHO IS IN NEED

X

THE EVOLUTIONARY PERSPECTIVE

GIFTS FROM AN EVOLUTIONARY PERSPECTIVE

Embracing an evolutionary perspective of life empowers me to live responsibly with integrity.

If you were to make a valiant effort to climb to the highest point of a tall mountain,
You could then gaze in all directions and, thus, enjoy a wider view of your surroundings.

When we study history, we gain greater awareness of the glories and defeats of humanity,
And, therefore, learn much about ourselves and our key relationships with one another.

If a child places its hand on a hot stove, the child will get "a bigger picture" of what a stove is,
For this direct experience usually provides a whole new perspective about fire and heat.

Over the last few centuries, science has revealed a wealth of information
Offering us brand new perspectives of how the evidence-based knowledge of evolution
Is now becoming *the Universal Creation Story* that clarifies our cosmic origins,
For it's a genesis story about how everything in the Universe came to be.

Archeological science has given us vast fossil evidence regarding the evolving Tree of Life,
Biological science and DNA research has established the interrelationships of species,
Geological science has confirmed the evolutionary journey
Of a four-and-a-half billion year planetary development of the Earth,
And cosmological science has presented us an expansive glimpse
Into the unraveling processes of the entire Cosmos
From the beginning of time.

Just like climbing a tall mountain, this **evolutionary perspective** of where we have come from
And the dynamic process of arriving where we are now in this epic interconnected story
Can empower us as human beings to perceive a much "Bigger Picture of reality"
And give us many insights regarding the purpose and meaning of our life.

By directly observing and comprehending how we are intimately connected
To every other creature, every diverse eco-system, and every facet of life on Earth,
We recognize the importance of taking **responsible and integrous actions**.

By deepening our understanding of how every person on our planet
Grows over a lifetime through various stages of expanding progress and development
(Just as you and I also grow through these same developmental stages),
We learn to foster **greater compassion** for the challenges of others.

By examining "the Big Picture of our world" from *an evolutionary perspective,*
We become aware of what strengthens the beneficent progression of life
As well as the dysfunctional aspects of ourselves that no longer support life
And, thus, acquire the inner **motivation to transform**.

By embracing a grander perspective of what really matters provided by this view of evolution,
We awaken a deep understanding of the benefits and **joys of self-development**.

A shift in our awareness occurs as "we climb this peak of understanding" and see life as a gift,
The kind of gift that inspires us to offer our own gift back to the perpetual evolution of life.

Circle of Gifts From An Evolutionary Perspective

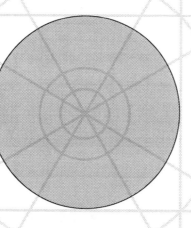

INTEGRITY
REALIZING EVERYTHING
IS AN INTEGRAL PART OF
A PERPETUALLY EVOLVING
UNIVERSE EMPOWERS ME
TO ALIGN WITH *LIFE*
AND LIVE WITH INTEGRITY
*+GIFT – CREATES A VISION
OF LIVING WITH INTEGRITY*

DEVELOPMENT
KNOWING THAT ALL
OF EVOLVING LIFE HAS
A NATURAL IMPULSE
TO LEARN INSPIRES ME
TO FURTHER DEVELOP
MY OWN POTENTIAL
*+GIFT – AWAKENS A JOY
TO DEVELOP MYSELF*

TRANSFORMATION
EMBRACING "THE BIG
PICTURE" PROVIDES ME
CLARITY CONCERNING
MY THOUGHTS WHICH
SUPPORT LIFE - AND
THOSE WHICH DO NOT
*+GIFT – MOTIVATES ME
TO TRANSFORM MYSELF*

COMPASSION
*THE EVOLUTIONARY
PERSPECTIVE* HELPS ME
FEEL EMPATHY
FOR ANOTHER - AND LIVE
A COMPASSIONATE LIFE
THAT SERVES OTHERS
*+GIFT – CULTIVATES IN ME
COMPASSIONATE SERVICE*

INTEGRITY

I live with integrity as I engage in actions that empower others and support ethical behavior.

Many people have hiked through an alpine valley and then came upon a flowing stream
Where they stopped for a moment to watch its bubbling water race down the slope
Effortlessly passing over rocks and other physical obstacles
As the stream followed its *path of least resistance.*

If a natural event, such as a landslide or an avalanche, should occur near a stream
And many large stones, branches, or logs obstruct the water's path,
Then the stream's normal flow would be fully or partially blocked.

Relating to our own life, the quality of **integrity** is like the moving current of a mountain stream
In which *authentic integrity* effortlessly circulates through us without resistance
When we are aligned with *the Infinite Presence of Love* at the core of our heart.

When we find ourselves out of alignment - because we somehow place our attention
On unloving thoughts such as selfishness or fear,
It's as if we're unconsciously accumulating "large stones or logs across our path"
Which impede the natural stream of *Life Force energy* that flows in us.

To live our life with *integrity* requires us to be consciously aware of any fear-based thoughts
Which habitually keep us from expressing our highest values and principles.

For *integrity* is the instinctual part of us that **courageously makes choices and takes action
Based on the highest values and beliefs we currently hold to be true**.

It is also the natural impulse in us to choose to make the everyday choices
Which are in the highest service to others - and to all of life.

Furthermore, *integrity* is expressed when **we choose to consciously live our life in a way
In which all of our actions generate life-supporting consequences**.

Integrity, like anything else we intentionally desire to develop in our life, takes practice
For we must consistently practice being mindful and aware throughout the day
To observe if there are any fearful thoughts blocking the flow of our intention.

In regards to the many choices we must formulate everyday,
We have the opportunity to learn to sustain this course of awareness
By making a conscious decision to only engage in actions that empower others
And **actions that support moral and ethical behaviors.**

One way to ensure a high level of *integrity*
Is to **each day align our awareness with *the Source of Life*
So we may feel and act on the guidance available to us in all that we do.**

When we are intentionally aligned in this manner, we become "a River of Awareness"
That effortlessly pours through the daily circumstances of our life
Guiding our thoughts and actions into a natural flow of *true integrity.*

Circle of Integrity

HIGHEST VALUES
INTEGRITY –
COURAGEOUSLY MAKING
CHOICES AND TAKING
ACTION BASED ON
THE HIGHEST VALUES
AND BELIEFS I CURRENTLY
HOLD TO BE TRUE

MORALITY
INTEGRITY –
CHOOSING TO MAKE
THE EVERYDAY CHOICES
AND ACTIONS
WHICH SUPPORT
MORAL AND ETHICAL
BEHAVIOR

LIFE-SUPPORTING
INTEGRITY –
CHOOSING TO LIVE
MY LIFE IN A WAY
IN WHICH ALL OF
MY ACTIONS GENERATE
LIFE-SUPPORTING
CONSEQUENCES

ALIGNMENT
INTEGRITY –
MAINTAINING
AN ALIGNMENT WITH
THE SOURCE OF LIFE
SO I MAY FEEL AND ACT ON
THE GUIDANCE AVAILABLE
TO ME IN ALL THAT I DO

THE FRACTAL NATURE OF EMERGENT EVOLUTION

The fundamental patterns within Nature point me to my own destiny of living an awakened life.

For many eons humans have explored a vibrant curiosity with Nature's majestic wonders
And have responded to an innate longing to understand and creatively express
The unique forms and patterns that are observed within all of life.

About 300 BCE, the Greeks invented a mathematical system we now call Euclidean geometry
Which attempted to describe the fundamental shapes of Nature
Using primary images such as the circle, triangle, and square,
And over time, these were expanded to more complex geometric concepts
Like the plane and the five platonic solids.

Euclidean geometry has been a numerical innovation used for over two thousand years,
Yet can only describe the most basic forms in Nature, and since Nature is so complex,
This type of math can't be used to describe a majority of its countless patterns.

In 1972, an important breakthrough in mathematics took place
When *fractal geometry* was discovered by the mathematician, Benoit Mandelbrot.

Fractal geometry is a numerical formulation that can mathematically describe
The more complex shapes and phenomena of Nature,
Such as the repeating formations of plants, organic systems, mountain ranges,
Cloud patterns, the irregularity of coastlines, and much more.

In general terms, **fractals** are specific geometrical forms with characteristics that allow them
To repeat slight variations of their original pattern over and over again at various scales.

For example, a full-grown tree has inherent fractal qualities embedded within its seed
For as a tree develops during its life, it first produces an initial large branch or trunk
From which it repeats a similar pattern by creating smaller branches off the trunk,
Which repeat again with the emergence of even smaller twigs,
And these patterns repeat as the veins inside each individual leaf.

The natural expression of this universal fractal geometry
Can be found in almost every aspect of life on Earth, including our human body.

The creation of planet Earth four-and-a-half billion years ago
Was also governed by these same fractal principles.

The Earth, as well as our entire Solar System, evolved from a massive supernova explosion
As a unique living organism demonstrating its own novel form of planetary intelligence.

Over billions of years *the Natural Intelligence* governing evolution repeated a similar pattern
Creating smaller forms of itself with **the emergence of early biological life**,
Which then developed another branch of intelligent expression
In the form of **the self-reflective human mind**,
And could it be that this fractal pattern is yearning to repeat itself
In the form of **spiritually awakened human beings**?

Circle of the Fractal Nature of Emergent Evolution
(In Relation to the Awakening Human)

THE EVOLUTION OF PLANET EARTH
THE EARTH, AS WELL AS OUR ENTIRE SOLAR SYSTEM, EVOLVED FROM A MASSIVE SUPERNOVA AND, OVER TIME, THE EARTH *AWAKENED* INTO A LIVING ORGANISM

THE EVOLUTION OF THE AWAKENED HUMAN
MODERN HUMANS ARE EVOLVING TOWARD NEW EMERGENT STAGES OF *AWAKENING*, REPEATING THE FRACTAL PATTERNS OF ALL LIVING SYSTEMS

THE EVOLUTION OF EARLY HUMANS
PRIMITIVE HUMANS EVOLVED FROM THE EARLY BIOLOGICAL LIFE OF PLANET EARTH, REPEATING A SIMILAR FRACTAL PATTERN OF EMERGENT *AWAKENING*

THE EVOLUTION OF THE SELF-REFLECTIVE MIND
THE HUMAN MIND EVOLVED AND BECAME SELF-REFLECTIVE, *AWAKENING* ANOTHER REPEATING EMERGENT FRACTAL PATTERN

THE INFINITE CREATIVITY OF THE UNIVERSE

The boundless creativity in me is the same Infinite Creativity that animates the entire Universe.

Each day people throughout the world make use of a boundless stream of creativity
  To help solve innumerable personal and collective challenges,
    Such as designing spacecrafts that will journey to distant planets,
      Cultivating sustainable societies that will end poverty,
        And even finding more innovative ways to deal with our garbage.

This wealth of unlimited creativity that dwells at the core of every human being
  Is the same essence of **creativity that animates all things within the Universe**
    And is *the Natural Intelligence* which has directed evolution for 13.8 billion years.

Cosmological science has postulated that at the beginning of the Universe
  The fullness of existence was unfathomably compressed into a *singularity*,
    One single tiny point containing an unimaginable amount of massive energy,
      And through a profound act of infinite creativity, it surrendered,
        In other words - it relinquished its "unity" with an explosion so large
          It formed all of the countless particles in the Cosmos
            Which now fill every corner of space.

These rudimentary particles, which initially consisted mostly of hydrogen, were drawn together
  By the evolutionary and gravitational **fields of attraction and repulsion**
    Until they slowly coalesced into immense **galactic clouds** of radiant energy.

Over billions of years, these galactic clouds surrendered, or let go of, their dispersed forms,
  And were condensed into colossal **stars** which became powerful nuclear furnaces
    Creating complex elements shaped by strong **electrical and magnetic forces**.

Eventually, these stars yielded their titanic power through magnificent supernova explosions
  That fashioned new solar systems where **biological life** could emerge on rocky planets
    Shaped by universal laws that included the **masculine and feminine polarities**.

In time, on our own planet Earth, evolving life forms surrendered their more simple expressions
  To gradually produce a plethora of diverse complex organisms
    (Such as **human life** with self-awareness, self-reflection, and conscious choices)
      That were shaped by certain emotional dynamics such as **love and fear**.

And now each and every day, this perpetual stream of *Infinite Creativity*
  Continues to help us resolve our ongoing dilemmas and challenges,
    Yet it also offers us the cognitive perspective and emotional capacity
      To become conscious of, and understand (for the very first time in history),
        The revelatory "Great Story of an intelligently evolving Cosmos"
          In which we humans are a small but integral part.

This key understanding of the evolving Universe inspires many to ask the existential question:
  What in my life must I now surrender, or let go of, at this unique moment in time
    So my open heart may receive Life's guidance regarding how I can serve others
      And collectively help create a more peaceful world?

Circle of the Infinite Creativity of the Universe
(In Relation to the Dualistic Forces of Evolution)

HUMAN LIFE
EVOLVING LIFE FORMS
SURRENDERED THEIR
SIMPLE EXPRESSIONS
TO PRODUCE COMPLEX
ORGANISMS WITH SELF-
AWARENESS THAT WERE
SHAPED BY EMOTIONS
SUCH AS *LOVE AND FEAR*

GALACTIC CLOUDS
IN THE BEGINNING, ALL OF
EXISTENCE SURRENDERED
ITS *SINGULARITY* SO AS TO
CREATE PARTICLES THAT
FORMED GALACTIC CLOUDS
OF HYDROGEN - SHAPED BY
*FIELDS OF ATTRACTION
AND REPULSION*

BIOLOGICAL LIFE
STARS SURRENDERED
THEIR VAST POWER WITH
SUPERNOVA EXPLOSIONS
TO FORM SOLAR SYSTEMS
WHERE BIOLOGICAL LIFE
EMERGED - SHAPED BY
*MASCULINE AND
FEMININE POLARITIES*

STARS
HUGE GALACTIC CLOUDS
SURRENDERED THEIR
DISPERSED FORMS TO
BECOME MASSIVE STARS
THAT CREATED PRIMARY
ELEMENTS - SHAPED BY
*ELECTRICAL AND
MAGNETIC FORCES*

EVOLUTIONARY EMERGENCE OF SPECIES

The Impulse of Evolution directs me each day to further cultivate my inner development.

If you are in the middle of a long journey - yet still have a considerable distance to travel,
    It's beneficial to have an appropriate map of the territory you intend to traverse
        So you can observe where you've been
            And plan the next route you might take toward your destination.

Similarly, exploring and understanding the evidence-based story of evolution
    (Our universal map of knowledge regarding the ever-unfolding Cosmos),
        Not only informs us about where we've come from - and how we got to this moment,
            But has the inherent gift of providing insightful clues
                To where we collectively, as a human species, may be headed.

Science has uncovered a wealth of information about the interconnected tapestry of life
    That has been weaving its way on our planet for billions of years.

These discoveries have revealed that life is in a constant process of evolutionary exploration
    Generating on our planet amazing diversity and creative innovations
        Which *the Infinite Intelligence* of the Universe has used for millennia
            To produce the first sensations of touch, sight, and hearing,
                To manifest the first impulses of instinctual knowing,
                    To feel the first emotional longings of the *heart*,
                        And to discern the very first primal thought patterns.

Over eons of time, we humans evolved into a unique species due to the complex interplay
    From all these various explorations of evolution within the diverse creatures of the world,
        And we're still evolving within the perpetual line of developing life forms.

The natural evolutionary tension of reptilian instincts, mammalian emotions,
    And primate brain functions
        Have all yielded to the sudden emergence of new and surprising life forms
            Producing the long progressing arc of myriad plants and animals.

At this present moment in evolutionary history, **there's a brand new creative tension**
    Pulling at the core of the human *heart* that yearns to spiritually awaken -
        And to collectively evolve into a more enlightened global society.

The Natural Intelligence of the Universe is weaving its threads of creativity into a new tapestry
    And traveling down one more uncharted road
        Where the boundless expression of life has never been before.

The evolutionary tension of a self-oriented ego yielding to the yearning of *spiritual awakening*
    May, at this time, be what is necessary for the emergence of an entirely new species.

One thing that differentiates our species from all other creatures on this planet
    Is that we have developed the unparalleled capacity, the unique "human spark",
        To be a self-reflective and consciously responsible participant of evolution
            In the co-creation of life's unlimited possibilities for the future of this world.

Circle of the Evolutionary Emergence of Species

HUMANS TO
" ??? "
THE EVOLUTIONARY
TENSION OF A SELF-
ORIENTED EGO YIELDING
TO THE NATURAL YEARNING
OF *SPIRITUAL AWAKENING*
ALLOWS FOR
THE EMERGENCE OF
AN ENTIRELY NEW SPECIES

REPTILES TO
MAMMALS
THE EVOLUTIONARY
TENSION OF REPTILIAN
INSTINCTS YIELDING
TO THE DEVELOPMENT
OF NEW IMPULSES
OF EMOTIONS ALLOWED
FOR THE EMERGENCE
OF MAMMALS

PRIMATES TO
HUMANS
THE EVOLUTIONARY
TENSION OF PRIMATE
BRAIN FUNCTIONS
YIELDING TO FORCES
OF MORE COMPLEX
THOUGHT ALLOWED FOR
THE EMERGENCE
OF HUMANS

MAMMALS TO
PRIMATES
THE EVOLUTIONARY
TENSION OF MAMMALIAN
EMOTION YIELDING
TO THE DEVELOPMENT
OF IMPULSES OF PRIMAL
THOUGHT ALLOWED FOR
THE EMERGENCE
OF PRIMATES

EVOLUTION OF THE HUMAN BRAIN

The natural impulse of evolution within me is always inviting me to serve the good of all.

During the last few hundred years, there have been many archeological discoveries
In which modern science has observed that the unfolding path of evolution
Does not always progress forward in a simple linear manner,
But instead meanders through a maze of experimentation and possibility
As it explores the many diverse branches of the Tree of Life.

Throughout evolution, various life forms on their journey of discovery have led to "dead ends"
Where, for varied reasons, the novel lineage of a particular species eventually died out.

At this present time in our planetary history, the evolutionary line of the human species
(Starting with single-celled amoebas that evolved into multi-celled organisms,
Which over time became reptiles, then various forms of mammals,
And ultimately emerged as our current human expression)
Continues its ceaseless exploration of cognitive development.

Neuroscientists have discovered that our human brain,
Which has been evolving for over two million years, consists of three principal regions.

At the base of our neck, the brain stem contains our **reptilian brain**,
Which, many eons ago, developed basic physical-body instincts
That mainly are focused on survival, acquisition of food, and procreation.

Located toward the mid-section of our head is our **mammalian brain**,
Which slowly evolved capacities for relational bonding, simple emotional responses,
And primitive thought processes that furthered chances for survival.

During the last 200,000 years, the frontal lobes of our **human neocortex** developed
Fostering complex thought processes, rational thinking, and creative self-expression.

Each of these three brain regions has their own specific needs, desires, and areas of focus,
Yet, sometimes, their individual functions aren't in sync - and work against one another.

As conscious self-reflective beings, it has now become our responsibility to discover ways
To align all three of these into one coherent stream of awareness that works together.

When we do this, we assist a whole new collective compassionate consciousness to evolve
Into what we can call **the awakened brain**, which (among other things)
Is focused on being in service to the wellbeing of others - and to all of life.

One of the major gifts of embracing *an evolutionary perspective* is to develop this awareness,
And we can cultivate this spiritual awareness by engaging in daily transformative practice.

Could it be that by becoming aware of the vast evolutionary journey all of life is embarked on,
We are more able to be consciously active in contributing our small, but meaningful part
Toward helping our world, integrated with the collective heart of humanity,
Develop its "next unique branch of the Tree of Life"?

Circle of the Evolution of the Human Brain

AWAKENED BRAIN
THE DEVELOPMENT
OF A COLLECTIVE
COMPASSIONATE
CONSCIOUSNESS
(INTEGRATED SELF)
+ FOCUS IS ON SERVING
THE WELLBEING OF OTHERS

REPTILIAN BRAIN
THE DEVELOPMENT
OF BASIC PHYSICAL-
BODY INSTINCTS
(INSTINCTUAL SELF)
+ FOCUS IS ON
SURVIVAL, FOOD,
AND PROCREATION

**MODERN HUMAN
BRAIN**
THE DEVELOPMENT
OF COMPLEX RATIONAL
THOUGHT PROCESSES
(CONSCIOUS SELF)
+ FOCUS IS ON SELF-
EXPRESSION AND
PERSONAL GROWTH

MAMMALIAN BRAIN
THE DEVELOPMENT
OF PRIMARY EMOTIONAL
RESPONSES
(PRIMITIVE SELF)
+ FOCUS IS ON
RELATIONAL BONDING,
POWER, AND CONTROL

INFINITE AWAKENINGS

Life is constantly inviting me to cultivate more compassion and empathy for others.

When some people ponder the words "awakening" or "enlightenment",
    A generalized meaning of these spiritual concepts can conjure up images
        Of a titanic, difficult, and profound liberating event
            That might possibly take place at some future time in their lives
                If they are "lucky" enough, or "spiritual" enough, to experience it.

Yet when we take into account "the Big Picture perspective" of a perpetually evolving world
    That's constantly manifesting new innovative forms of emergent life,
        We can begin to see that *spiritual awakening* is surely the most natural next step
            Of evolutionary development in humanity's continuum of unfolding.

In fact, from an evidence-based vantage using the vast knowledge of evolutionary science,
    Various forms of *"awakening"* have been ceaselessly occurring since the dawn of time.

Billions of years ago, during the early evolutionary history of the Cosmos, stars did not exist
    Until the conditions in the Universe were just right - then suddenly the first star appeared.

Also planets didn't exist until external conditions were just right - then the first planet appeared,
    And for eons, no form of life existed - then the first structure of evolving life appeared.

Eckhart Tolle, a contemporary spiritual author, describes in his book, "The New Earth",
    About how numerous and diverse expressions of *"awakening"* have taken form
        Throughout different stages of Earth's evolutionary history.

Eckhart explains that, millions of years ago, no flower had yet appeared in the world,
    But *the Natural Intelligence of Life* eventually found a creative and innovative way
        To set the scene for this brand new emergent expression to arise
            By suddenly and mysteriously transforming simple green vegetation
                Into the delicate form of **the first flower**.

For the first flower to discover a way to suddenly take shape on Earth,
    A radical leap in consciousness within Nature was required.

Therefore if we expand our definition, a new and emergent expression of the initial flower
    Can be thought of as the *"enlightenment"* - or *"awakening"* - of the plant kingdom.

This radical leap of *"awakening"* also occurred in other realms, such as the mineral kingdom
    As carbon was transformed into crystals and, thus, *"awakened"* into **the first diamond**,
        And in a similar way, an *"awakening"* took place within the animal kingdom
            As a land reptile was transformed into **the first bird that took flight.**

The same vital evolutionary impulses are happening right now in you and me and everyone
    As they have been steadily expressing within all form from the beginning of the Universe.

Could it be that each one of us is part of a perpetual spectrum of **infinite awakenings**
    In which we are (consciously or unconsciously) evolving into an **awakened human**?

Circle of Infinite Awakenings
(Progressive Images of Emergent Evolution)

FIRST AWAKENED HUMAN
THE TRANSFORMATION OF A FEARFUL SELF-ORIENTED PERSON INTO THE FIRST ENLIGHTENED HUMAN WAS
AN *"AWAKENING"* WITHIN HUMANITY

FIRST DIAMOND
THE TRANSFORMATION OF CARBON ATOMS INTO THE CRYSTALLINE FORM OF THE FIRST DIAMOND WAS
AN *"AWAKENING"* OF THE MINERAL KINGDOM

FIRST BIRD
THE TRANSFORMATION OF A LAND REPTILE INTO THE FIRST BIRD THAT TOOK FLIGHT WAS
AN *"AWAKENING"* OF THE ANIMAL KINGDOM

FIRST FLOWER
THE TRANSFORMATION OF GREEN VEGETATION INTO THE DELICATE FORM OF THE FIRST FLOWER WAS
AN *"AWAKENING"* OF THE PLANT KINGDOM

PRIMARY STAGES OF EVOLUTION

I am "the eyes of the Universe" gazing into the vast Cosmos and observing my own evolution.

Some people have homes surrounded by yards that are decorated with colorful flowers
    And these flowers are intended to bring enjoyment and a touch of beauty to the setting.

Yet in order for anyone to take pleasure in their beautiful blossoms,
    Each flower must first grow through a series of natural stages.

In due course, there must be a tiny bud that's produced on the stem
    From which the actual blossoms of the flower emerge.

And before this stage, a stem and set of leaves must grow, preceded by a sprouting seedling
    Which originally bursts forth from a germinated seed buried in moist soil.

It makes sense that if we want to build a strong stable structure, such as a house or a bridge,
    We must first prepare the proper foundation on which to construct the rest of the stages.

Likewise, because of the various discoveries of evolutionary science in the past 150 years,
    We can observe that the evolution of the Cosmos has gone through progressive stages
        Which were necessary to physically unfold in proper sequence
            In order to have manifested the complexities of this magnificent Universe.

Our Universe required billions of years of constantly unfolding evolution
    For galaxies with their massive stars to coalesce from vast amounts of hydrogen
        In order to create the suitable conditions and primary physical elements
            So biological life could ultimately emerge.

Over time, **individual planets were shaped from the residual material of exploding stars**
    Which created the proper environment for life to emerge on a planet we call Earth
        From these prime elements (the basic building blocks of "stardust")
            Producing a rich bio-diversity of myriad plants and animals.

Evolution then needed three-and-a-half billion years of further exploration
    To generate the ideal conditions for **the emergence of intelligent life**
        That was birthed from the advance of complex emotions and thought processes
            Responding to an impulse to expand and express individual potential.

Approximately two-and-a-half million years ago,
    The first hominids, our human ancestors, appeared on the scene.

A most monumental event took place within the Universe
    When these early hominids eventually demonstrated more advanced cognitive abilities,
        Developed into humans, learned to be consciously aware of their own evolution,
            And thus began to realize their unique place in *The Great Cosmic Story.*

Could it be that our collective development as **a global family of conscious humans**
    Is like a tiny bud on the perpetual growing stem of *Life* poised to burst forth and blossom
        Into "the flower of the next great *awakening* of the human species"?

Circle of the Primary Stages of Evolution

**THE STAGE
OF CONSCIOUS
HUMAN LIFE**
THE DEVELOPMENT
OF BEINGS WITH SELF-
REFLECTIVE MINDS AND
COMPASSIONATE HEARTS
THAT ARE AWARE
OF THEIR OWN EVOLUTION

**THE STAGE
OF GALAXIES
TO PLANETS**
THE EARLY FORMATION
OF MASSIVE GALAXIES
WITH EXPLODING STARS
THAT CREATED PLANETS
WHERE PRIME ELEMENTS
WERE THE BASIS FOR LIFE

**THE STAGE
OF INTELLIGENT
LIFE FORMS**
SOME LIFE FORMS EVOLVE
COMPLEX EMOTIONS AND
THOUGHT PROCESSES,
RESPONDING TO IMPULSES
TO EXPAND AND EXPRESS
INDIVIDUAL POTENTIAL

**THE STAGE
OF BIOLOGICAL
LIFE**
THE EMERGENCE
OF BIOLOGICAL LIFE
ON EARTH - PRODUCING
A RICH BIO-DIVERSITY
OF THE MYRIAD FORMS
OF PLANTS AND ANIMALS

XI

ARCHETYPES OF LIFE MASTERY

ARCHETYPES OF LIFE MASTERY

Today I envision myself creating a life of inner freedom that serves the good of all.

In the well-known story about the mythical city of Camelot,
>There was a wise and just king named Arthur, a kind queen named Guinevere,
>>A powerful magician who lived in the forest called Merlin,
>>>And many loyal and brave Knights of the Round Table.

This longstanding saga describes how all of these individuals joined together
>To offer their unique gifts and talents to the collective community
>>In a valiant attempt to rid their kingdom of darkness and oppression,
>>>And, as a group, take decisive action toward building a better world.

Each and every morning the voice of *Life* whispers softly in our ears
>And invites us to take a similar journey, to reach for a more expanded horizon,
>>To discover "the king or queen" of higher wisdom in us,
>>>To explore "the magician" within us who can help transform our life,
>>>>And to stand as a "spiritual warrior" for the truth we feel in our heart.

There is a particular group of symbolic images called **the Archetypes of Life Mastery**
>Which are mythological and visionary representations of our greater human potential
>>And, over time, accessing these archetypes can help us gain mastery of our life,
>>>The mastery of living a life of inner freedom that serves the good of all.

The archetype of **the Peaceful Warrior** is a visionary image that can be thought of
>As one who expands spiritual awareness by practicing mindfulness,
>>Who confronts the challenges of life with conscious responsibility,
>>>Who has a heart and mind that's open to unlimited possibilities,
>>>>And who, through personal discipline, strives for excellence.

The Mystical Lover is an archetypal template of one who has a passion and love for life,
>Who is able to be gracefully flexible with life's changes and challenges,
>>Who lives authentically with a compassionate heart,
>>>And who has discovered the sublime gift of caring for others.

The Spiritual Magician can be thought of as one who demonstrates "the magic of miracles"
>By aligning with *the Source of Life, the Infinite Creativity* of the Universe,
>>So as to help manifest what *Life* inwardly directs every person to achieve
>>>Using the marriage of conscious intention and elevated emotions.

Living with generosity from "the royal throne of heart wisdom",
>Making awakened choices that serve all people,
>>Empowering and supporting every facet of life,
>>>And taking benevolent action which is guided by *Love*,
>>>>Is the noble realm of **the Enlightened King or Queen**.

Together these four archetypes hold a common vision of a more enlightened society,
>An image of extraordinary possibilities for a more evolved future,
>>And a collective dream of transforming fear into the mastery of unconditional love.

Circle of Archetypes of Life Mastery

**ENLIGHTENED KING
OR QUEEN**
IT IS THE PART OF ME
THAT CULTIVATES
GENEROSITY AND HEART
WISDOM, LIVES MY LIFE
IN SERVICE TO OTHERS,
EMPOWERS ALL PEOPLE,
AND TAKES ACTION
WHICH IS GUIDED BY *LOVE*

**PEACEFUL
WARRIOR**
IT IS THE PART OF
ME THAT DEVELOPS EACH
DAY THROUGH THE
PRACTICES OF MIND-
FULNESS, CONSCIOUS
RESPONSIBILITY,
AND BY BEING OPEN TO
UNLIMITED POSSIBILITY

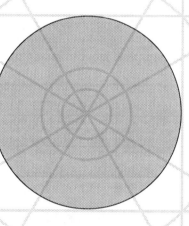

**SPIRITUAL
MAGICIAN**
IT IS THE PART OF ME
THAT ALIGNS WITH
*THE SOURCE OF LIFE,
THE INFINITE CREATIVITY*
OF THE UNIVERSE,
SO AS TO MANIFEST
WHAT *LIFE* INWARDLY
DIRECTS ME TO ACHIEVE

**MYSTICAL
LOVER**
IT IS THE PART OF ME
THAT LIVES
AUTHENTICALLY WITH
A PASSION FOR LIFE,
IS FLEXIBLE TO CHANGE,
QUESTIONS EVERYTHING,
AND CARES FOR THE
WELLBEING OF OTHERS

ENLIGHTENED KING OR QUEEN

Life is always inviting me to envision and create the next expression of who I intend to be.

Some people like to keep the curtains drawn over their bedroom windows
> So they can sleep late into the morning
>> Without the glaring light of the Sun disturbing their slumber.

When they finally wake up - the room is still dark, for the light has not been able to enter
> Until they open the curtains to let the outer luminance pour in.

Darkness is not eliminated from a room by attempting to physically remove the *dark*,
> But by simply bringing *light* into the space.

There is a natural stirring deep within us, the perpetual whisper of an inner guiding impulse
> Which constantly invites us to bring "more light into the space of our heart",
>> Live with greater compassion and empathy for others,
>>> And transform our life from living in the bondage of fear
>>>> To living with the radiant freedom of *Limitless Love*.

The Source of Life, the Infinite Intelligence of the Universe, is always inviting us
> To meet the present moment with "the light of possibility"
>> And to envision and create the next expression of who we intend to be
>>> So we can more effectively participate in helping to build a better world.

Through the powerful practice of archetypal visualization
> Using the focused stream of our creative imagination,
>> We can draw on the visionary image of **the Enlightened King or Queen**
>>> To imagine embodying within ourselves the qualities of **heart wisdom,**
>>>> **As well as greater compassion and empathy for the suffering of others**.

We can also use this specific visionary template to envision how it feels
> To **make the most benevolent choices that serve the wellbeing of others,**
>> **Promote greater cooperation,**
>>> **And aid others in the realization of their *Eternal Nature*.**

As we heighten our awareness of the authentic goodness, inner beauty,
> And true creative potential of all people, it becomes easier to experience
>> **The gift and blessing of empowering each person** we come in contact with.

There is "a seed of awakening" that can begin to expand within us
> When we intentionally **visualize each day - as a day of living with integrity,**
>> **A day of contributing our creative gifts and talents,**
>>> **And a day of being guided by *the Infinite Intelligence of Life*.**

At times we may feel as if we're asleep, as if we're living our life within a darkened awareness,
> Yet using the symbol of **the Enlightened King or Queen** as a transformative practice
>> Can be like opening the window shades in the morning to the radiant Sun
>>> So the light of expanded awareness may come pouring into our heart and mind.

Circle of the Enlightened King or Queen
(An Archetype of Life Mastery)

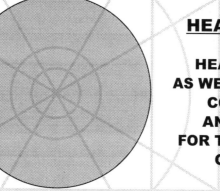

EMPOWERMENT
I EMPOWER
THE PEOPLE IN MY LIFE
BY CONSCIOUSLY
SUPPORTING THEIR
AUTHENTIC *GOODNESS*,
INNER *BEAUTY*, AND *TRUE*
CREATIVE POTENTIAL

INNER GUIDANCE
I TAKE ACTION WITH
INTEGRITY THAT'S
GUIDED BY *THE INFINITE
INTELLIGENCE OF LIFE*
AND THAT CONTRIBUTES
MY CREATIVE GIFTS
AND TALENTS TO OTHERS

HEART WISDOM
I FOSTER
HEART WISDOM,
AS WELL AS GREATER
COMPASSION
AND EMPATHY
FOR THE SUFFERING
OF OTHERS

SERVICE
I SERVE THE WELLBEING
OF OTHERS,
PROMOTE GREATER
COOPERATION,
AND AID PEOPLE
IN THE REALIZATION OF
THEIR *ETERNAL NATURE*

FEBRUARY 18

HEART WISDOM

I am aligned with Life and relax as the heart wisdom within the Universe easily flows through me.

Take a moment to imagine an eagle soaring through the sky high above the ground
Looking down at the land below from its lofty point of view
And perceiving a much broader vantage of the world than most other creatures.

When this majestic bird flies over trees and meadows, or mountains and valleys,
It uses its towering perspective to hunt for unsuspecting prey.

This grand perspective provides the eagle with the benefit of taking in "the Big Picture"
Allowing it to observe a wider and more expansive outlook of the terrain
Which is a great advantage regarding its survival.

Over eons of time, the human species has evolved a highly developed brain
Which enables each of us to have the capacity to take in "the Big Picture of life",
To observe the various *parts* of reality in relationship to the *whole* of reality
And to gain greater understanding of what our life is truly about.

It's very natural to attempt to discover the best and most virtuous choice in every situation
Based on the highest perspective we've attained from all we've previously experienced,
And so every day, we make simple or, sometimes, incredibly difficult choices
In which we must respond with either wisdom - or react with fear.

Heart wisdom is the natural insight we acquire from an attunement with our heart
(Our authentic alignment with *the Source of Life)*
In which we use this wisdom to deal with, and face, the challenges of each day.

It develops from taking decisive action and then learning from the consequences of that action,
While at the same time, discovering how to be more mindful in everything we do.

**This wisdom is also the inner guidance we receive as a natural consequence
Of aligning our awareness with our *Eternal Nature*.**

Another expression of **heart wisdom can be described
As *the deep communion of the heart* that streams through us
Offering us the kind of sublime knowing
That's far beyond our limited personal mind.**

When we spend time in sacred silence and align our awareness with "the Big Picture of life"
(In other words, with *"the Heart of the Universe"),*
It becomes effortless for us to hear **the Infinite Intelligence
That's always guiding us in everything we do**.

Like an eagle in flight gazing down upon the world from the sky above,
As we continue to cultivate more inclusive perspectives of what really matters,
Gain greater empathy of other people's points of view, and stay aligned with *Life,*
We eventually learn to soar with the kind of **heart wisdom**
That constantly whispers to us from "the corners of the Cosmos".

Circle of Heart Wisdom

INFINITE INTELLIGENCE
HEART WISDOM – THE INFINITE INTELLIGENCE THAT GUIDES ME EACH DAY WHICH I'M ABLE TO HEAR AS I ALIGN MY AWARENESS WITH *"THE HEART OF THE UNIVERSE"*

NATURAL INSIGHT
HEART WISDOM – THE NATURAL INSIGHT THAT I EXPERIENCE WHICH IS ACQUIRED FROM AN ATTUNEMENT WITH MY *HEART* - MY CONNECTION TO *LIFE*

INNER GUIDANCE
HEART WISDOM – THE INNER GUIDANCE I RECEIVE AS A NATURAL CONSEQUENCE OF ALIGNING MY AWARENESS WITH MY *ETERNAL NATURE*

SUBLIME KNOWING
HEART WISDOM – A DEEP COMMUNION OF *THE HEART* THAT STREAMS THROUGH ME WITH A SUBLIME KNOWING THAT'S FAR BEYOND MY LIMITED PERSONAL MIND

EMPOWERMENT

I empower and support the people in my life - and accept them just as they are.

When young children play with a couple of small magnets for the first time,
    They are usually mesmerized by the strange unseen forces
        Which seem to magically tug and interact between these metallic objects.

Magnetism is a force that's exerted on magnetic materials
    Bringing a magnet and an object together, or pushing them apart,
        Because of a phenomenal interaction with an invisible field of energy.

Two magnets that are brought close together have a magnetic influence on one another,
    Either attracting or repelling the other
        From the power and intensity of this mysterious imperceptible force.

Like magnetism, our daily thoughts also project a subtle field of invisible energy
    That has an influence on the world, and especially on the people around us,
        Either positive or negative based on our mental focus of attention.

When we develop the conscious awareness to **empower the people in our life**
    With thoughts focused on what is possible for them to envision and achieve,
        We help magnetize to them a field of nourishing life-affirming energy
            That can be thought of as "food for their *Souls*".

As we share the gift of **expressing supportive words**
    And holding the energetic space for another's growth and development,
        These thoughts can influence their *personal field of what they believe is possible*
            And **encourage** their beliefs of what they can attain in their life.

When we **inspire our children (which in reality includes all the children of the world)**
    To access and express their wealth of innate creativity and potential,
        We contribute a simple, yet magnificent offering to our global family.

One of the most potent and effective ways to empower someone
    Is to fully accept them just as they are without judgment,
        Honoring their uniqueness and individuality.

It can be a very transformative experience to feel fully embraced, radically accepted,
    And seen with eyes of compassion and love for who you are.

Whatever new seeds we plant today in "the garden of someone's heart",
    And then nourish with the blessings of our support and encouragement,
        Can provide an abundant harvest of creative possibilities
            In "the days of their tomorrows".

As we learn to become mindful to plant seeds of empowering thoughts
    In "the fertile soil of the gardens of our family, friends, and co-workers",
        Their *future selves* will magnetically attract
            A bounty of new wonders and gifts that will bless the world.

Circle of Empowerment

ENCOURAGEMENT
I EMPOWER OTHERS
BY ENCOURAGING
THEM TO EXPAND
THEIR PERSONAL
BELIEFS OF WHAT
IS POSSIBLE
TO ACHIEVE

SUPPORT
I EMPOWER OTHERS
BY SUPPORTING,
AND HOLDING
THE ENERGETIC
SPACE FOR,
ANOTHER'S GROWTH
AND DEVELOPMENT

ACCEPTANCE
I EMPOWER OTHERS
BY FULLY
ACCEPTING THEM
JUST AS
THEY ARE
WITHOUT
JUDGMENT

INSPIRATION
I EMPOWER OTHERS
THROUGH MY OWN
EXAMPLE BY INSPIRING
THEM TO ACCESS
AND EXPRESS THEIR
INNATE CREATIVITY
AND UNIQUE POTENTIAL

INNER GUIDANCE

Today I receive inner guidance that comes from life's perpetual stream of Natural Intelligence.

Each night as we go to bed and gently close our eyes,
  Our sleeping awareness (whether we're conscious of it or not)
    Experiences a seemingly magical realm of dreams
      Filled with symbolic imagery and scenarios
        That may take us on an enchanted adventure.

Yet in order for us to experience these nightly dream-adventures,
  We must, temporarily, stop our external active life and become still and quiet
    So, through sleep, we can enter a domain of internal pictorial voyages.

Of course, many people have discovered that the symbolic images of their dreams
  Can, sometimes, be used to gain insight or guidance
    Concerning the daily events of their external waking world.

However there's also another realm of *inner guidance*
  That's continually available to us during each moment of the day
    When we're able to stop the ongoing whirl of our activities and thoughts
      So we can receive the perpetual stream of *Natural Intelligence* from within.

Inner guidance is the intuitive clarity we can attune ourselves to
  Which, for each situation of life, is informing us to travel down a particular path.

It is **a silent insightful message felt within our heart**
  That inwardly tells us it's good to further a precise action or choice.

This internal communication from our *Eternal Self (the voice of our True Nature)*
  Is a powerful gift that's always available to all people at all times.

Yet in order to gain proficient access to this gift, we must learn to cultivate our experience of it
  By taking opportunities to stop, quiet our mind, and align with this *Natural Intelligence.*

The daily experience of our *inner guidance* can be further developed
  By engaging in certain transformative practices such as prayer and meditation,
    And by consciously attuning our awareness with *the Source of Life.*

Inner guidance is also **our interior knowing that helps us make a specific decision,**
  As well as **the emergence of an inner certainty to move ahead in a given direction**.

As children, we all probably remember singing the well-known song,
  "Row, Row, Row Your Boat".

Maybe when we maintain an alignment with *the Infinite Intelligence* of the Universe,
  Inner guidance eventually becomes so much a part of our life that it's second nature
    And, with this clarity, we flow effortlessly "down the stream" of each day's events
      Naturally celebrating that "life is but a dream", a beautiful earthly delight,
        As we "sail beyond the dream" into the vast *Ocean of Limitless Love.*

Circle of Inner Guidance

INTUITIVE CLARITY
INNER GUIDANCE –
THE INTUITIVE CLARITY
I ATTUNE MYSELF TO
WHICH IS INFORMING ME
TO TRAVEL DOWN
A PARTICULAR PATH

INSIGHTFUL MESSAGE
INNER GUIDANCE –
A SILENT INSIGHTFUL
MESSAGE FELT
WITHIN MY HEART
TO FURTHER A PRECISE
ACTION OR CHOICE

INWARD KNOWING
INNER GUIDANCE –
MY INWARD KNOWING
THAT COMES FROM THE
NATURAL INTELLIGENCE
WITHIN ME TO MAKE
A SPECIFIC DECISION

INTERNAL CERTAINTY
INNER GUIDANCE –
THE EMERGENCE OF
MY INTERNAL CERTAINTY
TO MOVE SOME ASPECT
OF MY LIFE
IN A GIVEN DIRECTION

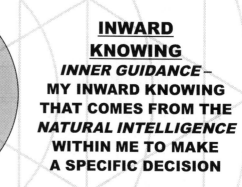

147

CONSCIOUS CHOICES

Throughout the day I make choices, which are guided by my heart - and serve the good of all.

When people are locked up in a prison
    They are forced against their will to remain in a building or cell behind bars
        Which, obviously, restricts their movements and limits their choices.

Of course, at the time when someone is set free and able to leave the constraints of the prison,
    His or her choices regarding movement in the outer world are greatly expanded.

Every person experiences both an exterior world of outward activities and outside influences,
    And an interior world of personal intuitions, thoughts, emotions, and bodily sensations,
        An internal reality that is not under the control of the external world.

Other people may confine our physical body within a prison or restrict our outer movements,
    But only we have the power to create an "internal prison for ourselves"
        By focusing our thoughts on fear, which restricts the freedom of our inner world.

For example, if we don't fully feel the emotions that arise in us each day, we limit our freedom
    By allowing fear to impede the flow of *Life Force energy* that wants to surge through us.

The more we choose to allow our emotions to be freely channeled and fully expressed
    (In other words - the more we completely experience our feelings as they happen),
        The more we're able to experience true **happiness** and vibrant **health**.

Also, when we look at ourselves in restrictive ways or diminish how we think of ourselves,
    We limit our ability to experience the freedom that's possible for us in every moment.

The more we choose to cultivate a greater understanding of life - and our relationship to it
    And, thus, gain a greater perspective of what our life is truly about,
        The more **heart wisdom** we develop.

We are all on a *journey of awakening* that's about consciously realizing our *True Nature*
    And, in time, as we learn to free ourselves from the self-made prison of our fears,
        We awaken to a new paradigm of *loving all of life more fully.*

This emerging paradigm invites us to maintain an alignment with *the Infinite Presence of Love,*
    The Natural Intelligence that's available to us at all times,
        The tranquil voice within our heart perpetually directing all of our choices.

Could it be possible that when we align our awareness with *the Source of Life*
    We are intuitively guided from within to consciously choose
        The exact choice that brings the health, happiness, and wisdom we seek
            And the **inner freedom** that is our ultimate destiny to realize?

Each day as we valiantly break more of the shackles within our habitual fear-oriented nature,
    We transform ourselves by removing our self-imposed walls and imprisoning thoughts
        Allowing *Infinite Intelligence* to make the most benevolent choices through us
            Which benefit every aspect of our world - and every facet of our life.

Circle of Conscious Choices

INNER FREEDOM
**THE MORE I MAKE
CHOICES BASED
ON ALIGNING
MY AWARENESS WITH
THE SOURCE OF LIFE,**
THE MORE
I EXPERIENCE
INNER FREEDOM

HEALTH
**THE MORE I CHOOSE
TO SUPPORT
LIFE FORCE ENERGY
TO FLOW UNIMPEDED
THROUGH MY BODY,**
THE MORE
I EXPERIENCE
VIBRANT HEALTH

HEART WISDOM
**THE MORE I CHOOSE
TO CULTIVATE
A GREATER PERSPEC-
TIVE OF WHAT MY LIFE
IS TRULY ABOUT,**
THE MORE
I EXPERIENCE
HEART WISDOM

HAPPINESS
**THE MORE I CHOOSE
TO COMPLETELY
FEEL MY EMOTIONS
WHILE THEY ARE
HAPPENING,**
THE MORE
I EXPERIENCE
TRUE HAPPINESS

XII

SPIRIT
AWARENESS
PRACTICES

CULTIVATING SPIRITUAL AWAKENING

I frequently question my core beliefs so as to deepen my understanding of what really matters.

Many city office buildings are built with several floors, or levels, one on top of the other,
    And before modern elevators were invented, if you wanted to ascend to a higher floor
        You would, of course, need to climb the stairs.

A stairway consists of a specific number of individual steps
    That, if we use them, will get us to the next higher level.

Similarly, if we desire "to ascend" to a higher, more awakened level of consciousness,
    Then we must take the necessary steps that will get us to our intended goal.

There are many things we can do to **cultivate our spiritual awakening**
    But right now, let's look at four practices that are key to expanding our awareness
        And to supporting us in the attainment of our next higher level.

To further our inner development, **it is beneficial to frequently question our beliefs**
    Which helps us deepen our understanding of what really matters in our life.

Our beliefs about our self-identification (who we believe we are) and how we relate to the world
    Are what establish how we largely respond to life, other people, and our environment.

Our current belief system can both empower us - or keep us locked in an old way of thinking
    That doesn't allow us the freedom to grow and move to elevated levels of awareness.

Daily transformative practices can be likened to valuable nutrients for a healthy garden
    And are *useful tools* that can nourish the ongoing expansion of our development.

As we practice consistently while maintaining an alignment with *Life*, we supply our inner being
    What it needs to move along our ascending path toward a more awakened awareness.

Another important facet of spiritual awakening
    Is discovering how to **live a life that's in service to the good of all.**

There can be numerous stumbling blocks along the way caused by the illusions of the mind
    As we journey on our spiritual path of *learning how to live a life of loving service.*

Yet as we discover who we are, not as a separate self, but as a unique part of *the Unity of Life*,
    It becomes natural to offer "the gift of who we really are" to the service of others.

Our next step in conscious awakening invites us to go beyond the limiting thoughts of our mind
    And embrace certain notions that are paradoxical to our understanding of life.

We can utilize our mind to point us to key insights that help us learn to **embrace paradox**
    So we may use these insights to go beyond our mind - and realize our *True Nature*.

As we courageously take important steps on "our ascending stairway of awakening",
    We "climb to our next horizon" along our perpetual journey of Infinite Awakenings.

Circle of Cultivating Spiritual Awakening
(Transformative Practices)

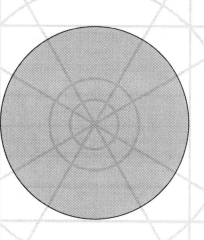

**QUESTION
EVERYTHING**
IN ORDER TO FURTHER
MY DEVELOPMENT,
IT IS BENEFICIAL
TO FREQUENTLY QUESTION
MY BELIEFS TO HELP ME
DEEPEN MY UNDERSTANDING
OF WHAT REALLY MATTERS

**SERVICE TO
THE GOOD OF ALL**
IN ORDER TO BE
OF GREATER SERVICE
TO ALL OF LIFE,
I OFFER "THE GIFT
OF WHO I REALLY AM"
TO OTHERS
AND TO THE WORLD

**DAILY
PRACTICE**
IN ORDER TO CON-
SCIOUSLY TRANSFORM
TO HIGHER LEVELS
OF DEVELOPMENT,
I ENGAGE IN DAILY
TRANSFORMATIVE
PRACTICES

**EMBRACE
PARADOX**
IN ORDER
TO CULTIVATE
THE NATURAL AWAKENING
CURRENTLY TAKING
PLACE WITHIN ME,
I EMBRACE THE SPIRITUAL
PARADOXES OF LIFE

CULTIVATING AWARENESS OF ONE'S *ETERNAL NATURE*

I experience the vast Universe as a natural extension of my physical body.

We live in a world that's full of paradox,
  A reality in which there are numerous examples of dual contradictory aspects of life
    Where both aspects mysteriously appear to be happening at the same time.

Generally, we attempt to understand the outer phenomenal experiences of our daily lives
  From what we've learned of scientific laws, or what we think we know of material reality.

Yet sometimes, paradoxically, a surprising "miracle" occurs from out-of-the-blue
  Which seems to inexplicably arise beyond the accepted rules of science.

Many religions recognize God as "The Beloved", as a God of love and compassion,
  As a God who created everything in a manner that only expresses *absolute perfection.*

Yet people who trust these religions live in a world where they also experience grief and pain
  While, paradoxically, they live within the *Perfect Love* of God's perfect creation.

Another paradox some people experience is that each person has both a human nature,
  Which is physical, impermanent, changing, and exists in time and space,
    And yet, simultaneously, each person has a *Transcendent Nature*,
      Which is non-physical, eternal, and beyond the realms of time and space.

Just like anything we desire to improve or develop in our life,
  If we want to **cultivate an awareness of our non-physical *Eternal Nature***,
    We must consciously place our attention on it through disciplined practice.

With transformative practices, we're able to foster an authentic realization of our *True Nature*
  And directly experience the part of us that's eternal and unbounded.

One powerful practice that deepens our awareness of our *Eternal Nature* is **being grateful**
  For the recognition that who we really are is *the Essential Nature of the entire Universe*,
    Understanding we're intimately connected to every atom within the Cosmos.

We can also **cultivate the attribute of surrender** as we let go of, and attempt to see beyond,
  All of our human concepts of duality
    Using the practice of aligning with our Unity, the Oneness in everything and everyone.

Another practice is to **accept and embrace** (from an absolute "Big Picture perspective")
  That our life is in *perfect order* just as it is
    And that from the vantage of *the Eternal Self*, the Universe is unfolding perfectly.

Furthermore, we can imagine that the vast Universe is a natural extension of our physical body
  And, in truth, **we are one with *All That Is* - for literally, *we are the Universe***.

Many people are now awakening to the transformative gift of embracing paradox,
  For authentically embracing life's spiritual paradoxes opens an important door
    Into a vibrant world of "miracles" - and a profound discovery of who we really are.

Circle of Cultivating Awareness of One's *Eternal Nature*

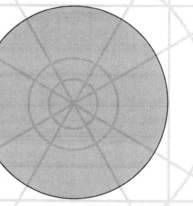

ONENESS
PRACTICE EACH DAY
IMAGINING
AND EXPERIENCING
THAT THE VAST
UNIVERSE IS
A NATURAL EXTENSION
OF YOUR PHYSICAL BODY

GRATITUDE
PRACTICE EACH DAY
BEING GRATEFUL
FOR THE RECOGNITION
OF WHO YOU REALLY
ARE AS *THE ESSENTIAL
NATURE OF*
THE ENTIRE UNIVERSE

ACCEPTANCE
PRACTICE EACH DAY
ACCEPTING
THAT YOUR LIFE
IS IN *PERFECT ORDER*
JUST AS IT IS - AND
THAT THE UNIVERSE IS
UNFOLDING PERFECTLY

SURRENDER
PRACTICE EACH DAY
LETTING GO OF,
AND SEEING BEYOND,
ALL CONCEPTS OF DUALITY
BY ALIGNING WITH THE
ONENESS IN EVERYTHING
AND EVERYONE

SELF-OBSERVATION

Today I expand my awareness of what I feel and think so I may deepen my peace of mind.

When you stand on a sandy beach and look far out upon the pulsing waves of the ocean,
　　You know deep below its surface, it is teeming with many forms of life you cannot see.

If you are hiking in the woods and take time to gaze at the beauty of a stately forest,
　　You know below the ground, there is a network of hidden roots that sustain it.

All myriad expressions of life, such as microorganisms, algae, plants, animals, and humans,
　　Intrinsically have both a visible exterior component and an invisible interior component.

For us humans, our exterior realm is, of course, our bodies and the environment around us,
　　While our interior realm is all that we sense, feel, think, and intuit.

Because of each person's unique experiences of their outer world
　　As well as humanity's sustained quest for science-based knowledge,
　　　　Most people are generally familiar with their exterior physical aspects.

Yet in regards to what people know concerning the realm of their "internal landscapes"
　　By and large, there is little conscious awareness of the fullness of their inner world,
　　　　For many seem to be struggling to maintain balance and wellbeing in their lives
　　　　　　In part because they are not as familiar with their interior aspects of self.

Throughout human evolution which has been progressing for over two million years,
　　There was, first, a need to focus on the exterior part of life, in order to physically survive,
　　　　And then as time went on, to develop *individuation* in the form of a personal ego
　　　　　　So one could find better ways to survive emotionally as well as physically.

But now in modern times as our species continues its evolution, we are recognizing
　　That in order to further humanity's growth toward ever-higher stages of development
　　　　We must learn to transform our unloving, self-centered egoic nature
　　　　　　Into something that supports our ongoing evolutionary unfoldment
　　　　　　　　By becoming increasingly familiar with the interior part of our being.

Self-observation is a mindfulness practice that helps us expand our awareness
　　Of the various internal sensations experienced within our body,
　　　　The quality of our passing emotions and feelings within our heart,
　　　　　　And the nature of our thoughts constantly coursing through our mind.

The gift in this practice is derived from *becoming the observer*, yet observing without judgment,
　　Without resistance, without needing anything to be different than it is,
　　　　While at the same time, becoming aware of whether or not
　　　　　　What we're observing within us supports and serves our wellbeing.

Could it be that by simply expanding our awareness in relation to our **body**, **heart**, and **mind**,
　　The invisible *Ocean of Being (the Infinite Intelligence* within us)
　　　　Then mirrors and manifests greater visible expressions of our peace of mind
　　　　　　As individual waves of experience in the unfolding days of our lives?

Circle of Self-Observation
(A Mindfulness Practice)

SPIRIT
PRACTICE
BEING AWARE
OF "WHO AND WHAT
IS OBSERVING"
THE EVER-CHANGING
EXPERIENCES OF YOUR
BODY, HEART, AND MIND

BODY
PRACTICE
BEING AWARE
OF THE VARIOUS
PHYSICAL SENSATIONS
WITHIN YOUR BODY,
AND ANY RESISTANCE
YOU MAY EXPERIENCE

MIND
PRACTICE
BEING AWARE
OF THE NATURE
OF YOUR THOUGHTS
AS THEY PASS BY,
AND IF THEY SUPPORT
AND SERVE YOUR LIFE

HEART
PRACTICE
BEING AWARE
OF THE QUALITY
OF YOUR EMOTIONS
AND FEELINGS,
AND ANY JUDGMENTS
YOU HAVE ABOUT THEM

157

XIII

ARCHETYPES OF HIGHER KNOWLEDGE

"AN OCEAN JOURNEY"

I frequently examine and reflect on my life so I may cultivate peace of mind and inner freedom.

Imagine that a person is traveling on a small raft floating upon a vast ocean,
　　However the raft is without a sail for forward momentum - or a rudder for steering,
　　　　And he or she is being haphazardly tossed on the water by the wind and waves.

This individual would obviously have no control regarding the direction where the raft is going
　　And would be totally dependent on the external forces of Nature to determine its fate.

A raft like this drifting aimlessly without sail or rudder could be seen as analogous to a person
　　Who experiences their life without any conscious self-reflection or self-inquiry,
　　　　Someone who has not yet discovered the illuminating gift of self-examination.

The Greek philosopher, Socrates, expressed the importance of conscious awareness
　　In his famous statement, *"**An unexamined life** is not worth living"*.

If this phrase were turned around and stated in linguistically positive terms, it might read,
　　"An examined self-reflective life cultivates peace of mind and inner freedom".

As we continue this poetic metaphor, **a self-reflective life** could be thought of
　　As someone who navigates the ocean on a large sailboat
　　　　With its sails filled from a strong wind, symbolizing his or her inner development
　　　　　　Due to asking meaningful questions on a fervent search for what is true.

It is similar to a person who has become aware of a greater meaning and purpose for their life
　　Other than mere physical or emotional survival, or self-centered pursuits,
　　　　And who is actively engaged in fostering a more conscious heart-centered life.

Another stage on the arc of life's ever-unfolding journey
　　Is learning to surrender everything in our life to *a Power* greater than ourselves,
　　　　To the *Source of All That Is*, to *the Infinite Intelligence* of the Universe,
　　　　　　To *the Ultimate Power* directing the perpetual evolution of the Cosmos.

This is the stage of a developed individual who has learned to live **the surrendered life**
　　And could be analogous to one who navigates the ocean on a majestic schooner
　　　　Where all commands come from the guidance of *"an Inner Benevolent Captain"*.

It's a sublime experience of *"Life* navigating life", or stated in the language of *The Great Circle*,
　　It's a *journey of awakening* - in which we realize our daily choices are inwardly directed
　　　　Which are then outwardly expressed as our contribution and service to the good of all.

All of life seems to be continuously evolving toward "some far off point on a distant horizon",
　　As if each form of life is trying to reach *an ultimate place of Unity* or *Absolute Oneness*.

This "horizon point" represents our destiny of a life of inner freedom - our **fully integrated life**,
　　The stage where we recognize that *"The One"* who truly navigates the schooner,
　　　　And *"the Inner Captain"*, as well as *"the one who journeys upon the Ocean"*,
　　　　　　Have always been one and the same.

Circle of "An Ocean Journey"
(A Metaphor for the *Journey of Awakening)*

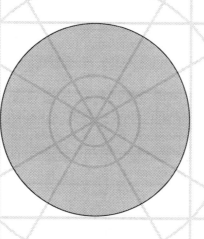

**THE FULLY
INTEGRATED LIFE**
KNOWING *"THE ONE"* WHO
TRULY NAVIGATES THE
SCHOONER, *"THE INNER
CAPTAIN"*, AND *"THE ONE
WHO JOURNEYS UPON THE
OCEAN"* HAVE ALWAYS
BEEN ONE AND THE SAME

**THE UNEXAMINED
LIFE**
ONE WHO DRIFTS UPON
THE OCEAN OF LIFE
ON A RAFT WITHOUT
A SAIL OR RUDDER,
AND IS HAPHAZARDLY
TOSSED BY THE WIND
AND WAVES

**THE SURRENDERED
LIFE**
ONE WHO NAVIGATES
THE OCEAN OF LIFE ON
A MAJESTIC SCHOONER
WHERE ALL COMMANDS
COME FROM THE
GUIDANCE OF *"AN INNER
BENEVOLENT CAPTAIN"*

**THE SELF-REFLECTIVE
LIFE**
ONE WHO NAVIGATES
THE OCEAN OF LIFE
ON A LARGE SAILBOAT, HAS
CLARITY OF DIRECTION,
AND ASKS MEANINGFUL
QUESTIONS ON A SEARCH
FOR WHAT IS TRUE

THE QUEST FOR HIGHER KNOWLEDGE

I am constantly being invited by Life to expand my awareness of truth, goodness, and beauty.

Anyone who has spent time watching infants has observed how they are naturally curious
And how they're fascinated with exploring brand new sensations, colors, and shapes.

Deeply embedded in the human mind from birth is *the natural impulse of curiosity,*
The instinctual longing to discover - the innate yearning to attain greater knowledge.

"The spiritual map of an awakening life" referred to as **The Great Circle** - reminds us
That life involves both an **inward expanding consciousness** (always reaching higher)
And an **outward expression of creativity** (always revealing new creative forms).

For all of the myriad phenomenal forms that exist within the evolving Universe,
There is both an interior and exterior component.

This impulse of curiosity at the core of each person fuels the flame of humanity's basic desires,
Which at its most primal external level is to survive and procreate,
And at its most primal internal level is to learn and develop.

During their primitive pursuit to overcome the hardships and challenges of a hostile world,
Early humans used their expanding brain capacities
To learn how to fashion tools and develop effective strategies
That would increase their chance of survival.

The last five thousand years of humanity's investigative pursuit of ongoing development
Has led to a vast field of empirical knowledge we now call **science**.

Over many millennia, humans gradually evolved from small clans - to villages - to nation states
And then organized themselves into more civil and peaceful environments
That they hoped would foster greater safety for their families and offspring.

This pursuit involving better systems of proper conduct and improved structures of governance
Greatly benefited human survival,
And eventually developed into the field of ethical knowledge called **philosophy**.

The search for how to deepen one's experience of the endless creations of natural beauty
Emerged from an innate yearning to explore the myriad forms of pattern within Nature,
And this human enterprise to express *the beautiful* is what we refer to as **art**.

Spirituality is the natural human longing to experience inner peace and wholeness,
Discover what life is truly about, and realize sublime Oneness with *the Transcendent*.

At this crucial time in our history, spirituality is possibly humanity's greatest promise
To move us progressively forward on the ever-unfolding arc of evolution.

As each of us continues to expand our awareness of **truth**, **goodness**, and **beauty**
As well as consciously cultivate these four essential quests for knowledge,
We must empower the curiosity of our children to help them foster a better world.

Circle of the Quest for Higher Knowledge

SPIRITUALITY
(A QUEST FOR ABSOLUTE TRUTH)
THE SEARCH FOR
INNER PEACE, FOR WHAT
MY LIFE IS TRULY ABOUT,
AND FOR ONENESS WITH
THE TRANSCENDENT

SCIENCE
(A QUEST FOR EMPIRICAL TRUTH)
THE SEARCH FOR HOW
THE WORLD AND THE
UNIVERSE WORKS, AND
WHAT MY RELATIONSHIP
WITH THEM TRULY IS

PHILOSOPHY
(A QUEST FOR GOODNESS)
THE SEARCH FOR HOW
TO BEST LIVE TOGETHER
USING SYSTEMS
OF PROPER CONDUCT
AND GOVERNANCE

ART
(A QUEST FOR THE BEAUTIFUL)
THE SEARCH FOR HOW
TO EXPRESS, AND DEEPEN
MY EXPERIENCE OF,
THE ENDLESS PATTERNS
OF NATURAL BEAUTY

ARCHETYPES OF HIGHER KNOWLEDGE

Today I consciously align my awareness with the field of unlimited universal knowledge.

The human mind has an astonishing capacity to perceive and process information
And, like a flower opening its petals and reaching toward the Sun,
The mind is always yearning to blossom by expanding its range of knowledge
And is constantly being illumined through our daily experience of *learning*.

Developmental psychologists have observed that humanity's *quest for knowledge*
Has centered around three primary areas of discovery:
Science, the acquisition of empirical facts about what is believed to be **true**,
Art, the enjoyment and expression of what is thought to be **beautiful**,
And **philosophy**, the collective investigation of what is **good**.

A fourth essential area of *subjective knowledge* is our natural quest for **spirituality**,
Our innate longing to find inner peace so we can better serve the wellbeing of others.

For thousands of years, a plethora of people have formulated numerous methods
To assist us in our passionate intention to cultivate greater knowledge.

Books, libraries, and the Internet contain massive quantities of evidence-based information,
Accomplished teachers motivate students to develop their unique cognitive abilities,
And primary schools and universities provide systems of disciplined learning.

Another more esoteric means by which we can access what is called **higher knowledge**
Is to consciously align our awareness with *the field of unlimited universal knowledge*
That exists everywhere within the Universe and, therefore, within you and me.

This vast *field of knowledge* can be tapped into using certain transformative practices,
Such as meditation, contemplation, and self-inquiry.

Another way to access this *field* involves the practice of envisioning specific archetypal images
So as to connect us with the rich consciousness of a particular *sphere of knowledge*.

The archetype of **the Awakened Scientist** represents one who dedicates his or her life
As a living experiment to discover greater awareness of what is undeniably true.

The Awakened Artist can be used to help us cultivate the abundant ways
To enjoy and experience everything we do as a creative expression of beauty and art.

Gaining the wisdom of how to establish the most harmonious, good, and compassionate ways
To live with others is embodied in the symbolic template of **an Awakened Philosopher**.

The Awakened Mystic is one who maintains an alignment with *the Source of Life*
So as to live in ways that truly serve the wellbeing of others.

These **Archetypes of Higher Knowledge** can be used to expand our natural abilities to learn,
To plant seeds of awareness within our heart and mind of what is good, true, and beautiful
So we may reap a bountiful harvest of *Life's* heart wisdom in all that we sow.

Circle of the Archetypes of Higher Knowledge

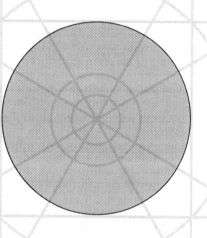

**AWAKENED
MYSTIC**
IT IS THE PART OF ME
THAT USES EFFECTIVE
WAYS TO MAINTAIN
AN ALIGNMENT WITH
THE SOURCE OF LIFE
SO I CAN TRULY BE
OF SERVICE TO OTHERS

**AWAKENED
SCIENTIST**
IT IS THE PART OF ME
THAT DEDICATES MY LIFE
AS A LIVING EXPERIMENT
SO I MAY GAIN GREATER
AWARENESS OF THE
TRUTH (WHAT IS BELIEVED
TO BE UNDENIABLY TRUE)

**AWAKENED
PHILOSOPHER**
IT IS THE PART OF ME
THAT FOSTERS HEART
WISDOM SO I MAY
ESTABLISH THE MOST
HARMONIOUS, *GOOD*,
AND MEANINGFUL WAYS
TO LIVE WITH OTHERS

**AWAKENED
ARTIST**
IT IS THE PART OF ME
THAT CULTIVATES
ABUNDANT WAYS TO
ENJOY AND EXPERIENCE
"LIFE AS AN ART
- AND AS A CREATIVE
EXPRESSION OF *BEAUTY*"

AWAKENED MYSTIC

Today I maintain an alignment with the Source of Life - and relax into an experience of peace.

Before the days of modern GPS systems, if someone decided to embark on a road trip
    To a destination where they had never traveled before,
        It was advantageous to have a map of the territory
            So they could discern, ahead of time, the best route to take.

If circumstances were such that they didn't have a map of where they wanted to go,
    They still could arrive at their destination without it
        But they might need to arduously discover their own path
            Through "the uncharted jungle" or "the maze of possible side roads",
                And it might take them much longer to get there.

Generally, the same notion that it's helpful to have a map is true regarding our *spiritual journey*
    (Our internal quest to maintain an alignment of our awareness with *the Source of Life*)
        So we may experience peace of mind - and live a life of inner freedom.

Most likely, it would benefit us if we had "an established map" to use
    Accurately drawn and offered by "a spiritually developed individual"
        Who had already *awakened* to the realization of loving all of life unconditionally.

Thus, it can be helpful for our own journey to bring to mind images of other "mystic travelers"
    Who have come before us - and have shown others *the way*
        (Those spiritual pioneers who have crafted experiential maps we can now utilize).

A few examples of these *"mystic mapmakers"* are the revered spiritual wayshowers
    Such as Jesus and Buddha, Krishna and Lao Tzu,
        Or anyone who has lived an authentic awakened life.

The visionary archetype of the Awakened Mystic can also function as a spiritual map
    By using its expansive qualities to point us to the sacred sanctuary that dwells within us,
        The place within our heart where we yearn to **fully love** all of life unconditionally,
            Where we long to be **completely present** in each moment,
                Where we sense **a life of serving the good of all**,
                    And where we cultivate **higher stages of awareness**.

The symbolic image of this archetype is a transformative tool we can use in our daily life
    To hold these intentions in mind, to passionately envision these goals with clarity,
        And to embody the exquisite feelings of fulfilling our destiny
            So we may more easily traverse the path of our *spiritual journey*.

Any spiritual map is only a temporary device to assist us in getting to where we intend to go
    And then can be set aside when it's no longer needed.

Yet there will always be brand new maps for humanity to investigate
    That will be "artfully sketched by the future explorers of consciousness"
        Who will march through the uncharted territories and unknown spheres of life
            Which are awaiting the human family to explore.

Circle of the Awakened Mystic
(An Archetype of Higher Knowledge)

LOVE
I CHOOSE TO
ALIGN MY AWARENESS
WITH *THE NATURAL
INTELLIGENCE OF LIFE*
SO I MAY LEARN TO FULLY
LOVE UNCONDITIONALLY

TRANSCENDENCE
I CHOOSE TO
QUIET MY MIND
SO I MAY TRANSCEND
TO, AND ABIDE IN,
MORE ELEVATED STAGES
OF CONSCIOUSNESS

PRESENCE
I CHOOSE TO
CORRECT ANY
UNLOVING THOUGHTS
SO I MAY LIVE MY LIFE
COMPLETELY PRESENT
IN EACH MOMENT

SERVICE
I CHOOSE TO
MAINTAIN A HEART-
CENTERED CONNECTION
WITH *THE SOURCE
OF LIFE* SO I MAY
SERVE THE GOOD OF ALL

PERSPECTIVES OF ONENESS

As I expand my perspectives regarding the inclusion of others my compassion for others grows.

Everyday we communicate with one another through a common language,
    A set of agreed-upon sounds, or written symbols, that make up individual words
        Which we assemble and use to share ideas, beliefs, and worldviews.

Over the centuries, it has been suggested by "many of the great wisdom holders"
    That in order to maintain a greater level of balance and harmony in one's life,
        It is beneficial to consciously embrace *the proper perspective*.

If we observe most of the world's modern languages, we see they have developed in ways
    Which are linguistically constructed around multiple perspectives.

For example in the English language, when we speak about ourselves - "I or me",
    We are sharing a **first person perspective**.

When we speak to another person - "you" (singular), or to other people - "you" (plural),
    We talk in the **second person perspective**.

And when we speak about others or some object- "he, she, they, or it",
    We are communicating in the **third person perspective**.

Just from the everyday use of our native language,
    We experience the dynamics of life from many different perspectives.

Over decades of research and clinical studies, developmental science has discovered
    That the more perspectives of inclusion we learn to embrace in our everyday lives
        (And then, in due course, embody within our own experience),
            The more empathy and compassion for others we're able to feel.

"I am one with God" is a powerful spiritual affirmation of connection to *a Transcendent Unity*,
    Referring to, and pointing us to, a first person perspective of our alignment with *Life*,
        Our direct experience of Oneness with *the Source of All That Is*.

As our awareness expands and, thus, as we're able to expand our **perspectives of Oneness**
    To embrace a wider circle regarding the inclusion of others,
        We learn to embody a second person perspective that includes more people
            Which is expressed in the affirmation, "**We are one with God**".

And, in time, with further expansion of our awareness in relation to every person on the planet,
    We achieve the even greater collective perspective, "**All is one with God**".

Yet with surrender, a grateful heart, a deepening of acceptance, and through the gift of *grace*,
    We are ultimately destined to experience the sublime knowing of **Perfect Oneness**,
        Realizing the separate illusory states of "I", "we", and "all" do not exist.

This profound blessing is the realization - there is only Oneness, the Unity of All That is,
    Where every previous perspective of the mind simply melts away.

Circle of the Perspectives of Oneness
(Ever Increasing Levels of Coherence)

PERFECT ONENESS
IN THE ABSOLUTE REALM,
THE SEPARATE ILLUSORY
STATES OF *"I"*, *"WE"*,
AND *"ALL"* DO NOT EXIST,
SINCE THERE IS ONLY
PERFECT ONENESS,
THE UNITY OF ALL THAT IS

INDIVIDUAL
"I AM ONE WITH GOD"
IS THE AFFIRMATION OF
MY DIRECT EXPERIENCE
OF *THE TRANSCENDENT,
THE SOURCE OF LIFE
(PERSONAL
COHERENCE)*

COLLECTIVE
"ALL IS ONE WITH GOD"
IS THE AFFIRMATION
OF A COLLECTIVE
GLOBAL EXPERIENCE
OF TRANSCENDENCE
*(PLANETARY
COHERENCE)*

RELATIONSHIP
"WE ARE ONE WITH GOD"
IS THE AFFIRMATION
OF AN EXPERIENCE
OF TRANSCENDENCE
THAT INCLUDES ANOTHER
PERSON OR PERSONS
(GROUP COHERENCE)

THE NATURAL STATE OF PRESENCE

As I maintain an alignment with Life, living in the present moment is natural and instinctual.

All creatures within the natural world, from the smallest amoebas to the largest whales,
   Live their lives within an instinctive state of *presence*.

It's a state of total surrender and acceptance of everything they experience just as it is
   With no attachments to the way it was in the past - or expectations regarding the future,
      While being fully present to what's taking place in each *eternal moment*.

For example, the flowers in our gardens effortlessly unfold in this instinctual field of *presence*,
   As do trees, birds, and the animals that live in the wilds of Nature.

Yet we humans seem to be one type of animal that is currently an exception to this rule
   For we, at times, are habitually immersed in our past or future thoughts,
      But, fortunately for us, there's a quiet voice of *Infinite Intelligence* within
         Always guiding us to return to this natural state - if we choose to listen.

As we awaken to our **natural state of presence** (also called *present moment awareness)*
   Something deep within our very core begins to profoundly shift.

From a state of *awakened awareness*, we can surrender all of our "doing" to *the Source of Life*,
   For every action we initiate is then experienced as (what is referred to as) **non-action**.

Because when we're truly present, everything we "do" or achieve
   Becomes a natural flow of "non-doing" guided by *Life* - rather than by our self-oriented agenda.

As we authentically experience *presence*, we're able to fully feel every emotion that arises
   Allowing each spectrum or quality of emotion which we embrace
      (Whether it be sorrow, anger, joy, happiness, etc.)
         To be experienced as an expression of **Limitless Love**.

Living in our busy contemporary world while, at the same time, abiding in *presence*
   Allows each of our thoughts, and the conscious act of choosing a thought,
      To be experienced as an elevated stream of **choiceless awareness**
         In which we relinquish all control of our thinking
            And let our thoughts be directed by *the Natural Intelligence* within.

For choiceless awareness dwells within *eternity,* which intersects the time of our human world
   Only in the timeless gift of the present moment.

When we learn to mindfully dive into the fullness of *presence*,
   Our intuition dissolves into the sublime experience of **inner guidance**,
      Which is the natural and perpetual communication from our *Eternal Nature*.

It seems that each of us is on a *journey of awakening* "to spiritually blossom like a flower",
   "To reach for the limitless sky like an oak tree",
      "To soar through the heavens of possibility like a majestic bird",
         And to live in a *natural state of presence* as an awakened human.

Circle of the Natural State of Presence
(In Relation to Action, Emotion, Thought, and Intuition)

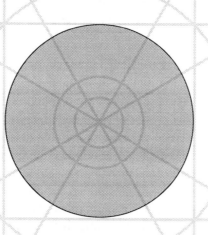

INNER GUIDANCE
WHEN I LIVE IN A STATE
OF *PRESENCE*,
MY *INTUITION*
IS EXPERIENCED AS
INNER GUIDANCE
- THE PERPETUAL
COMMUNICATION FROM
MY *ETERNAL NATURE*

HIGH CREATIVITY
WHEN I LIVE IN A STATE
OF *PRESENCE*,
ALL OF MY *ACTIONS*
ARE EXPERIENCED AS
NON-ACTION
AS I SURRENDER
ALL OF MY "DOING"
OR ACTIONS TO *LIFE*

**ELEVATED
AWARENESS**
WHEN I LIVE IN A STATE
OF *PRESENCE*,
ALL OF MY *THOUGHTS*
ARE EXPERIENCED AS
CHOICELESS AWARENESS
AS I RELINQUISH
CONTROL OF MY MIND

LIMITLESS LOVE
WHEN I LIVE IN A STATE
OF *PRESENCE*,
ALL OF MY *EMOTIONS*
ARE EXPERIENCED AS
LIMITLESS LOVE
AS I FULLY FEEL EVERY
EMOTION AND LET GO
OF MY ATTACHMENTS

"A FLOWING RIVER" (A METAPHOR FOR TIME)

I recognize that there is no area of my life where the flow of Limitless Love is not present.

Imagine for a moment that you're all alone
    Standing in the sunshine on the green banks of a flowing river
        Gazing with awe as the churning water rushes by,
            Feeling the tremendous power of its current
                As if it were a long freight train journeying towards its destination.

Picture the incessant movement and mesmerizing dance of the water
    As it sends your mind into a deep tranquil state, until you become very quiet,
        So quiet that you begin to hear "the voice of the river" speak to you
            Telling you its mythic story, a simple tale about both time and eternity.

Now imagine that the river invites you to look upstream so you can gaze into your **future**
    And, as the water flows toward you, observe **there is an *Infinite Source of Creativity***
        Continuously bringing what you are about to encounter in your life,
            The myriad experiences that are heading "down the river"
                Which symbolize all of your desires, intentions, and possibilities
                    Regarding how you see *the days of your future* unfolding.

Then visualize that "the voice of the river" is now asking you
    To direct your attention to the flowing current directly in front of you
        Inviting you to fully embrace your ***present***
            As you observe **the *River of Life* is always renewed in every moment**,
                Reminding you that *the Source of All That Is*
                Is also renewing you in every moment.

Next, place your awareness downstream that you might completely celebrate your **past**,
    And notice **the perfect experiences and moments that have occurred in your life**
        Which, like the waters of a constantly flowing river, have already passed by.

Downstream represents all the memories and lessons acquired from prior encounters,
    Every desire you have previously manifested,
        And the blessings you feel from what you learned with every event just as it was,
            For what has happened can never be changed.

Finally, imagine that "the river's voice" brings its ever-unfolding story to completion
    Inviting you to picture an image of the entire river, including its *past, present*, and *future*,
        And try to feel the fullness and totality of its perpetual flow
            So you may truly recognize that in your life -
                There is no place where the flow of *Limitless Love* (the "*Water*") is not.

Wherever we're standing in the world and whatever challenges we may experience,
    We are constantly being invited to awaken to a new possibility for our life,
        The possibility to boldly dive into the flow of *Limitless Love*,
            To courageously ride the perpetual train of this *Mighty Current*,
                To merge as one with the endless movement of *the River of Life*,
                And to ultimately surrender to **the Mystery of Eternity**.

Circle of "A Flowing River"
(A Metaphor for Time)

ETERNITY
NOW OBSERVE
THE PERPETUAL MOVEMENT
OF THE ENTIRE RIVER
AND RECOGNIZE THAT
THERE IS NO PLACE WHERE
THE FLOW OF *LIMITLESS LOVE*
(THE "WATER") IS NOT

THE FUTURE
AT A FLOWING RIVER,
LOOK UPSTREAM
AND OBSERVE THAT
THERE IS ALWAYS
AN INFINITE SOURCE
OF *"WATER"* HEADING
TOWARDS YOU

THE PAST
AT A FLOWING RIVER,
LOOK DOWNSTREAM
AND OBSERVE THAT IN
EACH MOMENT, THERE
IS A PERFECT FLOW
OF *"WATER"* THAT HAS
JUST PASSED YOU BY

THE PRESENT
LOOK AT THE CURRENT
OF A FLOWING RIVER
DIRECTLY IN FRONT OF YOU
AND OBSERVE THAT
THE *"WATER"* - AS WELL AS
YOU - ARE BEING RENEWED
IN EVERY MOMENT

XIV

SPIRIT
AWARENESS
PRACTICES

"DOORWAYS" TO THE PRESENCE

I accept that, in the present moment, my life is unfolding perfectly just as it is.

Every now and then when we watch the beginning of a TV drama or feature film,
  The experience can feel like we're passing through "a doorway into a brand new world",
    Because our complete attention with the unfolding story causes us to be very present
      And our total focus on the theatrical event in front of us makes us feel we're there.

For all people, an experience of *the state of presence* is fundamentally natural and simple,
  But in this busy fast-paced modern world,
    It seems it's a state of awareness that's not easy to maintain
      And it's certainly not the norm for most people.

Our dynamic contemporary lifestyles have, sometimes, led to patterns of dysfunctional thinking
  In which our minds can be habitually fixed on loveless thoughts,
    Such as resentments of the past, or fears of the future,
      Or attachments to the preferred outcome of our desires.

At times, it can feel like the present moment is far away, in another location out of reach,
  Or is some foreign dimension that's difficult to personally experience.

Even though the present moment is always here and always now, we can think of *presence*
  As a sublime "doorway" to enter, a unique "portal" we must pass through,
    In order to get from our current thoughts of past or future to *a state of presence*.

"Portals" are openings from one place to another, or from one dimension of reality to another,
  That allow us passage from one space of awareness into a new space of possibility.

There are four "portals" or **"doorways" to the presence** listed on the following page
  That are mindfulness practices we can use in our daily lives
    To help us "enter" into a state of *present moment awareness*.

First, if you desire to deepen your awareness of *presence*, consciously bring your attention
  To **the physical sensations of your body** (any pain, skin temperature, heartbeat, etc.)
    Which helps you align your awareness with the reality of what is.

You can also stop to become quiet, in order to notice *the inner aliveness*, or *Life Force energy*,
  That's always radiating within your ***inner body***.

The inner body is the invisible field of radiant energy that constantly pulsates within you,
  In other words - it's the pathways where *Life Force energy* circulates through your body,
    And with practice and attention, you can become aware of this radiant field.

Another powerful, yet simple exercise is to **focus your full attention**
  On the rhythmic pattern of your breathing and be *the Silent Witness* of your breath.

And **accepting that, in the present moment, your life is unfolding perfectly just as it is**
  Is also an effective practice to deepen *presence*
    And help catapult you through "a sublime doorway into a fully radiant world".

Circle of "Doorways" to the Presence
(Mindfulness Practices)

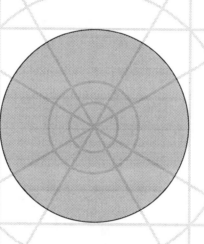

THE BREATH
AS AN EXERCISE
TO DEEPEN *PRESENCE*,
FOCUS ATTENTION ON
THE RHYTHMIC PATTERN
OF YOUR BREATHING
AND BE *THE SILENT
WITNESS* OF THE BREATH

SENSATIONS
AS AN EXERCISE
TO DEEPEN *PRESENCE*,
CONSCIOUSLY PLACE
YOUR MENTAL
AWARENESS ON THE
PHYSICAL SENSATIONS
OF YOUR BODY

ACCEPTANCE
AS AN EXERCISE
TO DEEPEN *PRESENCE*,
FULLY ACCEPT THAT,
IN THIS MOMENT,
YOUR LIFE IS
UNFOLDING PERFECTLY
JUST AS IT IS

THE INNER BODY
AS AN EXERCISE
TO DEEPEN *PRESENCE*,
FEEL *THE ALIVENESS*,
OR *LIFE FORCE ENERGY*,
THAT RADIATES
AND CIRCULATES WITHIN
YOUR *INNER BODY*

CULTIVATING SPIRITUAL WELLBEING

I use daily transformative practice as a way to help me stay aligned with the Source of Life.

If you decide to learn something new, such as become skilled at playing the piano,
  Then usually an effective system of disciplined practice needs to be employed.

For example, you might find a good piano teacher to study with,
   Or you may use a popular self-teaching program for the keyboard
      So, over time, your musical abilities can be developed and refined.

If you intend to commit to becoming an accomplished pianist,
   Then, most likely, you will never stop the fundamental need for practice,
      Because there's no point in time when one becomes "the ultimate piano player",
         Since the possibilities of developing this creative skill are virtually endless.

Even a master concert pianist at the top of his or her career
   Always practices every day in order to attain the next level of proficiency.

If we apply this as an analogy for *life mastery*, then we can use daily transformative practice,
   Not as a means of fixing ourselves or arriving at a supreme point of spiritual perfection,
      But as a means of, each day, keeping us aligned with *the Source of Life*,
         Of constantly developing our unlimited potential,
            And of persistently stretching the limits of what we can achieve.

The older traditional concept of *enlightenment* or *awakening*,
   Defined as an ultimate goal we can one day attain
      If we want to realize a state of Oneness with God, is being reevaluated by many.

A newer, more contemporary understanding of this state of being is now emerging
   Defining *enlightenment* as a level of awareness in which one lives with inner freedom,
      Experiences life in a way where one continues to expand and evolve spiritually,
         And compassionately dedicates one's life to the loving service of the good of all.

Even though the specific form of the practices may change over the years,
   Transformative practice can become a joyous life-long activity
      Helping us more fully participate with the ceaselessly unfolding path of our life
         And supporting us to contribute our creative gifts to the wellbeing of others.

On the following page, there's a short summary of a number of practices,
   Such as **meditation**, **mindfulness**, and **prayer**,
      That we have already explored in previous narratives
         Which can assist us to cultivate **spiritual wellbeing**.

The practice of listening to, and acting on, **inner guidance** is also included in this list
   For courageously following the graceful flow of *the Natural Intelligence* within us
      Makes it so much easier to experience peace of mind.

There have been a few great classical pianists that were mysteriously gifted child prodigies,
   But most gained their high level of excellence through a lifetime of devoted practice.

Circle of Cultivating Spiritual Wellbeing
(Transformative Exercises)

MEDITATION
I ENGAGE IN DAILY
MEDITATION
OR PERIODS OF SILENCE
SO I MAY DIRECTLY
EXPERIENCE AND MAINTAIN
AN ALIGNMENT WITH
THE SOURCE OF LIFE

INNER GUIDANCE
I LISTEN TO,
AND ACT ON,
THE GRACEFUL
AND EVER-PRESENT
FLOW OF *THE NATURAL
INTELLIGENCE*
THAT'S WITHIN ME

MINDFULNESS
I SUSTAIN A PRACTICE
OF DAILY MINDFULNESS
THAT SUPPORTS
CULTIVATING
MY AWARENESS OF WHO
I REALLY AM - AND WHAT
I AM IDENTIFIED WITH

PRAYER
I SPEND TIME
FREQUENTLY SENDING
PRAYERFUL THOUGHTS
TO OTHERS SO AS
TO HELP THEM RESTORE
THE FLOW OF WELLBEING
IN THEIR LIVES

THE GREAT CIRCLE OF THE BREATH

I frequently use my breath to help align myself with the sublime sanctity of the present moment.

Certain native tribes of North America have used the symbol of the stone medicine wheel
    To honor their sacred connection with Nature - and to revere the Circle of Life.

They observed the image of the circle in the Sun, the Moon, the eyes of animals and people,
    The shape of fruit, the blossoms of flowers, as well as the turning of the seasons.

The cycle of the breath can also be pictured as an invisible wheel or circle,
    Such as a waterwheel, that turns within the central area of the body,
        Utilizing the breath as a powerful tool for spiritual development.

For thousands of years, the breath has been thought of as "a doorway or portal",
    That a spiritual seeker could use to align with God, *the Source of All That Is.*

Many spiritual traditions from around the world incorporate the conscious practice of breathing
    As one of the most natural ways to become present
        And to expand an individual's awareness of his or her connection with *Life.*

As a transformative practice, we can visualize the cycle of our breathing
    As an inner circular movement of *Life Force energy* throughout our body,
        Imagining the **inhalation** rising up the back of our spine,
            Experiencing a point of **stillness** at the top of the head,
                Then **exhaling** down the front of our torso
                    And feeling a place of stillness at the base of the spine,
                        Repeating the visualization over again and again.

The natural *cycle of the breath* is a physical manifestation of *the Great Wheel of Life,*
    Also known as **The Great Circle**, "a spiritual map of an awakening life".

It has been speculated that all the information from 13.8 billion years of cosmological evolution
    Is contained and organized within the majesty of the human body,
        For the Universe is the grand macrocosm of existence,
            And the human body directly mirrors the Universe as the microcosm.

We can use the inhalation of each breath to connect us to *the Source of Life,*
    To this universal ascending impulse of our expanding **consciousness**
        Which is always yearning to develop, awaken, and be aligned with **"The One".**

Our exhalation aligns us with the descending impulse of our unlimited **creativity**
    As we feel *Life Force energy* manifesting our intentions into the world -
        "The Many" forms, expressions, and contributions of our creative potential.

As we learn to cultivate our breath as a means to mindfully expand our awareness,
    It's like entering into "the portal of an *invisible stargate* or *cosmic wormhole*"
        That can magically transport us to a more expanded reality
            Where we swiftly travel from the mundane and the ordinary
                To the sublime sanctity of the present moment.

The Great Circle of the Breath
(A Transformative Practice)

STILLNESS
I IMAGINE AT THE TOP
OF MY HEAD
THERE IS A SUBLIME
POINT OF STILLNESS
AS I FEEL MY AWARENESS
ALIGNED WITH
THE SOURCE OF LIFE -
"THE ONE"

INHALATION
I INHALE DEEPLY
IMAGINING
LIFE FORCE ENERGY
RISING UP
THE BACK OF MY SPINE
AS I VISUALIZE
THE EXPANSION OF MY
CONSCIOUSNESS

EXHALATION
I EXHALE SLOWLY
IMAGINING
LIFE FORCE ENERGY
MOVING DOWN
THE FRONT OF MY TORSO
AS I VISUALIZE
EXPRESSING UNLIMITED
CREATIVITY

STILLNESS
I IMAGINE AT THE BASE
OF MY SPINE
THERE IS A SUBLIME
POINT OF STILLNESS
AS I FEEL *LIFE FORCE*
ENERGY MANIFESTING MY
CREATIVE INTENTIONS -
"THE MANY"

XV

NAVIGATING THE JOURNEY OF *THE GREAT CIRCLE*

THE GREAT CIRCLE OF THE UNIVERSAL MASCULINE AND FEMININE

My life is the blessed merging of both the universal masculine impulse and feminine impulse.

The Great Circle is "a spiritual map of an awakening life"
That points to and describes *the universal dynamics at play in the world - and in our life.*

It visually illustrates the balancing streams of two essential polarities at the core of reality,
Both **an inward expansive impulse** which is the developing awareness in all life forms
And **an outward expressive impulse** which then manifests within the world
The unique creative gifts that each life form contributes to its environment.

In order to understand these opposite, but complimentary, universal dynamics more clearly,
We can describe these two polarities in a number of ways.

Previously in these narratives, we've explored these polarities
In terms of *the inward expansion of our <u>evolving consciousness</u>*
Being mirrored in the world as *the outward expressions of our <u>evolving creativity</u>.*

We've also portrayed these impulses as *the expansion of our <u>inner growth and development</u>*
Being mirrored in our lives as *the expression of our <u>outer transformation and healing</u>.*

Two other polarities (which can aid our understanding of these dynamics that are active in us)
Are **the fundamental principles of the masculine impulse and feminine impulse**.

So as to be clear, these *two ubiquitous and natural impulses that exist in all expressions of life*
Are not to be misunderstood as the physical bodies that take form as male or female,
But as essential and fundamental *universal principles*
Which exist at the center of all ordered structures throughout the Cosmos.

The masculine principle is *the <u>inward</u> expansive impulse* within every structure in the Universe
That's always yearning to expand beyond its limits, develop its highest potential,
Constantly learn how to be better, and become more of what is possible.

The feminine principle is *the <u>outward</u> expressive impulse* depicted in **The Great Circle**
That manifests novel creative forms, gives birth to diversity, transforms and heals,
Contributes to greater cooperation, and celebrates the wonders of life.

The masculine impulse in us (also referred to as *an inner yearning for spiritual awakening*)
Constantly invites us to reach for a higher stage of awareness
Which, in time, is mirrored by *the Infinite Intelligence of the Universe*
And then, through **the feminine impulse**, is creatively brought into form
As an embodied manifestation within the world.

Every person, each blade of grass, every exquisite flower,
Each form of animal, every exploding star, and each spinning galaxy
Is a unique merging, an unparalleled combination,
A sublime co-creation of these two fundamental principles,
An interweaving fusion and synchronized dance
Of the universal masculine and feminine impulses.

The Great Circle of the Universal Masculine and Feminine
(Fundamental Expansive and Expressive Impulses In My Life)

"THE ONE"
THE SOURCE OF LIFE, INFINITE INTELLIGENCE, THE TRANSCENDENT, THE LIMITLESS WOMB OF CREATION FROM WHICH ALL MATERIAL FORMS EMERGE

MASCULINE IMPULSE
THE INWARD IMPULSE OF EXPANSION EXISTING AT THE CORE OF EVERY FORM OF LIFE WHICH YEARNS TO REACH BEYOND ITS LIMITS, DEVELOP ITS HIGHEST POTENTIAL, AND BECOME MORE OF WHAT IS POSSIBLE

FEMININE IMPULSE
THE OUTWARD IMPULSE OF EXPRESSION WHICH MANIFESTS NOVEL CREATIVE FORMS, GIVES BIRTH TO DIVERSITY, TRANSFORMS AND HEALS, AND CONTRIBUTES TO GREATER COOPERATION

"THE MANY"
THE MANY UNIQUE FORMS OF EMBODIED MANIFESTATION (STARS, PLANETS, PLANTS, ANIMALS, HUMANS) THAT ARE EVOLVING AND UNFOLDING PERFECTLY

MARCH 7
UNIVERSAL MASCULINE IMPULSE

I feel a natural yearning within me that constantly invites me to love more fully.

Everything we experience in this material world of shapes, textures, and colors,
    And all that exists within the vast physical realm of phenomena
        Is made of a blending, or system, of two fundamental and universal opposites,
            The masculine expansive impulse and the feminine expressive impulse.

The masculine impulse, when viewed as a fundamental polarity of *the Impulse of Evolution*,
    Is the instinctual yearning within all of life that strives to develop its creative potential,
        And is also referred to as *the expansive principle of Nature within every human being.*

There are multiple ways to describe the **universal masculine impulse**,
    But for our purpose here, we will look at only four of the more prominent qualities.

The masculine principle is the intrinsic longing within every phenomenal form in the Cosmos
    To perpetually develop its unlimited potential,
        To **transcend** its current limitations so as to reach beyond them,
            And to attempt to ascend to its next higher stage of awareness.

Metaphorically, it yearns "to explore new horizons that have not yet been attained",
    And "to climb the next mountain that has not yet been conquered".

The universal masculine impulse (as it's felt within each of us)
    Is the yearning that inspires us to be self-reflective, to cultivate our creative imagination,
        To **expand** our awareness of what really matters, to love more fully,
            And to maintain an alignment with the transcendent nature of reality.

Other natural drives of *the masculine impulse* (in relation to our human awareness)
    Are discovering new life experiences, exploring more compassionate perspectives,
        And desiring "to soar higher than ever before"
            So we may gain a deeper understanding of what our life is truly about
                And, thereby, foster the kind of **heart wisdom**
                    That will be the foundation for our daily choices.

The masculine principle longs for us to conceive new patterns and opportunities,
    Is perpetually urging us "to plant new seeds of promise"
        That will, in time, blossom into higher stages of **consciousness**,
            And higher consciousness is the initiating source
                Of unparalleled creative potential for the future.

The universal masculine impulse is the instinctive force within our being
    That propels the continual expansion of our awareness,
        Of our inner growth and development,
            And of our natural process of spiritual awakening
                That constantly invites us to discover who we really are.

It's like an eagle soaring to a high apex in the sky
    To acquire a greater vantage of where next it intends to fly.

Circle of the Universal Masculine Impulse
(The Expansive Principle of Nature Within Every Human Being)

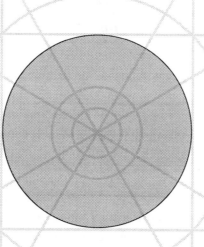

CONSCIOUSNESS
INITIATES CREATIVE
POSSIBILITIES
FOR THE FUTURE
+ + +
+ CONSTANTLY PLANTS
NEW SEEDS
+ YEARNS FOR GREATER
DIVERSITY

TRANSCENDENCE
PERPETUALLY STRIVES
FOR HIGHER STAGES
OF AWARENESS
+ + +
+ REACHES FOR NEW
HORIZONS
+ CLIMBS THE NEXT
MOUNTAIN

EXPANSION
EXPANDS AWARENESS
OF WHAT REALLY
MATTERS
+ + +
+ DESIRES TO SOAR
HIGHER
+ FORMULATES NEW
IDEAS

HEART WISDOM
GAINS LARGER PERSPECTIVES
SO AS TO FOSTER
GREATER WISDOM
+ + +
+ DEVELOPS FROM
LIFE EXPERIENCE
+ LONGS FOR A BETTER
POINT OF VIEW

UNIVERSAL FEMININE IMPULSE

I feel a natural yearning within me that constantly invites me to express my unlimited creativity.

There is a palpable *chemistry of communion* generated between a man and a woman
　　When they are both immersed in deep connection while dancing the Argentine tango.

"It takes two to tango" is a well-known contemporary phrase
　　Describing that in a dynamic relationship of connection and interaction
　　　　There are two individual forces that collaborate, merge, or "dance" together.

The feminine impulse, when understood as a fundamental polarity of *the Impulse of Evolution,*
　　Is the universal expressive principle of Nature within every person
　　　　That mirrors in the outer world, one's inner development *(the masculine impulse).*

It is the natural response to an inner yearning that governs one's outer transformation,
　　As well as the motivation to contribute one's creative gifts to the wellbeing of others.

Again, just like *the universal masculine principle,*
　　There are numerous ways to describe the **universal feminine impulse**,
　　　　But for our purpose here, we will look at four of the more prominent qualities.

First, *the feminine impulse* is vitally **creative**
　　Depicted by the poetic images of "harvesting the abundant fruits of the garden",
　　　　"Birthing the latent potentials of new life" into physical expression,
　　　　　　And manifesting ways to bring its newly discovered inner revelations
　　　　　　　　Into the outer world of phenomenal form.

From the perspective of all human beings, another quality of the feminine is **compassion**,
　　The essential innate pull within everyone to embrace, include, and honor others,
　　　　As well as a natural longing to restore the flow of wellbeing and harmony
　　　　　　Into the lives of those who suffer or experience pain.

The feminine principle gives birth to an inborn yearning
　　To **express** our feelings, ideas, thoughts, and desires,
　　　　To generate in us greater levels of transformation and healing,
　　　　　　To manifest our unique creative gifts and talents,
　　　　　　　　Which we've explored and developed inwardly
　　　　　　　　　　And now desire to contribute outwardly within the world.

And *the feminine impulse* also has an inherent affinity
　　To experience deep states of **presence**
　　　　Through its innate ability "to enjoy and celebrate the journey",
　　　　　　To fully participate in each moment of life,
　　　　　　　　And to simply take time "to stop and smell the flowers".

The feminine impulse can be thought of as "the artistic hand of *the Divine"*
　　Sculpting and fashioning the visions within our heart,
　　　　While harmoniously dancing in step with our *masculine impulse*
　　　　　　To the sublime *Music of the Infinite.*

Circle of the Universal Feminine Impulse
(The Expressive Principle of Nature Within Every Human Being)

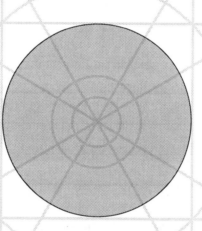

CREATIVITY
CREATES NOVEL WAYS
TO BRING ORIGINAL
IDEAS INTO FORM
+ + +
+ HARVESTS THE
GARDEN
+ BIRTHS NEW LIFE
INTO THE WORLD

PRESENCE
ENJOYS, AND FULLY
PARTICIPATES IN,
EACH MOMENT OF LIFE
+ + +
+ CELEBRATES THE
JOURNEY
+ STOPS TO SMELL
THE FLOWERS

EXPRESSION
EXPRESSES UNIQUE
MANIFESTATIONS AS
A WAY OF CONTRIBUTING
+ + +
+ TRANSFORMS AND
HEALS
+ EXPRESSES FEELINGS
AND THOUGHTS

COMPASSION
LONGS TO RESTORE
THE FLOW OF HARMONY
TO THOSE WHO SUFFER
+ + +
+ YEARNS TO EMBRACE
AND INCLUDE
+ WELCOMES THE
CHALLENGE

RELATIONSHIP OF THE UNIVERSAL MASCULINE AND FEMININE

Today I plant seeds of my creative visions and trust they will blossom in the garden of my life.

There is a fascinating scientific experiment that demonstrates the interdependent relationship
Between frequency and physical structures.

If you were to take a percussive drum and evenly pour a cup of sand over the skin of the drum,
As well as attach a variable-speed electronic oscillator to the drumhead
That sends a specific frequency through the drum and sand,
The sand lying on the drumhead will begin to move with the oscillations
And the grains of sand will rearrange into a visual ordered pattern.

If you were to then adjust the oscillator output so as to send a different frequency to the drum,
The pattern of sand would begin pulsating to the new vibration and change accordingly,
Because the oscillator frequencies and visual ordered patterns are interrelated.

With each adjustment of the invisible interior frequency from the oscillator,
The visible exterior pattern of sand will produce a corresponding new form.

All of life works in the same way, for there is an inward **expansive** impulse (consciousness)
That initiates every new unique pattern of a related outward **expressive** form (creation).

Consciousness is always yearning "to explore new horizons" and "to reach beyond limitations",
And can also be referred to as *the universal masculine principle* of **transcendence**.

The masculine impulse is analogous to the internal frequency of the oscillator,
While the changing patterns of sand on the drumhead represent *the feminine impulse*
Symbolizing the manifestation of the forms and shapes of everything in our world,
As well as a longing to celebrate life (*the feminine principle* of **presence**).

Everything in the Cosmos is a complimentary blend of these two seemingly opposite polarities,
The merging of the essential qualities within these two internal and external realms,
The sacred marriage of *the universal masculine and feminine principles.*

Our life consists of both our inner **consciousness** that "plants the seeds of new possibilities"
Mirrored as the expressions of our outer **creativity** manifesting as "the fruits of our life".

It's the blending of our **heart wisdom** that inwardly develops from our life experiences
(As well as all we learn regarding what our life is truly about - and what really matters),
With our **compassion** that urges us to outwardly embrace and include all beings,
And welcome the challenges and opportunities for personal growth.

The entire "uni - verse" is essentially "one - song" played by *the Symphony of "The One"*
Made up of "an unlimited array of celestial musical instruments"
(I.e. *"The Many"* creative forms within the Cosmos all "conducted" by *the Source of Life).*

Each "instrument" emits a unique melody, a blended frequency of the masculine and feminine
That fashions the myriad patterns of stars, planets, diamonds, flowers, and animals,
And, of course, the novel and magnificent patterns of every human being.

Circle of the Relationship of the Universal Masculine and Feminine

CONSCIOUSNESS AND CREATIVITY
M- CONSTANTLY PLANTS NEW SEEDS
F- HARVESTS THE GARDEN
+ + +
M- YEARNS FOR GREATER DIVERSITY
F- BIRTHS NEW LIFE INTO THE WORLD

TRANSCENDENCE AND PRESENCE
M- REACHES FOR NEW HORIZONS
F- CELEBRATES THE JOURNEY
+ + +
M- CLIMBS THE NEXT MOUNTAIN
F- STOPS TO SMELL THE FLOWERS

EXPANSION AND EXPRESSION
M- DESIRES TO SOAR HIGHER
F- TRANSFORMS AND HEALS
+ + +
M- FORMULATES NEW IDEAS
F- EXPRESSES FEELINGS AND THOUGHTS

HEART WISDOM AND COMPASSION
M- DEVELOPS FROM LIFE EXPERIENCE
F- YEARNS TO EMBRACE AND INCLUDE
+ + +
M- LONGS FOR A BETTER POINT OF VIEW
F- WELCOMES THE CHALLENGE

THE GREAT CIRCLE OF INNER AND OUTER PURPOSE

I consciously cultivate my inner purpose - "to learn", as well as my outer purpose - "to create".

Elephants communicate with one another, sometimes miles apart, by stomping on the ground,
   Whales signal their pods with sounds carried through the sea for a hundred miles,
      And a human child will frequently ask its mother, *"Can I go outside and play?"*

As intelligent life on Earth slowly evolved over millions of years
   Certain species began to develop unique systems of communication
      Producing resourceful advantages which aided their survival.

Numerous types of animals, such as birds, elephants, dolphins, whales, apes, and humans,
   Have cultivated sophisticated communication systems,
      Yet it is we humans who have evolved language to the kind of highly honed skill
         That has enabled our species to develop rational thought.

Over time, acquiring complex language allowed humans to explore the existential questions:
   What is **truth**? - in the search for understanding the nature of reality and what is true,
      Or what we now call the investigation of **science**,
         What is **goodness**? - in the quest for how to best live together in harmony,
            Or what we now refer to as the study of **philosophy**,
               What is **beauty**? - in the yearning to express forms of creativity,
                  Or what we now define as a longing to cultivate **art**.

The development of intricate languages has also provided humanity with the means
   To ask other powerful questions which have the ability to creatively shape our future:
      Who am I? – Why am I here?
         What really matters in my life? – What is my life truly about?

Many people have interpreted the diverse variations of these four perennial questions
   By simply wrapping all of them into one fundamental personal inquiry and statement:
      What is the purpose of my life?

Yet, since every form in the Cosmos has both an expansive and an expressive component,
   A constant dance of interconnected dual impulses,
      We can think of our life with both *an inner purpose* - as well as *an outer purpose*.

The collective inner purpose shared by every human is to discover the true nature of reality,
   To develop one's potential, which then leads to learning how to love all of life unconditionally
      And thus, it's the yearning for a sublime experience of knowing who we really are.

For each human being **one's individual outer purpose**, or *mission*, takes many different forms
   As each person on Earth finds unique ways to use their particular gifts and talents
      To create, manifest, and contribute to, more cooperative communities,
         A more enlightened society, and a more peaceful world.

We are a global tribe of diverse humans all exploring life together on our beautiful planet
   As we attempt to communicate the best ways to live with the existential paradox
      That we all have <u>one purpose</u> - as well as <u>many purposes</u> - at the same time.

The Great Circle of Inner and Outer Purpose
("To Learn" and "To Create")

THE PURPOSE OF
"THE ONE"
THE ONE SOURCE OF LIFE,
INFINITE INTELLIGENCE,
HAS NO PURPOSE - FOR
TIMELESS UNBOUNDED
CONSCIOUSNESS
SIMPLY IS

INNER PURPOSE
MY *"COLLECTIVE*
INNER PURPOSE" IS TO
<u>LEARN</u> TO LOVE ALL OF
LIFE UNCONDITIONALLY,
DEVELOP MY POTENTIAL,
AND DISCOVER
WHO I REALLY AM

OUTER PURPOSE
MY *"INDIVIDUAL*
OUTER PURPOSE", OR
MY *PERSONAL MISSION*,
IS TO <u>CREATE</u> AND
MANIFEST MY UNIQUE
GIFTS AND TALENTS SO
THEY MAY SERVE OTHERS

THE PURPOSE OF
"THE MANY"
SINCE THE BEGINNING
OF TIME - THE PURPOSE
OF THE UNIVERSE, AND
OF THE MANY FORMS OF LIFE,
HAS ALWAYS BEEN
TO FURTHER EVOLUTION

THE MANY INTERPRETATIONS OF INNER PURPOSE

Today I expand my awareness, develop my potential, and learn to love unconditionally.

A mighty river may travel the journey of a thousand miles or more
Before it steadily winds its way through the natural world to its final destination.

The river's long trek may start by running down a steep mountain slope,
Then pass tall green forests spotted with open meadows,
Meander through flat grassy plains,
May even carve out a rocky desert canyon,
Before it eventually merges with, and becomes, the ocean.

The many interpretations of our inner purpose understood by different individuals
Can be thought of as *a flowing river* traveling a similar kind of journey,
As if "the river of our life" passes through several phases of interpretation
Depending on the current stage of our personal development.

Yet ultimately each person's version of our life's collective inner purpose
Is a different form of reaching for the same supreme goal
Of learning to love all of life unconditionally - and realizing who we really are.

When a person's individual conscious development is at early stages of maturity,
One's inner purpose can be interpreted as a natural longing to simply *be happy.*

The innate desire within every person to experience **happiness** can be seen
As a fundamental human need to feel safe, loved, empowered, and connected with *Life.*

At this stage of our inner purpose, a yearning is felt to discover what really matters
Empowering us to live a more conscious life - and to let go of our personal suffering,
In other words - the beginning stages of accepting, and being grateful for,
Our experiences of life just as they are.

As we progress further over time, we gain a different understanding of our inner purpose
Which transforms to expanding our awareness of what is true, developing our potential,
And finding new **creative skills and talents** that we desire to express.

As we continue our development, the interpretation of our inner purpose changes even further
And is eventually understood as the emergent **awakening** that takes place in us
From cultivating a life of inner freedom - which is in service to the good of all.

From "a Big Picture perspective", all of these various interpretations are different forms
Of the same natural yearning in us to awaken to who we really are,
To reach for higher stages of spiritual consciousness,
To learn to love all of life unconditionally,
And to be the greatest expression of ourselves that we can be.

Each individual stage of our inner purpose is a different leg of "the same mighty river of our life"
Winding its way through the landscapes of our everyday experiences
So as to ultimately realize our **Oneness** with *the Infinite Ocean of Limitless Love.*

Circle of the Many Interpretations of Inner Purpose
(Different Versions of the Collective Purpose of Life)

ONENESS
AT EACH STAGE OF LIFE,
MY INNER PURPOSE
HAS ALWAYS BEEN:
*"TO LEARN TO LOVE
UNCONDITIONALLY
AND TO REALIZE
MY ONENESS
WITH ALL OF LIFE"*

HAPPINESS
INITIALLY,
MY INNER PURPOSE MAY
BE INTERPRETED AS:
*"TO LEARN TO FULFILL
MY NATURAL LONGING
TO EXPERIENCE A LIFE
OF HAPPINESS - AND TO
LET GO OF SUFFERING"*

AWAKENING
AS I PROGRESS FURTHER,
MY INNER PURPOSE MAY
BE INTERPRETED AS:
*"TO LEARN TO LIVE
AN AWAKENED LIFE
OF INNER FREEDOM
WHICH IS IN SERVICE
TO THE GOOD OF ALL"*

CREATIVITY
AS I PROGRESS IN LIFE,
MY INNER PURPOSE MAY
BE INTERPRETED AS:
*"TO LEARN TO EXPAND
MY AWARENESS
OF WHAT IS TRUE
AND TO DEVELOP
MY CREATIVE POTENTIAL"*

EVOLUTION OF OUTER PURPOSE

Contributing my gifts to the wellbeing of others advances the life-affirming arc of evolution.

When we look at the amazing diversity of Nature's life forms on our planet,
It may be difficult to see that everything is made of "the same fundamental stuff".

Modern science has revealed that the central components of all living things in this world
Consist of the same basic atomic building blocks,
Which, at the smallest quantum scale, is simply *pure universal energy*.

In some unfathomable manner, this same *radiant essence of universal energy*
Is mysteriously sculpted in countless distinct and unique ways,
And takes form in the world as minerals, microbes, plants, animals, and human beings.

Similarly, our collective inner purpose of learning to love all of life unconditionally
Is the same for everyone (though much of humanity is unaware of this purpose),
Yet the outer purpose for each person on Earth (one's individual mission in life)
Is as different as the myriad expressions of the people on this planet.

Our **outer purpose** (our mission in life) is found in the ways we contribute our gifts to the world
That changes, over time, as we develop and mature through the unfolding stages of life.

For example, some of these stages are basic survival, expression of personal creativity,
As well as the transformation required to cooperatively manifest the common good,
And are defined and interpreted based on our current level of inner development.

We all have a variety of creative ways to express our individual mission
Which emerges from our authentic interests, innate talents, and unique passions.

Ultimately, all expressions of our outer purpose are, at their essential core,
About discovering more creative ways to **contribute to the wellbeing of all of life**
Which naturally advances the life-affirming arc of evolution.

Contribution can be thought of as similar to a house we are building over a long period,
Slowly adding one brick at a time, until the entire structure is complete.

At birth, **our primal impulse to survive** became "the foundation of our house of contribution",
And once our basic survival needs were met, the foundation was established.

Then, based on our development, we began "adding more individual bricks to the foundation"
Each formed from **our creative explorations of what is *true*, *good*, and *beautiful***,
As well as the "bricks" we fashioned from **transforming our inner being**
So we could use our unique gifts and talents to help build a better world.

Of course, this "house of contribution" is a living structure that's never really complete,
Because *the Source of Life* constantly invites us to keep finding more creative ways
To augment "the additional bricks of our infinite potential"
In order to build a never-ending tower of possibility
That reaches high into the heavens.

Circle of the Evolution of Outer Purpose
(The Unfolding Expression of One's Individual Mission)

CONTRIBUTION
THE HIGHEST EXPRESSION
OF MY OUTER PURPOSE
HAS ALWAYS BEEN:
*"TO ADVANCE THE LIFE-
AFFIRMING ARC OF
EVOLUTION BY SERVING
AND CONTRIBUTING
MY GIFTS TO OTHERS"*

SURVIVAL
WHEN I WAS BORN,
MY OUTER PURPOSE
WAS SIMPLY:
*"TO ENSURE MY
BASIC SURVIVAL
SO MY BODY WOULD
CONTINUE TO THRIVE"*

TRANSFORMATION
AS I CONTINUE TO
DEVELOP, MY OUTER
PURPOSE BECOMES:
*"TO TRANSFORM MYSELF
SO I MAY USE MY
TALENTS TO HELP BUILD
A BETTER WORLD"*

CREATIVITY
BASED ON MY INNER
DEVELOPMENT, MY OUTER
PURPOSE CHANGES INTO:
*"TO CULTIVATE
AN ABUNDANCE OF WAYS
TO EXPRESS
MY NATURAL CREATIVITY"*

XVI

THE ART OF TRANSFORMATION AND HEALING

THE GREAT CIRCLE OF DEVELOPMENT AND TRANSFORMATION

As the love in me grows more fully, my experiences of transformation and healing grow as well.

In a turbulent wind such as a tornado, a willow tree will severely bend from its dynamic force,
But then later, will return to its normal upright position when the raging wind stops.

In a violent storm out at sea, the agitated water will form high wave crests and shallow troughs,
But the tranquil equilibrium of the ocean surface will return when blue skies reappear.

Chaos, disturbance, and change are regular occurrences within the unfolding of the Cosmos,
Yet at the same time, there's a natural innate force always striving to return to homeostasis,
Which is a state of balance.

The external physical world we experience each day is brimming with the *effects* of constant change
And, sometimes, these *effects* take the form of affliction, distress, or imbalance.

These kinds of challenging situations "cry out within us" with an intrinsic desire to be healed
Which can be thought of as a natural yearning to be made whole again.

In other words - it is the innate impulse in us that longs to return to balance
By alerting us that the *source* or *cause* of the problem must be corrected.

In order for us to feast on the bountiful fruits of the harvest,
We must first plant the appropriate seeds.

In order for us to smell the delicate fragrance of any flower in our garden,
We must first nourish its tiny seedling.

In order for us to enjoy the magnificent vista from the summit,
We must first climb the mountain.

And in order for us to most effectively manifest our creative vision of what's possible for our life,
We must first align our awareness with *the Source of Life, the Infinite Presence of Love.*

Similarly, the transformation and healing of the exterior reality of our body is much the same,
Because for authentic transformation to occur, we must first develop our interior self
Through the dedicated practice of spiritual growth, **inner development**,
And discovering who we really are.

The inward expansion of our awareness (i.e. learning how to love more fully and be at peace)
Is outwardly expressed and out-pictured by *the Source of Life*
In our body as our **outer transformation**,
Which can come in many forms of physical, emotional, or mental healing.

As we continue to develop our consciousness within our inner world *(source* or *cause),*
The expansion we inwardly experience is correspondingly mirrored in our outer world
As a natural expression of creativity, healing, or wellbeing *(outcome* or *effect)*
In the form of "the fruits of the harvest", "the blossoming of our garden",
Or "the spacious view from the mountaintop".

The Great Circle of Development and Transformation
(The Transformative Dynamics of Healing)

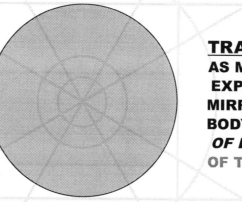

"THE ONE"
THE ONE SOURCE,
INFINITE INTELLIGENCE
+ + +
WITHIN THE REALM OF
ABSOLUTE ONENESS,
I AM ALWAYS ALIGNED
WITH THE INFINITE
PRESENCE OF LOVE

INNER
DEVELOPMENT
I CONSTANTLY EXPAND
MY AWARENESS OF
WHAT IS TRUE, LEARN
TO LOVE MORE FULLY,
AWAKEN TO WHO I AM,
AND DEVELOP MY
CREATIVE POTENTIAL

OUTER
TRANSFORMATION
AS MY DEVELOPMENT
EXPANDS, IT IS THEN
MIRRORED WITHIN MY
BODY BY THE SOURCE
OF LIFE IN THE FORM
OF TRANSFORMATION
OR HEALING

"THE MANY"
I AM A PERFECTLY
UNFOLDING EXPRESSION
OF THE MANY
UNIQUE FORMS OF LIFE
+ + +
IN THE PRESENT
MOMENT, I AM ALREADY
HEALED AND WHOLE

THE SPIRITUAL JOURNEY IN RELATION TO HEALING

Every moment offers me an opportunity to further my quest of learning to love unconditionally.

Every morning when we first open our eyes to the dawning light of a new day,
    The existential quest "to reach for a grander horizon" sets in motion once again.

As we expand our scientific understanding through a wealth of evidence-based knowledge
    And cultivate a greater comprehension of what our life is truly about,
        We can more easily accept that we're an integral part of an evolving Universe
            That's perpetually directed to increase our compassion and inclusion of others.

And as we begin to observe the daily unfolding of our life from *an evolutionary perspective*,
    This vantage helps us perceive our diverse life experiences, successes, and challenges
        (As well as every choice we make) from a much more expansive point of view.

This "Big Perspective" helps us understand that we're all "travelers on a grand cosmic quest"
    Which is about learning to live a life of inner freedom - and to love unconditionally.

The daily journey of our life is a constantly evolving quest, an ever-unfolding *spiritual journey*,
    For it reveals how we can make our unconscious adventure into a conscious adventure
        In which we eventually learn to be in service to the wellbeing and good of all.

The process called *healing* has also been described as a *journey*, a *journey of wholeness*,
    And if we examine our inner emotional landscapes deep enough,
        We can see that both <u>our spiritual quest</u> and <u>our search for healing</u>
            Have always traveled similar parallel paths - heading to the same destination.

Our *spiritual journey* is our path of discovering how to truly experience lasting peace of mind
    As our life "moves through a labyrinth" of conscious inner growth and development.

Because many people begin their spiritual search based on their need to relieve their suffering,
    One's *spiritual journey* may start out as *a search for healing*
        Attempting to restore a physical or emotional imbalance with specific modalities.

Yet *the healing journey* of our body and mind is essentially about re-establishing *wholeness*,
    And so to authentically return to *wholeness* we must know *the truth of who we really are*
        Which ultimately takes us to the sacred place within our heart
            Where contributing to the lives of others becomes a key step on our spiritual path.

Through the myriad twists and turns, trials and tribulations, and interior struggles of life,
    This *healing journey* eventually steers us down a path of *spiritual discovery*
        Where we learn to live a compassionate life of contribution and service.

In the fullness of time, serving others becomes one of the most natural transformative practices
    Along our *spiritual journey* of *healing* and *wholeness*.

The spiritual journey and **the search for healing**
    Are like "two interwoven vines growing in the garden of the gods",
        Spiraling together and weaving their way up *The Tree of Life*.

Circle of *the Spiritual Journey* in Relation to *Healing*

I AM
THE WAY
ULTIMATELY, I REALIZE
THERE IS ONLY
UNFOLDING PERFECTION
IN EVERY MOMENT
AS I TRULY AWAKEN
TO LOVING ALL OF LIFE
UNCONDITIONALLY

I SEEK
THE WAY
INITIALLY, I SEARCH
FOR A HELPFUL
HEALING MODALITY
OR EFFECTIVE SPIRITUAL
PATH - SO I MAY HEAL
MYSELF OF A CERTAIN
DISEASE OR IMBALANCE

I LIVE
THE WAY
IN TIME, I TEACH OTHERS
TO HEAL THROUGH
MY OWN EXAMPLE
OF A COMPASSIONATE
LIFE OF SERVICE - WHILE
I CULTIVATE GREATER LEVELS
OF HEALING

I FOLLOW
THE WAY
I THEN BEGIN A JOURNEY
OF FOLLOWING THE PATH
OF A SPIRITUAL TEACHER
WHO TEACHES ME TO LOVE
AND SERVE OTHERS,
WHICH BECOMES A PATH
FOR ME TO HEAL MYSELF

VARIOUS FORMS OF HEALING

I recognize that only Love is real - thus in this present moment, I am healed and whole right now.

If you have a small bar magnet that generates a fixed level of magnetism
    And decide you would like to increase the strength (intensity) of its attractive force,
        There are a number of possible ways this might be achieved.

First, you might get a welder to physically weld together a second bar magnet of equal strength
    To one side of the original magnet, which would then double its magnetic power.

Another approach for increasing its magnetism would be to hire an electrical engineer,
    Or someone who knows how to construct *an electric wire coil* around the magnet,
        And then send a pulsed current of electrical charge through *the wire coil*
            Which would amplify the intensity of its magnetic field.

Next, in "an idyllic world of infinite possibilities", you might find a gifted wizard-like magician
    Who could, mysteriously and miraculously, increase its strength in "a magical instant".

Assuming that all of these diverse methods are actually viable and could achieve your goal,
    It's obvious that "the magician's method" is the quickest and easiest,
        And would work in all possible situations, no matter the size of the magnet.

The above illustration can be used as a metaphor to help clarify
    Some of the various expressions of healing we can potentially utilize to heal ourselves.

Just like a skilled welder who could outwardly modify the physical structure of the magnet,
    If we want to correct an illness or painful condition that we're experiencing,
        We can effectively modify our body through a variety of physical techniques
            That try to alleviate illness by temporarily altering specific symptoms.

A holistic form of healing that's similar to an engineer sending a charged current through a coil
    Would be to use techniques to restore the balanced flow of *Life Force energy*, or *Chi*,
        To freely circulate throughout our body, assisting our body's ability to heal itself.

An instantaneous form, or dimension of *emergent healing*, would be like that of a magician,
    Where, on a quantum level, we align with *Life's Intelligence* "to miraculously alter creation"
        Via a dynamic shift in our consciousness that "re-forms" our body's energy field.

Each one of these **various forms of healing** are potentially available to us at all times,
    But if our only base of knowledge is such that **physical healing** is all we're aware of,
        Then physical healing will be the only option we're currently able to explore.

Yet as we expand our awareness of what our life is about - including our understanding of healing
    And learn about **the expressions of vibrational and emergent healing**,
        Our options to promote balance within us suddenly become more expanded.

There is nothing wrong with learning to heal in ways analogous to "a welder" or "an engineer"
    For these modalities can compassionately serve many of the needs of those who suffer,
        But why not ultimately discover how to heal as "an awakened Spiritual Magician".

Circle of Various Forms of Healing

PERFECT WHOLENESS
AN AWAKENED AWARENESS THAT ONLY LOVE IS REAL, THE STATE IN WHICH THERE IS NO NEED FOR HEALING - SINCE ONLY *PERFECT WHOLENESS* EXISTS

PHYSICAL HEALING
AN EFFECTIVE - YET TEMPORARY FORM OF HEALING IN WHICH I ALLEVIATE PAIN OR ILLNESS BY MODIFYING OR COVERING UP THE SYMPTOMS OF MY BODY

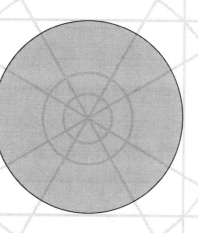

EMERGENT HEALING
AN INSTANTANEOUS FORM OF HEALING IN WHICH I'M ABLE "TO MIRACULOUSLY ALTER CREATION" THROUGH A DYNAMIC SHIFT IN MY CONSCIOUSNESS

VIBRATIONAL HEALING
A MORE SUBTLE AND HOLISTIC FORM OF HEALING IN WHICH I RESTORE THE BALANCED FLOW OF *LIFE FORCE ENERGY*, OR *CHI*, THROUGHOUT MY BODY

EMERGENT HEALING

As I awaken to the magnificence of who I really am, I open my heart to transformation and healing.

The exquisite process of *authentic healing* (*the restoration of wholeness and balance* in our life)
    Is directly related to *our spiritual awakening (our spiritual growth and development)*
        For it's a natural longing that always invites us to expand our awareness of what is true,
          And just like <u>spiritual awakening</u>, <u>healing</u> is also our search for what is true.

When *authentic healing* is insightfully understood from "a Big Picture view of life"
    (Or what some scientists and philosophers refer to as *the evolutionary perspective*
        By which we learn to perceive our reality and our relationship with the world
          From a more inclusive and expansive vantage of what our life is truly about),
          We realize that *true healing* isn't merely about fixing a specific problem.

From *an evolutionary spirituality perspective*, a deep understanding of *our personal healing*
    Is actually about using a challenging situation that's currently occurring in our life
        As a way to consciously awaken to the magnificence of who we really are
          So we can discover how to let go of loveless thinking, develop our creative potential,
          And ultimately learn to love all of life unconditionally.

From this "Bigger Picture of life", *true healing* is about *the Infinite Intelligence* of the Universe
    Using chaos and challenge as "a sacred gift" - so we may expand our awareness
        And, in time, cultivate more of our creative gifts and talents
          That may be used to serve the wellbeing and good of all.

The natural process of *healing* is one of the pathways the Universe uses
    To awaken its myriad forms of life into higher levels of consciousness
        So that, eventually from the steady building and expansion of awareness,
          A sudden or unexpected transformation can take place.

From this vantage, *emergent healing* can be described as **the spontaneous transformation**
    That instantaneously happens within our body, heart, or mind
        When we experience **a profound shift in consciousness**.

Emergent healing is an extraordinary change and sudden balance that occurs in our being
    When we experience an internal **"quantum leap"** to a **higher stage of awareness**.

At these higher stages of awareness where we embody a greater level of wholeness,
    Various forms of disease and imbalance, which we may have encountered previously,
        Can no longer exist within the elevated frequency of *Limitless Love*.

These imbalances may have taken the form of certain symptoms at lower stages of awareness
    But they cannot remain within a higher field of awakened awareness.

Emergent healing can be likened to shining a very bright light into a dark room
    And then simply watching the darkness that was once there - immediately disappear.

For the confusion of darkness can't exist when *the light of higher awareness*
    Is consciously radiating within the sanctuary of an open heart.

Circle of Emergent Healing

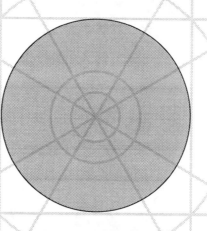

SHIFT IN CONSCIOUSNESS
EMERGENT HEALING –
THE INSTANTANEOUS AND
SEEMINGLY MIRACULOUS
WELLNESS THAT EMERGES
WITHIN MY BODY
FROM A PROFOUND SHIFT
IN MY CONSCIOUSNESS

QUANTUM LEAP
EMERGENT HEALING –
"A QUANTUM LEAP"
INTO A SUPERIOR
LEVEL OF WHOLENESS
WHERE PREVIOUS
FORMS OF DISEASE
OR IMBALANCE
CAN NO LONGER EXIST

HIGHER STAGE OF AWARENESS
EMERGENT HEALING –
AN EXTRAORDINARY
CHANGE AND SUDDEN
BALANCE IN MY BEING
THAT OCCURS FROM
ATTAINING A HIGHER
STAGE OF AWARENESS

SPONTANEOUS TRANSFORMATION
EMERGENT HEALING –
THE SPONTANEOUS
TRANSFORMATION OF
MY BODY, HEART, OR MIND
FROM EXPERIENCING
THE ELEVATED FREQUENCY
OF *LIMITLESS LOVE*

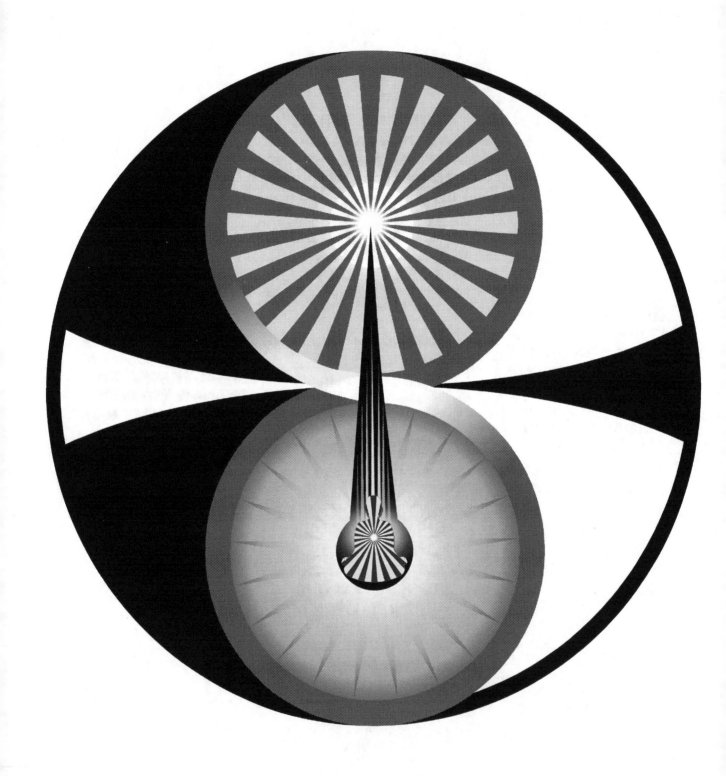

XVII

CONCLUSION
- SACRED
DESTINY

GIFTS OF *THE GREAT CIRCLE*

I am grateful for the blessed gifts of awareness I receive each day that help me love more fully.

If you want to build something from a store-bought kit such as a model sailboat,
    The kit would include an illustrated diagram of all the pieces and how they fit together.

When a building contractor erects a new house, he or she uses an architect's blueprint
    To help the construction workers understand how all of the parts fit into the whole.

Similarly when a person feels the yearning to create a more conscious and compassionate life,
    It's helpful to use a "blueprint", a "diagram", or in this case, a "spiritual map of an awakening life"
        That reveals the key dynamics for a life of inner freedom.

Through the sincere study of (what some spiritual philosophers have called) **The Great Circle**,
    In other words - *a map of the universal dynamics at play in the world and in our life*,
        We can open our heart and mind to receive its numerous gifts.

Contemplating **The Great Circle** helps us expand our awareness of what our life is truly about
    Which then assists us in developing greater compassion and empathy for others,
        As well as living our life with integrity and responsibility.

As we learn to perceive our life and the lives of others
    From more compassionate and expansive perspectives, we can more effectively
        Cultivate larger spheres of inclusion - and wider circles of cooperation.

Reflections on **The Great Circle** also provide us insights into the epic unfolding of the Cosmos,
    In other words - into the evolutionary dynamics of our life, our planet, and the Universe,
        Which helps us see that life is constantly evolving towards ever-greater creativity
            And, ultimately, reveals to us the blessed gift of being in **service** to others.

Through a wealth of evidence-based cosmological information and eons of spiritual knowledge,
    This *circle* brings to light an *evolutionary spirituality* with its universal creation story
        That leads to greater cooperation for all people - and the nations of the world.

Yet one of the most novel gifts of **The Great Circle** is a sense of clarity - so we can **embrace**
    The essential mystery and paradox of existence, the mystical nature of reality,
        Which helps us embrace a similar mystery and paradox within ourselves
            That's concerned with integrating both our eternal and temporal natures.

The Great Circle first portrays this parallel paradox from a larger "macro or cosmic vantage",
    Which then assists us in seeing that these same unfolding dynamics within the Universe
        Are also taking place within our own life, but from a "micro or human vantage".

Exploring these dynamics of **The Great Circle** can motivate us to contemplate
    "The Big Questions" of spiritual inquiry, the life-defining perennial questions
        That aid us in **expanding our awareness** of who we really are.

One of the expansive questions that **The Great Circle** constantly invites us to ask ourselves is:
    "Is there a more blessed gift than one that helps us to love all of life unconditionally?"

Circle of the Gifts of *The Great Circle*

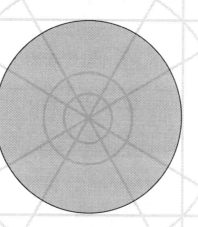

**EMBRACE MYSTERY
AND PARADOX**
THE GREAT CIRCLE GIVES
ME CLARITY SO I CAN
EMBRACE THE MYSTERIES
AND PARADOXES OF LIFE,
WHICH HELPS ME EMBRACE
THE MYSTERY AND PARA-
DOX OF MY OWN ETERNAL
AND TEMPORAL NATURES

**EXPAND
AWARENESS**
THE GREAT CIRCLE
HELPS ME MORE DEEPLY
CONTEMPLATE
"THE BIG QUESTIONS"
OF SPIRITUAL INQUIRY,
SO I MAY FURTHER
EXPAND MY AWARENESS
OF WHO I REALLY AM

**MORE INCLUSIVE
PERSPECTIVES**
THE GREAT CIRCLE
ASSISTS ME IN LIVING
LIFE WITH INTEGRITY,
CULTIVATING GREATER
COMPASSION, AND
GAINING A MORE INCLU-
SIVE VIEW OF WHAT MY
LIFE IS TRULY ABOUT

**SERVICE
TO OTHERS**
THE GREAT CIRCLE
PROVIDES ME SPIRITUAL
INSIGHTS INTO THE
EVOLUTIONARY DYNAMICS
OF LIFE, WHICH POINT
ME TO CONSCIOUSLY
DEDICATING MY LIFE
TO THE SERVICE OF OTHERS

RENEWAL

Today I renew myself by aligning with the Infinite Presence of Love in the sanctuary of silence.

We have arrived at the end of another winter season within our planet's annual journey
  And have reached the completion of a natural period of self-reflection and rejuvenation
    Which has given us many rich moments to ponder how all of Nature,
      As well as our own heart and mind, have had the blessed opportunity
        To be renewed during this season.

The air outside is now beginning to be visited by warmer winds,
  The buds on the deciduous trees are eager to burst forth,
    And the early spring flowers and grasses
      Are slowly making their appearance in the world.

The tiny seeds which have waited patiently for so long,
  Lying half-asleep within the dark cold soil,
    Are acutely listening to the ubiquitous *Song of Life*
      And are now aware that, very soon, it will be their time to awaken.

For the intrinsic vitality of the Earth has been renewed once again,
  Energized during the reflective quiet of winter,
    Restored within its meditative stillness,
      Integrated through its experiences of discovery,
      And attuned to a heightened **awareness**.

And for each of us as well, there has been the possibility to envision our life anew,
  Through a season of meaningful contemplations and revelatory insights,
    Through the intimate inquiry of "the Big Questions",
      Through the vigilant eyes of mindfulness,
        And through *Life's* magnificent power to transform and heal us.

Winter's quality of *renewal* is always accessible to us no matter what season is occurring,
  For as we continuously align our awareness with *the Infinite Presence of Love*,
    The renewal of our body, heart, and mind is available
      Within the "winter" of every single day throughout the year.

Renewal can be thought of as the strengthening and **rejuvenation** of our inner being
  By consciously reconnecting with *the Source of Life*.

Stated another way, *renewal* is the fostering of beneficial insights and revelations
  Through attuning with *Infinite Intelligence* in moments of **self-reflection**.

The perpetual Breath of Life, the endless cycle of seasons, is about to make another revolution
  From its in-breath to its out-breath, from inhalation to exhalation, from rest to activity,
    At this annual completion of winter - at this hallowed time of *the vernal equinox*.

This past winter has been "another inhalation" endlessly spiraling towards the emerging future,
  Yet in a curious way, the constant cycle of life seems to gently pause for a brief moment
    At this threshold of *the equinox*, just before it makes "its next exhale" into spring.

Circle of Renewal

SELF-INQUIRY
RENEWAL –
THE CULTIVATION
OF MY SPIRITUAL GROWTH
AND INNER DEVELOPMENT
THROUGH THE INQUIRY
OF ASKING PERENNIAL
LIFE-DEFINING QUESTIONS

SELF-REFLECTION
RENEWAL –
THE FOSTERING
OF BENEFICIAL INSIGHTS
AND REVELATIONS
THRU SELF-REFLECTION
AND ATTUNING WITH *INFINITE INTELLIGENCE*

REJUVENATION
RENEWAL –
THE STRENGTHENING
AND REJUVENATION
OF MY INNER BEING
THROUGH ALIGNING
MY AWARENESS WITH
THE SOURCE OF LIFE

INTEGRATION
RENEWAL –
THE EXPANSION OF MY
CONSCIOUS AWARENESS
BY CONTEMPLATING
AND THEN INTEGRATING
MY RECENT SIGNIFICANT
EXPERIENCES OF LIFE

This series of Contemplative Practices continues in

The Spring Volume: March 19 – June 19

The Summer Volume: June 20 – September 21

The Autumn Volume: September 22 – December 20

The Great Circle Mantra

My life is unfolding perfectly
Just the way it is
Because all that truly exists
Is *Perfect Love*
Yet I am here
To help the world become more perfect
By living my life
Perfectly guided by *Love*

Introduction To The Poem – *Infinite Awakenings*

This *story poem* was inspired by the first few pages of the book "The New Earth" by the spiritual teacher, Eckhart Tolle - and by a powerful personal transformative experience of epiphany.

It was written in the spring of 2008 when I traveled to Brazil with an open heart and an intention to receive a physical healing from the Brazilian psychic healer, John of God. While at the John of God Healing Center, I had a profound spiritual epiphany of Oneness - and wrote this poem as part of an embodiment of that sacred event.

In his book Eckhart describes how at one time, millions of years ago, there was a plethora of green vegetation on the planet that had developed and taken form, yet there were no plants in the form of flowers. The beautiful manifestation of simple flowers had not yet arrived on the evolutionary scene. But over time and with gradual biological development, *Life* eventually found a way to empower a brand new emergent form of plant to arise; the very first flower.

For the first flower to take shape on Earth, a radical shift in consciousness was required within the plant kingdom. This new expression of vegetative structure can be thought of as an "enlightenment" or "awakening" within the plant kingdom.

A similar kind of radical shift in consciousness also occurred over geological time within the mineral kingdom from the first formation of a diamond - and millions of years later, within the animal kingdom from the first flight of a primordial bird.

The same expansive evolutionary impulses in consciousness are happening right now throughout the world as they continuously have since the origins of the Earth. Each person on the planet is now, consciously or unconsciously, evolving and developing into his or her sacred destiny as an awakened human.

----- Oman Ken

This poem is an excerpt from Oman Ken's poetry book entitled
"Infinite Awakenings – Philosophical Story Poems Envisioning A More Glorious World".

Infinite Awakenings

A noble princess displays an audacious string of gems
Her jeweled necklace glistens against bronze skin
A primal ribbon of geology rests over her heart
As translucent diamonds reflect the crimson Sun

Yet a billion rotations of this solar light - long ago
Soon after the Earth was fashioned into spherical form
These crystalline jewels did not yet exist

Until primordial dancers of raw minerals and molecules
Heard the whispers of a new creation song
And choreographed themselves into fractal ordered lattices
By the unseen power of some mysterious sculptor's hand
Awakening the first diamond

Mythic kings and simple peasants alike
Adorn their regal palaces and pastoral mud huts
With ornamental gardens of speckled flowers
That drink daily the god-like nectar
Of the descending sunlight

Yet 100 million seasonal turnings - eons ago
These blossoming creatures of kaleidoscopic hues
Had not yet emerged

Until green leafy pioneers
Heard the hypnotic allurings of a new and unparalleled melody
In which they catapulted their way
Into visions of unexplored frontiers
Giving birth to a unique pattern of natural artistry
Awakening the first flower

Poets and traveling troubadours
Throughout the spinning of centuries
Have heralded the poetic majesty
Of the wondrous flight of birds
That ceaselessly point us inward
To a timeless freedom

These winged magicians of the skies
    With their interlaced feathers unfurled
        Glide with ease to the horizon's edge

Yet millions of fleeting winters - so long ago
    These heaven bound miracles
        Had not yet discovered the arcane secret
        To the unfathomable craft of flight

Until a host of scaly cold-blooded reptiles
    Morphed through time
        Into wings of promise
           And leaped off cliffs of yesterday
              To triumphantly soar with plumed wings
            Awakening the first bird

In every hallowed corner of the world
    It's happening once again
        Journeyers on a sacred pilgrimage
        Like you and me
           Saints and sinners
              The pious and irreverent
                Awakening to a natural call

Yet a thousand ephemeral lifetimes ago
    These humble mystic journeyers
        Had not yet arrived

Until brave visionary warriors
    Krishna, Buddha, Lao Tzu, Jesus
        And multitudes of the nameless ones
        Held high the sword of truth
        Poked their *Souls*
           Through the one great portal
           Would not take their eyes away
              From the sublime *Light* within
              And merged with the purest field
              Of unbounded stillness
                Becoming the first awakened humans

And the heavens rejoiced
    Each time a new chorus from creation's canticle was sung

As the first virgin diamond awakened
    For every princess to adorn her neck

      As the first dazzling flower awakened
        Adding splendor to the bounty of our gardens

        As the first feathered bird awakened
          That we might dream of our own flight one day

          As the first sentient human awakened
            Inviting us to sing verses of the One Song

I wonder - how some glorious future species
    Gazing up at a starstrung sky
      And asking brazen questions
        Will celebrate the infinite possibilities
        And the perpetual unfolding
          Within the frequencies of celestial starlight
          In the next awakening

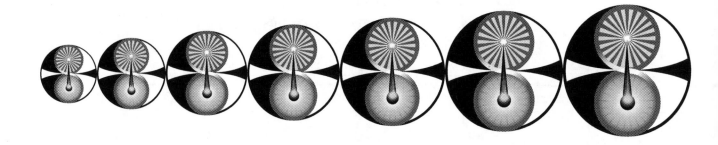

⁂ JOURNEY OF *THE GREAT CIRCLE* – GLOSSARY OF TERMS ⁂

Being defines the invisible and formless realm of *the Transcendent*. It is the sublime realm of existence in which all that exists is *Transcendent Oneness* - all that exists is *Absolute Perfection* - all that exists is *Unbounded Eternity* - all that exists is *Limitless Love*.

Becoming defines the natural process within any form of life that is developing its potential - which leads to manifesting more diverse creative expressions of itself or its environment. In relation to human beings, *Becoming* is one's *journey of awakening*. It is the *journey of discovery* or *spiritual journey* regarding one's inner development, the expansion of one's awareness, or one's spiritual awakening - which leads to greater contributions of one's creative gifts and talents employed in the service of others. *Becoming* can also be referred to as "one's creative actions and expressions to help make the world a better place".

Biosphere is *the Universal Consciousness* that gives shape to all biological life like microbes, plants, animals, which have evolved physical sensations and basic emotions.

Cause and Effect – The originating cause of everything within the phenomenal Universe is consciousness. The resulting effect from the creative intelligence of consciousness is the manifestations within the world of form (creation).

Consciousness is the invisible *Force of Natural Intelligence* which creates the visible world - the non-physical *Transcendent Power* which creates the physical Universe - an intangible internal *Awareness* which creates a tangible external reality. It is the invisible field of natural intelligence and information of any material or phenomenal structure that determines and gives creative shape to its visible form or pattern. Consciousness is the transcendent interiority of any structure of life which is the animating creative power that brings exterior form to its temporal body.

There is always some facet of consciousness (or natural intelligence) in every form of material expression within the Universe, such as the unique consciousness in every human being, animal, plant, micro-organism, rock, planet, star, galaxy, and beyond.

Consciousness is also the level or ability of a manifested form or structure within the Universe to be aware of, and respond to, experiences in its environment. A plant has a limited ability to respond to its environment. Whereas an animal has a greater, more developed ability. As far as is generally accepted, human beings have the greatest ability to be aware of, and respond to, experiences in their environment, and thus it is said that humans have the most evolved consciousness of all creatures on Earth.

Creation defines the phenomenal embodiment of the material realm. It is all expressions of the Universe - such as galaxies, stars, planets, microorganisms, plants, animals, and humans. Creation is also a word that represents the world of Nature.

In this book, the words Nature, Sun, Moon, Earth, Solar System, Universe, Cosmos are capitalized to represent that at a particular realm of consciousness, they are each a living entity of creation which is to be held in reverence, respect, honor, and is to be seen as sacred.

Emergent Healing is the spontaneous transformation that instantaneously happens within our body, heart, or mind when we experience a radical and profound shift in consciousness. *Emergent healing* is an extraordinary change and sudden balance that occurs in our being when we experience an internal "quantum leap" to a higher stage of awareness.

At these higher stages of awareness where we embody a greater level of wholeness, various forms of disease and imbalance, which we may have encountered previously, can no longer exist within the elevated frequency of *Limitless Love*.

Enlightenment is the sublime embodiment of inner freedom - which is living at a stage of spiritual consciousness where one abides in inner peace no matter what occurs. *Enlightenment* (from the perspective of this book) is not only about one's personal *awakening* or awareness of Oneness with God *(the Transcendent)*, but that any sustained individual alignment with *Ultimate Reality* must also be embodied and grounded within one's physical body and then shared collectively through the personal actions of serving the wellbeing of others.

In some contemporary spiritual groups, the concept of *enlightenment* is now perceived as an ongoing experience of loving others and loving self unconditionally while serving the good within all of life.

Evolution is the creative and natural development within all of life. It is the response within every phenomenon to *the Natural Intelligence* of the Universe which directs each facet of existence to further develop, expand its possibilities, create diversity, and express more of its potential.

The Evolutionary Impulse is *the Natural Intelligence* within the Universe that animates every material form along a path of perpetual creative unfoldment. It is the transcendent organizing principle within all of Creation. It can be thought of as *the Infinite Creativity* within all of existence that intelligently shapes and organizes higher expressions of manifested form such as galaxies, stars, oceans, myriad life forms, and every human being.

The Evolutionary Impulse is (from a religious perspective) the same as *the Universal Force of God* that guides development and manifestation within all forms of the natural world. It is the *Force* that "attracts together" sub-atomic particles, the planets in their solar orbits, all interdependent ecosystems, as well as two lovers who experience romantic passion.

Evolutionary Perspective – see Evolutionary Spirituality

Evolutionary Spirituality is a phrase that describes a "Big Picture Perspective" way of thinking about how our lives develop and transform. Evolutionary spirituality provides us with the gifts of a much larger perspective of reality inspiring us to further develop our higher potential, to motivate us to transform our fear-based self-oriented nature, to create the seeds of greater compassion for all of life, and to take responsible conscious actions toward building a more sustainable future.

Evolutionary spirituality merges both *the Transcendent Power of Consciousness* and the myriad forms of creation. It unifies God with evolution. It is the awareness which embraces a Oneness of an *Infinite and Eternal Intelligence* with an ever-unfolding Universe.

Existence is defined as the totality of the physical and the non-physical, the visible and the invisible, the Immanent and *the Transcendent*. It is the wholeness and merging of consciousness and creation, God and the Universe, Spirit and form, *"The One"* and *"The Many"*, *Being* and *Becoming*.

Fractals are natural objects or mathematical patterns that repeat themselves at smaller scales in which a reduced-size copy of the initial pattern is formed in succeeding generations, typically producing new emergent variations within each later generation.

There is also a group of *fractal patterns* that repeat themselves identically as they get smaller, yet the vast majority of *fractals* repeat their patterns with slight variations each time generating new and novel formations at different levels of magnification.

For example, trees grow in *fractal patterns* both above and below the ground, as well as the veins and arteries within the human body. Other *fractal patterns* that occur in the natural world are not as obvious - such as the way amorphous clouds slowly accumulate and form in the sky, how the ragged rock edges of mountain ranges are structured, the manner in which the coastlines of countries take shape, and how the patterns of galaxies and solar systems are created.

God – see *the Transcendent*

The Great Circle is "a spiritual map of an awakening life" which illustrates that our <u>internal awareness</u> creatively shapes the way our <u>external reality</u> is expressed and experienced within our daily life. In other words, it portrays the universal dynamics of <u>our inward expansion of consciousness</u> mirrored as <u>our outward creative expression</u>.

There are many examples of traditional iconic images that represent *The Great Circle* - such as the Yin Yang symbol, the Star of David, the medicine wheel, and the sacred cross.

The primary function of **The Great Circle** as a transformative tool is to simply portray a useful collection of words and phrases for the purpose of deeply comprehending the nature of existence. With this awareness we can develop a greater understanding of what our life is truly about and what really matters - and thus, cultivate an unconditional love for each expression of life.

Holiness and Magnificence is another way of describing our *True Eternal Nature*, our *Transcendent Self*, who we really are. In religious language, it is our sacred divinity.

Infinite Awakenings represents the perpetual evolution and constant development that occurs in every phenomenal structure in the Universe - including galaxies, stars, planets, animals, plants, micro-organisms, and humans. "Awakening" describes a natural process of "developing to a higher level of awareness" or "expanding to a more elevated stage of consciousness" or "evolving to a new species". "Infinite" points to the awareness that *Life's* "awakenings" continue on and on without end.

Infinite Intelligence – see *The Transcendent*

The Infinite Presence of Love – see *The Transcendent*

Inner Freedom is when one consciously realizes the perfection that's always unfolding within - and within all of life. Living with this awareness allows the natural states of peace, happiness, joy and harmony to effortlessly arise. It is a life of one who has devotedly learned to love others and all of life unconditionally - and who has gained the joyful awareness of serving the wellbeing of others. In these writings, one who attains this level of mastery is referred to as a **Master of Freedom**.

Therefore, when we are aligned with *the Source of Life* - and gratefully celebrate every experience we have while fully loving and accepting ourselves, as well as every part of life - we are free.

Journey of Awakening is the natural evolutionary journey of ongoing inner development that every person in the world is constantly embarked on (whether he or she is consciously aware of it or not). Over time, this *journey of discovery* becomes conscious and intentional through a process of expanding one's awareness, transforming one's beliefs, discovering how to master a life of inner freedom, and contributing one's creative gifts and talents to the wellbeing of others. This is also referred to as the *spiritual journey* or the *journey of self-mastery*.

Life (when italicized and spelled with a capital) is a word that represents *the Transcendent, the Source of All That Is, the Infinite Intelligence* of the Universe. It is a short way of referring to *the Source of Life*. When "life" is not italicized and capitalized, it represents our human existence in the physical world.

Limitless Love – see *The Transcendent*

"The Many" can be defined in a number of ways, such as the myriad forms of life, the countless expressions of natural creativity on the Earth and throughout the Universe, all that is created, the endless manifestations of creation, etc. In relation to human beings, *"The Many"* is the totality of all humans that exist on the planet. Every person is a unique creative expression of *"The Many"*.

Master of Freedom is a visionary archetype that represents our *Fully Awakened Self,* one's *True Eternal Nature* completely experienced and lived within one's physical body. It is the embodied realization of a person who lives a life of inner freedom, loves all of life unconditionally, and serves the good of all with their creative gifts and talents. It is every person's sacred destiny to embody the *Awakened Self* and fully experience their life as a **Master of Freedom.**

Morphogenetic Field is a phrase used in developmental biology and consciousness studies that proposes there is a tangible field of energy that's generated by all things, both physical structures and even mental constructs, which serves to organize the structure's characteristics and patterns.

When we consciously align ourselves to *the morphogenetic field of a specific visionary archetype*, we begin a process of personally resonating to the archetype - and bringing into our awareness the expansive qualities and visionary characteristics which the archetype symbolizes.

Noosphere is *the Universal Consciousness* that gives shape to both the individual and collective mind, which resides within all intelligent life forms.

"The One" – see *The Transcendent*

Oneness is Ultimate Reality in which every form of creation is a unique expression of one *Unity*. It can be described as Infinite Reality in which each expression of life is an integral part of *one unfolding never-ending spiral of Consciousness*. Oneness can be thought of as Quantum Reality in which all of the manifest world of form is made of the same *universal energy (Light)* in constant motion. It can also be described as Transcendent Reality in which the Universe and everything in it is comprised of *one Universal Love*, and many people simply call this *Love* - "God".

Paradox is the perception that two discrete realities which contradict each other both exist at the same time. It is the notion that two expressions of reality which are complete polar opposites can both take place at once.

In the writings of **Journey of The Great Circle**, embracing the existential paradoxes of life is a key to the cultivation of spiritual awakening. Embracing certain paradoxes enables us to merge consciousness with creation - God with the Universe - *Heaven* with Earth.

Physiosphere is *the Universal Consciousness* that gives shape to all material structures in the Universe - such as atoms, galaxies, stars, mountains, etc.

The Source of Life (The Source of All That Is) – see *The Transcendent*

Spiritual Journey – see *Journey of Awakening*

The Transcendent is the *Supreme Ubiquitous Intelligence* that is beyond form. It represents the invisible and formless *Natural Intelligence* throughout the Universe. *The Transcendent* is the sublime organizing principle which fashions everything in the manifested world of the material realm.

For millennia, this *Natural Intelligence* has been referred to in many ways throughout the world (The Thousand Names of the Divine) - such as *the Source of Life, Universal Consciousness, Pure Awareness, God, Allah, Tao, the Creator, the Great Spirit, the Great I Am, the Infinite Presence of Love, the Unbounded Ocean of Being, "The One", Infinite Intelligence, Limitless Love*, and so many more exquisite names for this sublime *Transcendent Power*. In many religious traditions this *Natural Intelligence* is simply referred to as "God".

(Note: Words that represent *"The Transcendent"* within **Journey of *The Great Circle*** are capitalized and italicized)

The Transcendent Impulse is defined as a constant spiritual yearning that we become aware of in our lifetime. It is the natural impulse to expand our awareness of what our life is truly about, to develop our potential, and to awaken to who we really are (an ascending impulse).

At the same time, it is the constant spiritual yearning of our expanding inner development to manifest ever-new expressions of creativity in our life (a descending impulse). This intrinsic and constant yearning (which is both the longing for spiritual awakening and for spiritual embodiment) that perpetually exists within us and within all forms of life - is called *the Transcendent Impulse*.

True Eternal Nature is the invisible transcendent consciousness of who we really are. It is the part of us that is eternal, unbounded, and limitless. Our *True Nature* is the aspect of who we are that guides and directs our life when we have learned to be aware of it.

There are numerous names for our *True Eternal Nature* - such as *the Higher Self, the Transcendent Self, the Authentic Self, the Essential Self, the Divine Self.* In many religious traditions, it is commonly referred to as the *"Soul".* Within **Journey of *The Great Circle*** it is also called our "holiness and magnificence".

The Unbounded Ocean of Being – see *The Transcendent*

The Unified Field is a term, which comes from quantum physics, that's defined as a limitless field of all possibilities that is formless and unbounded from which everything in the entire known Universe has emerged. Many religious traditions speak of this *Field* simply as "God" - or "The Kingdom of God" - or the Divine.

Unisphere is *Universal Consciousness* - which can also be referred to as *"The One", the Oneness within all of Consciousness, the Source of All That Is, Infinite Intelligence, The Unified Field, God.*

Universal Consciousness – see *The Transcendent*

Visionary Archetypes are poetic images of our greater potential or possibility. They represent qualities and virtues on ever-higher levels of human consciousness. Visionary archetypes are symbolic templates that point us to higher stages of inner development and to the qualities and realms of creative expression we strive to achieve. They can be thought of as pictorial representations of superior moral qualities which can empower and motivate us to express something greater in ourselves, a promise of a more positive future for our life.

THE STORY OF AWAKENING WITHIN THE FIRST NARRATIVES

IN THE CONCEPTUAL DESIGN of **Journey of *The Great Circle***, there is a poetic interweaving of themes within the first four contemplative narratives of each volume. Together these four narratives reveal "a hidden archetypal story" about every person's *spiritual journey of discovery*.

The first four narratives of the Winter Volume are:
1) Gifts of Winter
2) Qualities Within the Seasons of Life
3) The Great Story of Awakening
4) *Journey of Awakening*

The Transcendent Gifts of the Four Seasons

The first narrative of every volume depicts the transcendent gifts of each season, such as "Gifts of Winter" in this volume. Each season has four qualities listed that describe important interior aspects of our unfolding lives. Every quality has a particular placement either in the north, east, south, or west orientation.

Qualities Within the Seasons of Life

The second narrative within each of the four volumes is called "Qualities Within the Seasons of Life". This narrative lists all the transcendent qualities from the season on the previous page as well as all four qualities from each of the other seasons from the remaining volumes. Therefore, each of the four seasons displays four essential qualities (totaling sixteen individual qualities) that relate to our human developmental journey.

The Great Story of Awakening

The third narrative of each volume is called "The Great Story of Awakening". This narrative explains how the universal archetypal story of our spiritual awakening can be derived from organizing the four transcendent qualities from each of the four seasons into four specific chapters of a "story" that we are calling "The Great Story". These four chapters are the key components of the universal story of an awakening life (The Great Story) - and are listed as:

1) *The Great Circle*
2) Pillars of Awakening
3) Master of Freedom
4) Spheres of Contribution

"The Great Story of Awakening " can be thought of as "the spiritual portrayal of an awakening life" - and is the personal story of our conscious inner development and expansion of our awareness. It is our individual *journey of awakening*, our *journey of self-mastery*, in which we learn to awaken to a higher stage of spiritual consciousness.

The First Chapter: *The Great Circle*

The first chapter of "The Great Story of Awakening" is called **The Great Circle**. This chapter is formulated by gathering the first or top quality of each season from the previous narrative entitled "Qualities Within the Seasons of Life". The chapter of **The Great Circle** includes the following four qualities:

1) From **Winter:**   Align With *"The One"*   - (renewal and alignment)
2) From **Spring:**   Outward Expression   - (creativity and contribution)
3) From **Summer:**   Serve *"The Many"*   - (service to others and cultivating self-care)
4) From **Autumn:**   Inward Expansion   - (development and expanding awareness)

As we explore the daily narratives throughout this book, we will be introduced to the various dynamics at play in the world and in our lives. The first chapter called **The Great Circle** speaks to the natural invitation from *The Transcendent Impulse of Life* to learn what our life is truly about, discover what really matters, and cultivate an awareness of how to live a life of inner freedom.

The Second Chapter: Pillars of Awakening

In the first chapter, **The Great Circle** invites us to explore the Big Questions of *Life* and what our life is truly about. The personal inner development from this pursuit provides us with insights about the next segment of our unfolding story of discovery.

The second chapter, **Pillars of Awakening**, is created by gathering the second set of transcendent qualities from the narrative "Qualities Within the Seasons of Life". This includes the four following qualities:

1) **Winter:**   Oneness
2) **Spring:**   Acceptance
3) **Summer:**   Surrender
4) **Autumn:**   Gratitude

These four qualities are actually different ways to describe self-love and unconditional love - and are the personal attributes we develop using daily transformative practice to consciously transform our suffering into a life of inner freedom.

As an *artist of life*, we practice these spiritual attributes as a way to develop our highest expression of ourselves, as a means to cultivate our creative potential, and as a vehicle to reach for the next horizon of possibility of what we can become. Through our daily practice, we learn to maintain an ongoing alignment with *the Essence of Creation, the Source of Life, the Love of God*. And we reconnect with a natural transcendent yearning within us to feel this alignment in every moment of our life.

The Third Chapter: Master of Freedom

As we develop spiritual maturity and learn to maintain an alignment with *Life*, with *the Source of All That Is* we enter into the third chapter of our *awakening journey*, **Master of Freedom**.

Master of Freedom is the visionary archetypal image of an individual who is a fully integrated awakened being - and who experiences inner freedom, consciously maintains an alignment with *the Source of All That Is*, and uses his or her unique gifts and talents to serve the good of all. The chapter **Master of Freedom** is formulated by gathering the third set of transcendent qualities from the narrative "Qualities Within the Seasons of Life". This includes the qualities:

1) **Winter:**   Awakened Presence
2) **Spring:**   Endless Creativity
3) **Summer:**   Unconditional Love
4) **Autumn:**   Limitless Development

Through dedicated daily transformative practice these four qualities empower us to integrate our inner development into our everyday life as an embodied and anchored experience. These are the qualities of consciously cultivating the mastery of living a life of inner freedom - in other words, living an awakened life. Once this level of spiritual awareness has been realized, it becomes obvious that the most important way to use our creative energy is to offer our unique mission to the world through our personal contributions. Furthermore, we recognize how natural it is to follow the inner guidance of our heart as we share our novel contributions to help create a more glorious world.

The Fourth Chapter: Spheres of Contribution

The fourth chapter of "The Great Story of Awakening" is called **Spheres of Contribution**. As we explore this chapter, we discover ever-greater ways of living in this world and offering our creative gifts and talents. The chapter **Spheres of Contribution** gathers the fourth set of transcendent qualities from the narrative "Qualities Within the Seasons of Life". These include:

1) **Winter:**   Contributions to Oneself
2) **Spring:**   Contributions to Family
3) **Summer:**   Contributions to Community
4) **Autumn:**   Contributions to the World

When we learn to maintain an experience of living our life with peace of mind and inner freedom, the next obvious and intrinsic awareness is for us to serve the wellbeing of others - and to contribute our unique creative gifts and talents.

When these four chapters, ***The Great Circle*, Pillars of Awakening, Master of Freedom,** and **Spheres of Contribution** are placed together sequentially, they form the universal great story of our spiritual awakening, or what has been referred to in this book as **"The Great Story of Awakening"**.

Quadrant Directions	Gifts of Winter		Qualities Within the Seasons of Life		The Great Story of Awakening
NORTH Winter	Align With *"The One"*	* + − x	Align With *"The One"* Oneness Awakened Presence Contributions to Oneself	* * * *	**The Great Circle** Align With *"The One"* Outward Expression Serve *"The Many"* Inward Expansion
EAST Spring	Oneness	* + − x	Outward Expression Acceptance Endless Creativity Contributions to Family	+ + + +	**Pillars of Awakening** Oneness Acceptance Surrender Gratitude
SOUTH Summer	Awakened Presence	* + − x	Serve *"The Many"* Surrender Unconditional Love Contributions to Community	− − − −	**Master of Freedom** Awakened Presence Endless Creativity Unconditional Love Limitless Development
WEST Autumn	Contributions to Oneself	* + − x	Inward Expansion Gratitude Limitless Development Contributions to the World	x x x x	**Spheres of Contribution** Contributions to Oneself Contributions to Family Contributions to Community Contributions to the World

Journey of Awakening

The fourth contemplative narrative found within each volume is entitled *"Journey of Awakening"*. It has been written as another pragmatic version and additional way of understanding the preceding narrative **"The Great Story of Awakening"**.

"Journey of Awakening", with its four stages that describe our *spiritual journey*, form the foundation for our conscious exploration and inner development of self throughout the four volumes of **Journey of *The Great Circle*.** The four stages are:

1) Development = *The Great Circle*
2) Transformation = Pillars of Awakening
3) Mastery = Master of Freedom
4) Contribution = Spheres of Contribution

✳ THE DANCE, POETRY, AND SONG OF THE FRONT COVER ART ✳

THE FRONT COVER ART of **Journey of *The Great Circle*** is a visual representation of the relationship between three facets of reality: the transcendent aspect of life, one's *Eternal Nature*, and one's physical embodiment. In other words - it is a symbolic representation of the integration of *Spirit, Soul,* and body.

We are so much more than we appear to be. Our physical bodies are just a small part of the magnificent totality of who we really are. The realm of our physical body is like an iceberg that appears above the surface of the water. Yet ninety percent of the mass of an iceberg remains invisible underneath the ocean's waters. Similarly a vast part of who we really are remains invisible to our senses, yet it is present in, and determines, every aspect of our life.

Our physical body is obviously visible in the world of form, yet our *True Eternal Nature* and *the Infinite Intelligence within All That Is,* which created everything in the Cosmos, is invisible to our five senses.

The artwork of the front cover symbolically represents this awareness, and gives us a visual metaphor to use to deepen our understanding of it.

The black and white meditator represents our physical body that is embarked on a *journey of discovery* to learn to love all of life unconditionally.

The gold branches and roots of the Tree of Life represent our *True Eternal Nature,* our *Higher Self,* our *Soul,* which is eternal and unbounded - and is the consciousness that is mirrored in our physical body.

The circle around the Tree of Life, as well as the Universe of infinite stars, represent *the Transcendent, the Infinite Intelligence* of the Universe, *the Source of All That Is.*

✳ RESOURCES ✳

Braden, Gregg. *The Isaiah Effect + The Divine Matrix*

Brown, Michael. *The Presence Process*

Capra, Fritjof. *The Tao of Physics*

Chopra, Deepak. *The Path of Love + The Seven Spiritual Laws of Success + How To Know God + Quantum Healing*

Cohen, Andrew. *Evolutionary Enlightenment + What Is Enlightenment Magazine*

Davies, Paul. *The Mind of God*

Dispenza, Joe. *Becoming Supernatural + Breaking the Habit of Being Yourself + You Are The Placebo*

Dowd, Michael. *Thank God For Evolution*

Green, Brian. *The Fabric of the Cosmos*

Hawkins, David. *Power Vs. Force + Discovery of the Presence of God + The Eye of the I*

Houston, Jean. *The Possible Human + Life Force + A Mythic Life*

Hubbard, Barbara Marx. *Conscious Evolution*

Katie, Byron. *Loving What Is*

Lipton, Bruce and Steve Bhaerman. *Spontaneous Evolution: Our Positive Future and a Way To Get There From Here*

Mandelbrot, Benoit. *The Fractal Geometry of Nature*

McTaggert, Lynne. *The Field*

Millman, Dan. *Way of the Peaceful Warrior*

Ming-Dao, Deng. *365 Tao Daily Meditations*

Moore, Robert and Douglas Gillette. *King, Warrior, Magician, Lover*

Morter, Sue. *The Energy Codes*

Murphy, Michael. *The Future of the Body*

Patten, Terry. *A New Republic of the Heart*

Ra, Kaia. *The Sophia Code*

Reich, Robert. *The Common Good*

Rudd, Richard. *The Gene Keys*

Swimme, Brian. *Canticle to the Cosmos*

Swimme, Brian and Thomas Berry. *The Universe Story*

Teilhard de Chardin. *The Human Phenomenon*

Tolle, Eckhart. *The Power of Now + A New Earth*

Trott, Susan. *The Holy Man*

Tzu, Lao. *The Way Of Life*

Wilbur, Ken. *The Marriage of Sense and Soul + Sex, Ecology, Spirituality - The Spirit of Evolution*

Williamson, Marianne. *A Return To Love + Enchanted Love + The Healing of America + Everyday Grace*

Yogananda, Paramahansa. *Autobiography of a Yogi*

Spiritual awakening is the natural evolutionary journey
of constant inner development
that every person on the planet
is perpetually embarked on,
whether he or she is actually conscious of it or not.

✳ ACKNOWLEDGEMENTS ✳

I THANK THE FOLLOWING PEOPLE for helping me bring this creative project into form.

First, I thank my dear friend, Bob Sizelove, with whom I've shared many adventurous camping trips for over a decade. During one of these camping trips at a place we call "paradise", I received my first Contemplative Circle which became the springboard for **Journey of The Great Circle**. For years, Bob and I have discussed the primary themes of this book around a blazing campfire under a star-strung sky. Bob's deep devotion to God and his commitment to ongoing self-development and service has been an inspiring aspect for me in writing this book.

Next, I thank my friend, Jo Norris, for her constant support of my writings. Jo is a progressive and creative catalyst for change and has touched so many people with her loving presence and wisdom. She has touched and inspired me profoundly. Jo has been a supportive angel at many steps during the evolution of this book.

I thank my Beloved partner, Yana DiAngelis, for her unconditional love and perpetual support of seeing the holiness and magnificence within me. Her unwavering recognition of who I really am has been a powerful testament of the unconditional love and compassion that is possible for our glorious world. Her love gave me inner strength during the completion of this project.

I thank my Soul Friend and Anum Cara, Enocha Ranjita Ryan, for years of listening to me read each morning the daily contemplative narrative. She has been such a fervent and constant support of my creativity. Her steady love and the inspiring way she lives her life was so empowering to me in bringing these writings into manifestation.

Furthermore, I thank my dear friend, Maria Cavendish, for her loving support and encouragement all the many years as I spent time contemplating at the creek to bring through this body of work.

I thank my long time friend, Shambhu, who is a masterful guitar recording artist and creative wonder. Shambhu's consistent support and encouragement of all my creative endeavors has been a blessed gift in my life.

And I thank the following editing angels: Maureen Levy for her Amazonian feats, Chaka Ken-Varley, Robert Varley, Kathleen Haverkamp, Rhianne Teija Newluhnd, and those who have given me discerning feedback and assistance in various ways toward the polishing of this work: Shanti Norman, Karl Anthony, Mia Margaret, Charley Thweatt, and Iala Jaggs for showing me a magical place at the creek where I spent over 10 years downloading the inspiration for this book.

As a final note, I thank the following inspiring teachers of philosophical and spiritual viewpoints that have pointed me to embracing larger perspectives of what I believe my life is truly about and what really matters: Marianne Williamson, Jean Houston, Barbara Marx Hubbard, Deepak Chopra, Joe Dispenza, Dr. Sue Morter, Gregg Braden, Alan Cohen, Andrew Harvey, Ken Wilber, Michael Dowd, Brian Swimme, Andrew Cohen, Kaia Ra, and Paramahansa Yogananda.

✳ ABOUT THE AUTHOR ✳

Oman Ken has devoted his life to being a multi-instrumentalist and singer. He lives in a home filled with exotic instruments from around the world, and professionally has focused his musical presentations on the harp, guitar, piano, Native American and ethnic flutes, as well as the gift of his voice. He has performed hundreds of concerts and celebrations across the United States while creating 15 professional recordings of his original vocal and instrumental music.

Oman has also composed three Ritual Theater musicals which he directed and produced in Hawaii, entitled "Genesis: A Ritual of Transformation", "Starwheel: Journey of the Sacred Circle", and "The Mask and the Sword". Furthermore, he has produced myriad multi-media Solstice and Equinox Celebrations with a troupe of 25 people in Houston, Texas and Cincinnati, Ohio.

Oman has presented his transformational workshops: "The Ceremonial Art of Celebration", "Dance Movement as Spiritual Practice", and "The Power Within the Archetypes of the King, Warrior, Magician, and Lover", in various spiritual conferences and retreats around the United States.

After a challenging physical condition made it unfeasible to continue his musical travels, Oman deepened his spiritual quest for inner freedom by spending an abundance of time in Nature contemplating what life is truly about - and what really matters.

The result of his personal investigations was a host of poetic contemplative narratives that became the foundation for this book **Journey of The Great Circle**.

Oman now lives in the majestic Red Rocks of Sedona, Arizona.   JourneyOfTheGreatCircle.com

JOURNEY OF *THE GREAT CIRCLE*
DAILY AFFIRMATION STATEMENTS FOR WINTER

(Copy - then cut along the dotted lines to carry an affirmation with you each day)

----

1 - THE DANCE OF THE INFINITE SEASONS

DECEMBER 21 or 22   GIFTS OF WINTER
I expand my awareness of my True Nature and of what really matters through self-reflection.

DECEMBER 21 or 22   QUALITIES WITHIN THE SEASONS OF LIFE
Within the silent sanctuary of my heart Life is constantly inviting me to love unconditionally.

DECEMBER 23   THE GREAT STORY OF AWAKENING
My external reality mirrors my internal awareness and reveals to me my path to inner freedom.

DECEMBER 24   *JOURNEY OF AWAKENING*
The Infinitely Creative Impulse of Life constantly invites me to learn what my life is truly about.

DECEMBER 25   THE CELEBRATION OF CHRISTMAS
Today I offer prayers of peace and harmony so I may help to strengthen a global field of love.

DECEMBER 26   A NATURAL YEARNING FOR INNER DEVELOPMENT
I feel a natural yearning within constantly inviting me to develop my unique creative potential.

DECEMBER 27   *SPIRITUAL JOURNEY*
I am on an inner quest to learn to love all people - and all of life - unconditionally.

----

11 - <u>THE POETRY OF *THE GREAT CIRCLE*</u>

DECEMBER 28   *THE GREAT CIRCLE*

As I plant seeds of love in my inner awareness, they sprout forth out into the garden of my life.

DECEMBER 29   *THE GREAT CIRCLE* OF EXPANSION AND EXPRESSION

As I expand my awareness of what is true, it is expressed in my life as peace and inner freedom.

DECEMBER 30   *THE GREAT CIRCLE* OF THE TAO

Within every new cycle of birth and death there is a perpetual continuity of Absolute Oneness.

DECEMBER 31   COMPLETION

I let go of what limits me so I can receive the gifts of life that expand my awareness.

JANUARY 1   BIRTH OF NEW POSSIBILITIES

Each morning gives me another opportunity to birth new possibilities and miracles in my life.

JANUARY 2   NESTED SPHERES OF CONSCIOUSNESS

My consciousness is perpetually expanding along the arc of greater love and service to others.

JANUARY 3   THREE FACES OF GOD

I experience God as "The Transcendent" or "The Beloved" or "The Creation" - or all at once.

JANUARY 4   GOD AS "THE MYSTERY"

I revel in the Mystery of the Universe so I may deepen the meaning and purpose of my life.

III - <u>SPIRIT AWARENESS PRACTICES</u>

JANUARY 5   FOUNDATIONAL TRANSFORMATIVE PRACTICES
I use transformative practices to consciously transform the quality of my inner experience.

JANUARY 6   GIFTS OF MEDITATION
The practice of meditation naturally leads me to the sublime realization of my Eternal Nature.

JANUARY 7   SILENCE
I frequently renew and rejuvenate myself by spending time within the nurturing home of silence.

IV - <u>THE SONG OF EMBODIED LOVE</u>

JANUARY 8   THE NATURAL STATES THAT EMERGE FROM BEING
As I sustain an alignment with the Source of Life peace and joy naturally arise in my awareness.

JANUARY 9   THE NATURAL STATE OF PEACE
Today I live my life as a living expression of peace.

JANUARY 10   PILLARS OF AWAKENING
I am aware of my Oneness with all of life.

JANUARY 11   ONENESS
The world I perceive with all of its myriad forms of life is one expression of universal energy.

JANUARY 12   PILLARS OF SELF-LOVE
Loving myself unconditionally is the same as fully loving each unique expression of creation.

JANUARY 13   REVERENCE
Today I honor the sacredness and beauty of each unique expression within the Web of Life.

- -

V - SPIRIT AWARENESS PRACTICES

JANUARY 14   MEDITATION PRACTICES
I relax into the ocean of silence within me so I may directly experience my Eternal Nature.

- -

JANUARY 15   GOALS OF MEDITATION
In the spaciousness of silence lies my sacred communion with the Omniscient Source of Life.

- -

JANUARY 16   CULTIVATING AN AWARENESS OF ONENESS
I enter the sublime sanctuary of inner silence so I may directly experience my Eternal Nature.

- -

VI - ARCHETYPES OF SPIRITUAL AWAKENING

JANUARY 17   VISIONARY ARCHETYPES
Today I use my creative imagination to envision and embody the person I want to become.

- -

JANUARY 18   GIFTS OF THE ARCHETYPES
I use my imagination to envision greater possibilities for my future - and the future of the world.

- -

JANUARY 19   *THE GREAT CIRCLE* OF THE ARCHETYPES
I use my imagination to envision my life advancing to my next horizon of creative possibility.

- -

JANUARY 20   ARCHETYPES OF SPIRITUAL AWAKENING
I am on a quest to learn to love unconditionally - and to fully experience a life of inner freedom.

- -

JANUARY 21   MASTER OF FREEDOM
It is the destiny of all people, and thus my destiny as well, to live an awakened life.

JANUARY 22   UNCONDITIONAL LOVE
It is my spiritual destiny to love all people and every expression of life – unconditionally.

JANUARY 23   EVOLUTION OF AWAKENING
Evolution yearns for me to awaken to my True Nature as a vital part of a vast global awakening.

JANUARY 24   ENLIGHTENMENT
I realize inner freedom in the moments when I accept life just as it is and when I'm serving others.

VII – SPIRIT AWARENESS PRACTICES

JANUARY 25   MINDFULNESS
The thoughts I consciously focus on grow stronger – as the ones I ignore gradually fade away.

JANUARY 26   MINDFULNESS PRACTICES
Today I am mindful of the quality of my thoughts that I choose to focus my attention on.

JANUARY 27   WITNESSING AWARENESS
I witness without judgment the thoughts, emotions, and sensations that pass by my awareness.

VIII – ARCHETYPES OF CONSCIOUS CONTRIBUTION

JANUARY 28   SPHERES OF CONTRIBUTION
There is a natural yearning in me to serve and contribute to the wellbeing of others.

JANUARY 29   CONTRIBUTION TO ONESELF (PERSONAL WELLBEING)

Today I nourish my body, my heart, my mind, and my spirit so I'm truly able to serve others.

JANUARY 30   ARCHETYPES OF CONSCIOUS CONTRIBUTION

I consciously contribute my creative gifts and talents in ways that serve the good of all.

JANUARY 31   VISIONARY LEADER

Today I make conscious choices that support the vision of a better world for all people.

FEBRUARY 1   PRIMARY PERSPECTIVES OF THE WORLD

I constantly expand how I perceive the world so I may learn to love others more fully.

FEBRUARY 2   SPIRITUAL UNDERSTANDING

A greater understanding of what really matters leads me to a greater attunement with my heart.

FEBRUARY 3   VISION

Today I hold a vision in my mind that imagines the fully awakened person I am destined to be.

FEBRUARY 4   IMAGINATION

I use the unlimited power of my imagination to envision myself as the person I intend to be.

IX - <u>SPIRIT AWARENESS PRACTICES</u>

FEBRUARY 5   PRIMARY TRANSFORMATIVE PRACTICES

I use transformative practices to assist Life in creating its next expression of awakening in me.

FEBRUARY 6 CULTIVATING SPIRITUAL AWARENESS
Today I sit quietly in the silence of the present moment and align with the Source of Life.

FEBRUARY 7 PRAYER
I willfully align my awareness with the Infinite Presence of Love - thus every moment is a prayer.

X - THE EVOLUTIONARY PERSPECTIVE

FEBRUARY 8 GIFTS FROM AN EVOLUTIONARY PERSPECTIVE
Embracing an evolutionary perspective of life empowers me to live responsibly with integrity.

FEBRUARY 9 INTEGRITY
I live with integrity as I engage in actions that empower others and support ethical behavior.

FEBRUARY 10 THE FRACTAL NATURE OF EMERGENT EVOLUTION
The fundamental patterns within Nature point me to my own destiny of living an awakened life.

FEBRUARY 11 THE INFINITE CREATIVITY OF THE UNIVERSE
The boundless creativity in me is the same Infinite Creativity that animates the entire Universe.

FEBRUARY 12 EVOLUTIONARY EMERGENCE OF SPECIES
The Impulse of Evolution directs me each day to further cultivate my inner development.

FEBRUARY 13 EVOLUTION OF THE HUMAN BRAIN
The natural impulse of evolution within me is always inviting me to serve the good of all.

FEBRUARY 14　　　　　INFINITE AWAKENINGS

Life is constantly inviting me to cultivate more compassion and empathy for others.

- -

FEBRUARY 15　　　　　PRIMARY STAGES OF EVOLUTION

I am "the eyes of the Universe" gazing into the vast Cosmos and observing my own evolution.

- -

XI - <u>ARCHETYPES OF LIFE MASTERY</u>

FEBRUARY 16　　　　　ARCHETYPES OF LIFE MASTERY

Today I envision myself creating a life of inner freedom that serves the good of all.

- -

FEBRUARY 17　　　　　ENLIGHTENED KING OR QUEEN

Life is always inviting me to envision and create the next expression of who I intend to be.

- -

FEBRUARY 18　　　　　HEART WISDOM

I am aligned with Life and relax as the heart wisdom within the Universe easily flows through me.

- -

FEBRUARY 19　　　　　EMPOWERMENT

I empower and support the people in my life - and accept them just as they are.

- -

FEBRUARY 20　　　　　INNER GUIDANCE

Today I receive inner guidance that comes from life's perpetual stream of Natural Intelligence.

- -

FEBRUARY 21　　　　　CONSCIOUS CHOICES

Throughout the day I make choices, which are guided by my heart - and serve the good of all.

- -

XII - <u>SPIRIT AWARENESS PRACTICES</u>

FEBRUARY 22   CULTIVATING SPIRITUAL AWAKENING
I frequently question my core beliefs so as to deepen my understanding of what really matters.

FEBRUARY 23   CULTIVATING AWARENESS OF ONE'S *ETERNAL NATURE*
I experience the vast Universe as a natural extension of my physical body.

FEBRUARY 24   SELF-OBSERVATION
Today I expand my awareness of what I feel and think so I may deepen my peace of mind.

XIII - <u>ARCHETYPES OF HIGHER KNOWLEDGE</u>

FEBRUARY 25   "AN OCEAN JOURNEY"
I frequently examine and reflect on my life so I may cultivate peace of mind and inner freedom.

FEBRUARY 26   THE QUEST FOR HIGHER KNOWLEDGE
I am constantly being invited by Life to expand my awareness of truth, goodness, and beauty.

FEBRUARY 27   ARCHETYPES OF HIGHER KNOWLEDGE
Today I consciously align my awareness with the field of unlimited universal knowledge.

FEBRUARY 28   AWAKENED MYSTIC
Today I maintain an alignment with the Source of Life - and relax into an experience of peace.

FEBRUARY 29   PERSPECTIVES OF ONENESS
As I expand my perspectives regarding the inclusion of others my compassion for others grows.

MARCH 1   THE NATURAL STATE OF PRESENCE

As I maintain an alignment with Life, living in the present moment is natural and instinctual.

MARCH 2   "A FLOWING RIVER" (A METAPHOR FOR TIME)

I recognize that there is no area of my life where the flow of Limitless Love is not present.

XIV - SPIRIT AWARENESS PRACTICES

MARCH 3   "DOORWAYS" TO THE PRESENCE

I accept that, in the present moment, my life is unfolding perfectly just as it is.

MARCH 4   CULTIVATING SPIRITUAL WELLBEING

I use daily transformative practice as a way to help me stay aligned with the Source of Life.

MARCH 5   *THE GREAT CIRCLE* OF THE BREATH

I frequently use my breath to help align myself with the sublime sanctity of the present moment.

XV - NAVIGATING THE JOURNEY OF *THE GREAT CIRCLE*

MARCH 6   *THE GREAT CIRCLE* OF THE UNIVERSAL MASCULINE
                           AND FEMININE

My life is the blessed merging of both the universal masculine impulse and feminine impulse.

MARCH 7   UNIVERSAL MASCULINE IMPULSE

I feel a natural yearning within me that constantly invites me to love more fully.

MARCH 8   UNIVERSAL FEMININE IMPULSE

I feel a natural yearning within me that constantly invites me to express my unlimited creativity.

MARCH 9   RELATIONSHIP BETWEEN THE UNIVERSAL MASCULINE AND FEMININE

Today I plant seeds of my creative visions and trust they will blossom in the garden of my life.

MARCH 10   *THE GREAT CIRCLE* OF INNER AND OUTER PURPOSE

I consciously cultivate my inner purpose - "to learn", as well as my outer purpose - "to create".

MARCH 11   THE MANY INTERPRETATIONS OF INNER PURPOSE

Today I expand my awareness, develop my potential, and learn to love unconditionally.

MARCH 12   EVOLUTION OF OUTER PURPOSE

Contributing my gifts to the wellbeing of others advances the life-affirming arc of evolution.

XVI - THE ART OF TRANSFORMATION AND HEALING

MARCH 13   *THE GREAT CIRCLE* OF DEVELOPMENT AND TRANSFORMATION

As the love in me grows more fully, my experiences of transformation and healing grow as well.

MARCH 14   *THE SPIRITUAL JOURNEY* IN RELATION TO HEALING

Every moment offers me an opportunity to further my quest of learning to love unconditionally.

MARCH 15   VARIOUS FORMS OF HEALING

I recognize that only Love is real - thus in this present moment, I am healed and whole right now.

MARCH 16   EMERGENT HEALING

As I awaken to the magnificence of who I really am, I open my heart to transformation and healing

----

XVII - <u>CONCLUSION – SACRED DESTINY</u>

MARCH 17   GIFTS OF *THE GREAT CIRCLE*
I am grateful for the blessed gifts of awareness I receive each day that help me love more fully.

MARCH 18   RENEWAL
Today I renew myself by aligning with the Infinite Presence of Love in the sanctuary of silence.

Printed in the United States
by Baker & Taylor Publisher Services